MASS COMMUNICATION
Research and Analysis

MASS COMMUNICATION

Research and Analysis

Rajiv Saxena

CENTRUM PRESS
NEW DELHI-110002 (INDIA)

CENTRUM PRESS
H.O.: 4360/4, Ansari Road, Daryaganj,
New Delhi-110002 (India)
Tel: 23278000, 23261597, 23255577, 23286875
B.O.: No. 1015, Ist Main Road, BSK IIIrd Stage,
IIIrd Phase, IIIrd Block, Bangalore-560085 (INDIA)
Tel: 080-41723429
Email: centrumpress@gmail.com
Visit us at: www.centrumpress.com

Mass Communication: Research and Analysis

First Edition, 2010

ISBN 978-93-80836-21-8

PRINTED IN INDIA

Printed at Mehra Offset Press, Delhi

Contents

Preface

Mass communication is the term used to describe the academic study of the various means by which individuals and entities relay information through mass media to large segments of the population at the same time. It is usually understood to relate to newspaper and magazine publishing, radio, television and film, as these are used both for disseminating news and for advertising.

Mass communication research includes media institutions and processes such as diffusion of information, and media effects such as persuasion or manipulation of public opinion. In the United States, for instance, several university journalism departments degraded into schools or colleges of mass communication or "journalism and mass communication".

In addition to studying practical skills of journalism, public relations or advertising, they offer programs on "mass communication" or "mass communication research." The latter is often the title given to doctoral studies in such schools, whether the focus of the student's research is journalism practice, history, law or media effects. Departmental structures within such colleges may separate research and instruction in professional or technical aspects of mass communication.

With the increased role of the Internet in delivering news and information, mass communication studies and media organizations tend to focus on the convergence of publishing, broadcasting and digital communication. The term 'mass' suggests that the recipients of media products constitute a vast sea of passive, undifferentiated individuals. This is an image associated with some earlier critiques of 'mass culture' and Mass society which generally assumed that the development of mass communication has had a largely negative impact on modern social life, creating a kind of bland and homogeneous culture which entertains individuals without challenging them.

However, with the advancement in Media Technology, people are no longer receiving gratification without questioning the grounds on which it is based. Instead, people are engaging themselves more with media products such as computers, cell phones and Internet. These have gradually become vital tools for communications in society today.

Chapter 1

Research Methods in Mass Communication Research

Keeping tabs on the research produced in any given field is no small task. Such efforts range from discrete meta-analyses of specific concepts and topics to the ongoing maintenance of large bibliographic databases and informatics. Mass communication offers no exception to this variety of work as researchers in this field have regularly directed their efforts toward the research enterprise itself.

This work examines research in mass communication as far back as the 1930s and includes topics ranging from the content of specific journals to the use of specific methods, concept development, and broad trends in multiple journals spanning decades.

This chapter offers a unique element to the body of work examining the research in mass communication by providing a more detailed look at the use of research methods during the 1990s. This chapter also serves as a companion piece for two other published works. First, the material presented here is designed as a direct replication of Cooper, Potter, and Dupagne's 1994 "A Status Report on Methods Used in Mass Communication Research."

While a census is employed in this work rather than a sample as used by those authors, identical coding schemes are employed to provide a fairly direct comparison with the 1994 study. This allows examination of data spanning thirty-five years. second, this chapter serves as a comparison work for "Mass Communication Research Trends from 1980 to 1999" by Kamhawi and Weaver, providing support for some of the inferences made in their sample.

As in the previous work, an important focus of this chapter is on the use of quantitative versus qualitative methods. This chapter also directs additional attention to the use of mixed approaches in mass communication research. Some discussion of this phenomenon will be offered prior to describing the methods and results of this investigation.

MIXED METHODS

The epistemological frictions of this field, as described by Cooper, Potter, and Dupagne, have hardly disappeared over the last decade. As they point out, the issue goes much deeper than "to count or not to count." The quantitative versus qualitative distinction is only the surface representation of a spectrum of fundamental orientations toward how the world may be known and how truth might be approached. It is when such philosophical contrasts become politicized that the matter can become divisive. Perhaps as a consequence, we tend to see some degree of split in our journals, in the orientation of our academic units, and in our graduate instruction-all of which tend to be regarded as either quantitative or qualitative in orientation. Although purely qualitative or purely quantitative units, journals, and such are uncommon, truly ecumenical circumstances are certainly not the rule.

There has been some attention paid to the combining of quantitative and qualitative approaches. Weaver observed an increase in this variety of work in the 1980s and predicted that mixed approaches would increase in popularity. An underlying phenomenon that may be on the rise, as Cooper, Potter, and Dupagne suggested, is that of broader training in our graduate programs.

In order to improve their competitive edge, doctoral students maybe equipping themselves with a wider range of research tools, either through personal initiative or as a consequence of programmatic requirements. This question must be left to researchers surveying the field's graduate programs. But the presence of mixed research in our journals might serve as evidence of such training. At the very least, identification and examination of this domain of research could provide useful exemplars for graduate training.

Historically, attention to the mixing of quantitative and qualitative approaches has resided most strongly in the area of measurement. There, most references turn to Campbell and Fiske's development of the multitrait-multimethod matrix method for evaluating the construct validity of a given measure. While such mixed approaches may be embraced by those rigorously developing formal measurement tools, they are less strongly represented in the texts often used to introduce mass communication graduate students to research methods. When the mixed approach is discussed it is often referred to as triangulation and defined as "the use of both qualitative and quantitative methods to fully understand the nature of a research problem."

The term "triangulation" is borrowed metaphorically from the navigational technique in which a position can be geometrically fixed through its observation from two or more points. Triangulation is not a developed concept in the field of communication and can easily be argued to be a poor metaphor for the actual use of mixed approaches in research. But the term does appear across a number of other fields in social and behavioral research, where it at least offers an approach for categorizing various forms of mixed work. To that extent it will be given some brief attention here.

Triangulation was perhaps first conceptually described as a technique in the social sciences by Feigl, and is traced through Webb et al. to the primary reference typically given to Denzen. Denzen elaborates six specific forms of triangulation: theory, data, methods, investigator, analysis, and multiple. In an effort to make triangulation a more viable option for researchers, Kimchi, Polivka, and Stevenson provide a set of operational definitions.

Each specific approach to triangulation can be elaborated extensively. However, the primary focus of this chapter (and that of Cooper, Potter, and Dupagne, and most methods texts) is the examination of quantitative versus qualitative approaches. As Erzberger and Prein point out, the notion of combining quantitative and qualitative observations is hardly new, and is also described by such terms as micro-macro integration. They describe the origins:

The starting point for this discussion was the idea that the different research methodologies-interpretative analysis of qualitative data on the one hand and statistical analysis of numerical data on the other- each have specific weaknesses but also specific strengths: the weaknesses should be overcome by combining qualitative and quantitative data sources and methods of analysis in the same research project.

They develop three arguments for the use of quantitative-qualitative triangulation. First, researchers may be motivated to achieve convergence, to confirm (or disconfirm) results across methods. second, complementarity might be sought. The motivation for this approach lies in a desire to use multiple approaches to allow the development of various pictures of the same phenomenon and provide a broader view. Finally, dissonance may be desired. In this case, different methods are employed in order to find divergent results and provide a provocative analysis.

Examples of studies explicitly using the term triangulation can be found across a range of the social sciences, including communication, education, nursing, community health, and evaluation. Here we ask to what degree this approach is used in mass communication research, whether by the term triangulation or not. Cooper, Potter, and Dupagne estimated that 7.2% of the work in the eight journals they examined between 1965 and 9 199 89 used both qualitative and quantitative methods. Kamhwai and Weaver estimate that 2.5% of articles in ten journals they examined between 1980 and 1999 used such mixed approaches. Neither offers a closer examination of how the two approaches were combined. This study will again report the occurrence of mixed research, and will also examine those studies to detail how this approach is represented in mass communication research.

METHOD

In order to allow direct comparison, this study adopted with few exceptions the methods previously used by Cooper, Potter, and Dupagne.

The previous work examined a longer time period and used a sampling strategy to reduce the amount of coding. Since the present study is constrained to a shorter period of time it was feasible to undertake a complete census. It should also be noted that the numbers provided by Cooper, Potter, and Dupagne are estimates.

Direct comparisons between the studies must take that into consideration. Cooper, Potter, and Dupagne sampled approximately a third of the total population and had a sample size of 1,326, which would place their margin of error at about +/- 2.5%.

This study examines the same set of eight journals as did Cooper, Potter, and Dupagne: Communication Monographs, Communication Research, Critical Studies in Mass Communication, Human Communication Research, Journal of Broadcasting & Electronic Media, Journal of Communication, Journalism & Mass Communication Quarterly, and Quarterly Journal of Speech. These journals were originally selected because they had circulations over 20,0 000 and had high standards demonstrated by peer acceptance rates under 20%. This is still the case for these journals. Kamhawi and Weaver also selected seven of these journals in the set of ten they examined.

As before, only articles presenting original research are examined. Coding categories are also taken directly from Cooper, Potter, and Dupagne, and include the research focus, use of theory, the data source, and the analysis procedure. Each of these is detailed in turn.

The research focus involves "the portion of mass media phenomenon that authors attempt to explain or interpret." Cooper, Potter, and Dupagne elaborated ten categories through consideration of the classic Lasswellian model of "who says what to whom in what channel to what effect." The same set of categories were used in this study for research focus: media industry; personalities in the media; production of messages; message content; audience analysis; distribution of messages; effects of media on individuals or groups; effects of media on institutions, society, or culture; regulation of media; and other.

The most significant departure made from Cooper, Potter, and Dupagne involved coding for the use of theory. They admit, as must be admitted here, that the coding scheme may lean toward the quantitative hypothetico-deductive approach and slight some qualitative work in which theory is developed, or grounded, rather than tested.

In order to capture a clearer picture of theory, additional categories were added to account for the other possible ways that theory might be used, especially with respect to the application of research questions and hypotheses as they might appear in qualitative work. Thus, articles were coded as displaying no use of theory, presenting research questions or hypotheses, specifying a hypothesis without supporting theory, offering a research question without supporting theory, offering a theory-based hypothesis or research question, and evoking theory without the specification of either a research question or a hypothesis.

No changes were made from Cooper, Potter, and Dupagne in the categories used for procedures and sources for data. Procedures included experiments, surveys, observation (e.g., participant observation, interviews), content analysis, and secondary analysis. Data sources included direct contact with people, direct contact with media messages, direct contact with archival data, analysis of existing qualitative data, analysis of existing qualitative data, and analysis of the research of others (e.g., meta analysis, reanalysis of published results).

There is one minor departure from previous coding on these variables. Cooper, Potter, and Dupagne allowed for more than one procedure to be coded per case. Rather than use this approach, a category for "multiple" was added to both variables, providing some additional detail.

Three coders were trained based on the methods reported in Cooper, Potter, and Dupagne. All were graduate students who had completed coursework in both theory and methods in a journalism graduate studies programme. Coders had little difficulty understanding the categories employed. A total of 2,649 articles were coded. A subsample (N = 130, 5%) of the content was randomly selected and independently receded. Intercoder agreement was calculated by Holsti's method and corrected for chance and number of categories by Scott's pi: method 92% (pi = 85%), procedure 91% (88%), source 92% (87%), focus 82% (76%), and use of theory 84% (41% for the five-category scheme introduced here, 67% if collapsed to match Cooper, Potter, and Dupagne).

RESULTS

Tables and findings are presented in a manner generally matching Cooper, Potter, and Dupagne, and include their reported data to facilitate comparison. Here we see a clear quantitative versus qualitative distinction, at least as represented in the journals included in the analysis.

The 57% quantitative dominance seen in this study's census of the content is a very close match to the estimate made by Cooper, Potter, and Dupagne. Cooper, Potter, and Dupagne report a trend across their time span in which emphasis shifts from qualitative to quantitative. While this trend appears reasonable, the amount of variance is fairly substantial and could mitigate that finding. The data presented here are fairly uniform across the decade; 1993 was the only year in which there was more qualitative than quantitative work published.

The more striking distinction between these results and Cooper, Potter, and Dupagne's lies in the prevalence of studies using both quantitative and qualitative approaches. It is conceivable that the broader discussion of mixed studies that appeared in a number of journals in the 1980s played itself out and that over the last decade such approaches have become less popular. It should also be noted, though, that the difference between the two studies on this category is small in magnitude (about 5%). The most conservative assessment of these findings is that quantitative-qualitative integration is not now, nor has it ever been, an especially common approach in the journals examined. Given an estimate of a +/-2.5% margin of error it may also be reasonable to conclude that mixed approaches were less prevalent in the 1990s than in the previous 25 years.

The results of the examination of research focus shows some interesting parallels to the previous work as well. Audience, content, and individual-level effects remain the most common foci of quantitative studies. For qualitative studies, industry remained a popular focus, and the popularity of content studies seems to have increased while studies of regulation have decreased. Overall, within this study there is divergence in focus between qualitative and quantitative studies, with a weak correlation (Spearman's rho, r) of.34 for the ranking of foci by both methods. This contrasts with the Cooper, Potter, and Dupagne data, in which r = -.37.

Content dominated as the most common focus within the mixed category in both studies, accounting for about a quarter of all mixed studies.

This is reasonable as it might be argued that a content analysis offers the simplest domain in which to mix quantitative and qualitative methods. On one hand, a researcher might conduct a computer-aided analysis and enhance it with a discussion of a few excerpts.

On the other hand, a researcher might provide a few basic descriptive statistics to introduce an extensive discourse analysis. The consistency of the ranking of foci from Cooper, Potter, and Dupagne to this study is strongest for quantitative work (r =.88) and less so for the mixed (r =. 38) and qualitative (r =.14) categories. This may suggest that the topical interests of quantitative researchers vary less than those of their qualitative colleagues.

First, the percentage of atheoretical studies is likely to be smaller in the last decade than in the previous years, having dropped from Cooper, Potter, and Dupagne's estimate of 72% to this study's finding of 58% (summing the three atheoretical categories). This modest change is almost entirely in the realm of qualitative research, with the percentage of atheoretical work dropping from 97% to 59%. Cooper, Potter, and Dupagne do not elaborate this result by year, but we might presume a gradual change in this category.

This study does show a mild trend away from atheoretical work, with the high of 69% occurring in 1990 and the low of 51% in 1998, with only slight rebound in 2000 to 53%. The stronger trend is located in the qualitative work, but is also present in the mixed column, shifting from 90% atheoretical in Cooper, Potter, and Dupagne to 69% in this study.

Of the theoretical work done in the quantitative mode, the majority makes use of either a hypothesis or research question. Very likely this reflects the orientation of quantitative researchers toward a deductive approach and the use of inferential statistics.

The opposite is the case for the qualitative work, perhaps reflecting the stronger orientation toward induction. Closer examination, with categories collapsed to atheoretical, presentation of a hypothesis, and formal test of theory shows dependence between use of theory and methodology. Of the qualitative work, 58% is atheoretical with 32% presenting a hypothesis and only 11% formally testing. Of the quantitative work, again 58% is atheoretical but 8% presents a hypothesis while 38% formally test. Within the mixed category, 68% is atheoretical with 21% presenting a hypothesis and 10% formally testing.

Experiments, surveys, and content analysis-with their associated contact with people and media-remain the dominant approaches in quantitative work. It is more difficult to make comparisons with Cooper, Potter, and Dupagne in the qualitative column due to the low number of observations in the earlier study.

But in the 1990s we can see that qualitative studies rarely made use of experimental or survey approaches but do present more secondary analysis and reanalysis. Mixed research tended to involve content, with direct contact with people and media content as leading sources of data.

This study also allowed a category for multiple

procedures and sources. Of the 62 studies using multiple procedures (e.g., combining a survey with content analysis), 29 (48%) were quantitative, 28 (44%) were mixed, and 5 (8%) were qualitative. Alternately, of the 60 mixed studies nearly half (45%) employed multiple procedures. A similar pattern presents itself for data sources. Of the 37 studies using multiple sources 22 (60%) were quantitative, 9 (24%) were mixed and 6 (16%) were qualitative.

Looking more closely at the multiple categories for procedure and source also reveals their characteristics. For sources of data, 20 of the 37 instances of multiple sources involve the combination of people and media content. For mixed procedures, about a quarter (23%) combine survey and content analysis. These may be agenda-setting studies (data on that detail were not collected). Another quarter combine observation and content analysis.

Finally, while a number of additional cross tabulations could be done with these data, readers are probably most interested in details on the journals examined. Two such analyses were run.

Dependence was observed between journal and use of theory as well as journal and method. The journal in which atheoretical articles appear least (4%) is Critical Studies in Mass Communication, which is strongly qualitative (91%). This observation may provide some credibility to the present study at least to the degree that observations on qualitative work do not appear to be biased against identification of the use of theory.

The journals in which atheoretical work appears most commonly are Journalism & Mass Communication Quarterly and Quarterly Journal of Speech, both with about 85% of their content being atheoretical.

If combined with its dominance in terms of the number of articles published (27% of chapters in this study), Journalism & Mass Communication Quarterly makes the greatest contribution (40%) to the body of atheoretical research in this group of eight journals. Interestingly, Journalism & Mass Communication Quarterly is also the leading venue for research using mixed methods, accounting for just over half of those studies.

DISCUSSION

Very few studies were located in which methods were mixed. Each article listed combines quantitative and qualitative approaches and is indexed by the specific methods used. For example, the first chapter is an experiment and a survey combined, the second is an experiment and a content analysis, the third was survey only, the fourth begins a series of studies combining survey and observation, and so forth.

Not one of these chapters makes reference to triangulation or presents developed rationale for combining quantitative and qualitative approaches. And interestingly, an electronic search of Communication Abstracts for the term triangulation only returns five items, one of which is not relevant, and none of which appears in the eight journals examined here.

The overarching conclusion of this analysis seems to be that scholarship in these journals has reached a roughly 60/40 quantitative/qualitative split, rarely combines these approaches, and is almost devoid of triangulation as a formal approach to research.

To what degree might this argument be more broadly true of the field? It is certainly defensible that these journals represent our flagship outlets and are appropriately considered elite by virtue of their circulation and selectivity. But it is less clear what that actually means, especially in terms of influence over doctoral pedagogy. If these journals carry more credibility and exert more influence than other journals then the results of this study are more important than otherwise. A broader study of scholarship might paint a different picture and should be an invitation to further research.

To a limited degree a broader examination can be made by looking at the chapter described above by Kamhawi and Weaver, in which a sample of 889 articles in 10 journals were examined across the period 1980-1999. That study and the present one both report about the same proportion of articles using theory, 42% here and 39% in Kamhawi and Weaver. This is a useful concurrence given the differences between the studies in time span and journals examined. Kamhawi and Weaver found 70% of the articles in their sample using quantitative methods, while this study reports 57% (27% and 41% qualitative, 3% and 2% mixed, respectively). It is likely that these differences are largely due to the different journals examined, although some sampling and coding error must also be present.

Finally, there is good agreement between studies on the prevalence of experimental methods (15% and 13%), surveys (20% and 33%), content analysis (30% and 30%), and multiple approaches (2% and 3%). Due to differences in coding, these appear to be the only specific points of comparison for these two studies.

The original impetus for this chapter came from doctoral seminar discussions on the relative characteristics of quantitative versus qualitative research in this field, with some exploration of the characteristics of triangulation. Students in the seminar were required to write research proposals for their semester work, and were asked to integrate both quantitative and qualitative approaches to at least some degree.

While this N=1 observation is about as anecdotal as possible, most if not all seminar participants had considerable difficulty in conceptualizing studies with mixed methods. In fact, discussions over the course of the semester lead most participants to the conclusion that the additional difficulties of methods triangulation outweighed any potential benefits. This particular classroom observation seems to be reflected in the characteristics of articles published over the last decade in our leading journals.

In closing, readers are encouraged to consider the possibilities for their own research that might be embodied, especially in light of a broader trend in research. This broader trend involves the everincreasing encouragement for researchers to engage in interdisciplinary work that focuses on problems.

Major funding agencies are supporting such approaches and many universities are working to lower disciplinary boundaries. This is a world of research in which the kind of multiplicity parsed out cannot be avoided. In order for researchers in mass communication to join this world of research and take advantage of its opportunities it will be necessary to move away from descriptive studies that focus on quantitative puzzles and qualitative topics and embrace this multiplicity. Given mass communicaticn's roots in so many different disciplines and approaches, this should be natural.

Chapter 2

Mass Communication Research Trends

Scholars of mass communication-and indeed other fields-seem always to be interested in knowing research trends in their areas. Which methods are used most and least often? Which areas have been more or less studied? Which statistics are most and least in use? How does funding for research compare with that of other fields, and what kinds of studies are more or less likely to receive funding? Studies published in journals provide a good, but not entirely comprehensive, data source to answer these questions. Each year hundreds of articles on a wide range of topics are published in academic communication journals.

Viewing this literature from a distance, one can discern larger patterns and. trends in mass communication research. Knowing them can help researchers and students identify areas of strength and weakness, and of abundance and scarcity, in the research. Scholars may tackle topics that a meta-analysis shows have been ignored or they may refine a method to avoid problems identified in an analysis of dozens or even hundreds of individual studies.

One problem with generalizing from published journal articles to the whole mass communication field is that books, monographs, book chapters, and convention papers are excluded. Despite this drawback, many researchers argue that journal articles are a barometer of research trends1 and reflect the evolution of communication research. For most mass communication scholars, journal articles are the main channel for reporting current research after convention and conference papers.

Several systematic reviews or meta-analyses of mass communication journal articles have already been carried out, especially in the 1970s and 1990s. This monitoring has been important in a field that changes rapidly, but many of these studies have been limited in scope. Some have analysed only one topic or one journal. The present thematic meta-analysis is wider in scope to provide a larger and more representative picture of recent research trends in mass communication. This study analyses ten major mass communication journals during the decades of the 1980s and 1990s.

These journals were chosen based on circulation, acceptance rate, and blind review process as the most widely read and highly esteemed in the mass communication field. The twenty-year time period covered by this present study was chosen to provide a long enough span to observe trends and also because the last decade has not yet been examined in detail. This time period also enables us to evaluate predictions made by previous meta-analyses about the future of mass communication research, if one keeps in mind that our findings are limited to the major journals of our field, publications whose focus most likely changes more slowly than conference papers, newer journals, and possibly books and book chapters.

META-ANALYSES OF MASS COMMUNICATION RESEARCH

Previous meta-analyses of mass communication research have focused on the following topics. Qualitative versus Quantitative Methods, The emphasis on qualitative and quantitative research in mass communication journals has interested many researchers and scholars in general. Some studies have examined changes in methodology over time. Each has found an increase in the use of quantitative research.

Cooper, Potter, and Dupagne investigated the assumption that the amount of qualitative research has increased during the past decades. They studied eight journals during the 1965-

1989 period. A systematic interval of three years was used to choose the sample from a population of twenty-five years. They did not find an expected increase in qualitative research. Instead, they found that qualitative research was actually more common in the late 1960s, but in the 1970s and 1980s quantitative research far exceeded it.

They argued that this finding did not mean that qualitative research was losing favour with researchers, but rather that the journals sampled might not have been ones that qualitative mass media researchers sought out, considering that many of the high circulation journals were still heavily quantitative in orientation during this time period.

Weaver, surveying trends in the field, urged more studies that combine qualitative and quantitative methods. Previous research has shown that very few such studies have been published.

In those studies that combined more than one method, the combinations tended to be quantitative. Weaver argued that there was an increase in research combining the two approaches in the 1980s. This trend was expected to continue. But subsequent studies have shown that qualitative research has not increased, at least not in high circulation communication journals. Their primary focus is still quantitative research, even though more researchers continue to attest to the larger role that qualitative research should be playing.

THEORETICAL FRAMEWORKS

Several reviews of mass communication research have focused on whether there was an explicit theoretical framework evident in the articles. Riffe and Freitag found that only a fourth of the articles employing content analysis included an explicit theoretical framework, and fewer than half of them had clearly stated hypotheses or research questions that guided the analysis. Overall, research in mass communication has been found lacking in theoretical development by this and other reviews.

MEDIUM

Print media have been the focus of many research studies. Weaver and Gray found that 56% of the articles between 1955 and 1974 in Journalism Quarterly dealt with print media. Electronic media or a combination of electronic and print media constituted 26%.

They attributed this dominance to numerous historical articles on newspapers, magazines, and books. Other studies have also demonstrated the dominance of research on print media in mass communication journals. But these results were derived from only one journal-Journalism Quarterly. Since then the journal has widened its scope, and in 1995 it changed its name to Journalism & Mass Communication Quarterly.

One might ask today whether studies of print media still dominate. Television is the medium with the highest exposure among most groups in society. It is only logical that it will receive attention in proportion to its reach in society. There are newly discovered areas in television research that have drawn increased interest. In the past, visual aspects of television have not received a great deal of attention.

Television has mostly been studied in terms of its verbal messages (for theoretical and methodological reasons), but now there is an increased interest in studying visual images and how they interact with the verbal content of television to affect the audience. The Internet does not seem to have dethroned television yet as a focus for research, although there are increasing numbers of communication studies about the Internet.

FUNDING

Mass communication research has traditionally received less frequent funding than any of the other social sciences, according to studies by Weaver and Gray, and Zhi and Swiencicki. Weaver and Gray, studying the period from 1954 to 1978, found only one-fourth of the mass communication studies reported in Journalism Quarterly and Public Opinion Quarterly acknowledged funding, while the average funding rate for journals from the three disciplines of psychology, sociology, and political science was 55%. Zhu and Swiencicki studied the 1983-1993 period for these two journals plus Journal of Communication, Journal of Broadcasting & Electronic Media, Critical Studies in Mass Communication, and Communication Research.

They found only 22% of the sampled articles reported funding compared to 56% in the other disciplines. In their analysis of two major journals from 1954 to 1978, Weaver and Gray found that research funding was evenly balanced among university, government, and private sources. This present study checks on this balance during the 1980s and 1990s.

METHOD

The objective of this present study is to investigate trends in published mass communication research during the decades of the 1980s and 1990s in ten major journals. We were particularly interested in the use of qualitative and quantitative methods, the presence of theoretical frameworks, the medium (or media) being studied, and acknowledgment of funding (its presence or lack of, and sources of).

SAMPLE

As mentioned earlier, many meta-analyses have focused on single journals, but generalizing from one journal to most journals in the field is questionable. Studying more than one journal allows for wider generalization. We have analysed mass communication research published in the twenty years between 1980 and 1999 in ten major mass communication journals in the United States. We have excluded book reviews, essays, and commentaries as well as articles not dealing with mass communication. "Research-in-brief" articles also were not included.

Major mass communication journals were defined as those that have a circulation of more than 1,500, employ a blind review process, and have a typical acceptance rate under 20%. Based on these criteria, the selection was made from The Iowa Guide. Four of these journals-Journalism & Mass Communication Quarterly, Journal of Communication,

Journal of Broadcasting & Electronic Media, and Critical Studies in Mass Communication-are the official publications on mass communication research of four major professional societies.

We realise that the results of this study are influenced by the sample used. From the outset, for example, excluding "research in brief" meant that a certain line of research published in the selected journals was not included in our sample. We excluded these reports because they rarely included information on many of our key variables. The choice of "major" or "big" journals also restricts the kind of research we analysed, but we thought that studying the more general and larger circulation journals (as opposed to the more narrowly focused and smaller circulation publications) would be the most representative of mass communication research since these journals likely reach more scholars in the field than the newer journals. The fact remains that our findings can only be generalized to these journals and that different results would be likely from a wider selection of journals and publications than we analysed.

For each journal, one issue was selected randomly to represent each year. Thus there are a total of 196 issues analysed in this study. A table of random numbers was used to make the issue selection for each journal. A range was set (from 1 to 4 if the journal was quarterly, or 1 to 6 if it was bi-monthly). A random starting point was chosen, and then the researchers moved down the table taking the first number that fell within the range. Twenty numbers were selected for each journal, each representing a year. A total of 889 research articles related to mass communication published in the ten journals between January 1980 and December 1999 were included in this analysis.

CODING INSTRUMENT

Variables coded for each article included the general method of research (qualitative, quantitative, or a mix of both), the data gathering procedure (survey, content analysis, etc.), the theory behind the study (if any), the source of funding, and the time period from which data were gathered. If the method by which the results were determined involved numerical or counting procedures and statistics were used to report data, the chapter was classified as quantitative. Quantitative research included mostly content analyses, surveys, and experiments.

Qualitative research involves being closely involved with the subjects to increase depth of understanding. It does not convert what is observed into numerical form in order to perform mathematical procedures. It often includes focus groups, direct observation, in-depth interviews, and case studies, as well as legal, policy, and historical research. If more than one data gathering procedure was used, the method was coded as a mixture of quantitative if all the methods were quantitative, a mixture of qualitative if all the methods were qualitative, or a combination of both qualitative and quantitative when both kinds of methods were used. For example, a survey in addition to in-depth interviews would be coded as a combination of qualitative and quantitative methods.

We also coded the communication medium studied. An article was classified as print if it dealt exclusively with print media (newspapers, magazines, trade journals). It was considered broadcast if it dealt with television and/or radio. When print and broadcast were both studied, the article was coded as a combination. Studies of the Internet were coded separately. Some studies that did not mention any particular medium were coded as "media in general." Finally, an "others" option included other mass media studies too infrequent to have their own categories. These included videotext, cinema, wire services, public relations, and video games, as well as non-media studies (such as studies of mass communication students or faculty).

Theory was among the most difficult variables to code. We specifically looked for any theory mentioned. When no theory was specifically mentioned, we re-examined whether any theory was strongly implied but fell short of being mentioned. When more than one theory was mentioned, the dominant one was coded. When more than one seemed dominant, the first one mentioned was coded.

Funding source options included university, government, and private. More than one funding source could be checked for a single article; the category "combination" was included to be used for this situation. The funding status and funding source were coded based on the acknowledgment made by the author(s) in the text, footnotes, or the endnotes.

Study length was coded as an interval variable. It was later receded for ease of analysis. The categories created were (1) less than three months, (2) from more than three months to one year and (3) more than one year.

DATA COLLECTION

One mass communication doctoral student did the coding. An intercoder reliability test of a sample of 26 articles using Krippendorf's alpha showed 78% agreement. The lowest agreement was over data gathering method (65%) and the highest agreement was over the theory mentioned (100%).

STATISTICS

Considering the exploratory nature of this study, the statistical significance level was set at.05 to minimize Type II errors (overlooking real relationships). The statistic most employed was the difference of proportions test, mainly to examine whether the changes over the decades were significant or not. These tests are usually two-tailed.

FINDINGS

Methods. It has been widely asserted and assumed that qualitative methods have re-emerged in mass communication research. This assumption is evident in U.S. mass communication programs where the number of courses in qualitative methodologies appears to be growing. Contrary to expectations, however, qualitative research was not given as much attention as quantitative research in the 1980s in the 8 journals studied by Cooper, Potter, and Dupagne. They speculated that these journals might have been biased against publishing qualitative research, and that such research might have been published in other journals that were more qualitatively oriented. But their analysis included most of the leading journals with the largest circulations in the field. A reanalysis of the 1980s using our 10 journals (7 of which overlapped with those analysed by Cooper, Potter, and Dupagne), and an analysis of the 1990s, confirms their findings.

The use of qualitative methods did not increase significantly during the twenty-year period we analysed. There was a slight increase of 4% from the early 1980s to the late1990s. Even in the 1990s, non-qualitative studies clearly dominated in the 10 mass communication journals we analysed. Incorporating 1970s data from Cooper, Potter, and Dupagne, the gap between qualitative and quantitative research seems to have increased from the 1970s to the 1980s and then leveled off in the 1990s. The use of both methods jointly in single studies has been rare, especially in the 1980s and 1990s.

Experiments ranked third, nearly doubling in frequency from the early 1980s to the late 1990s. One reason that these three methods are used the most may be related to funding, considering that studies employing quantitative methods are more likely to have received funding than those not using such methods.

Increased use of experiments is consistent with the rise of the cognitive approach that uses experiments as the main method of data gathering and also with an increase in funding of experimental research.

USE OF THEORY

The use of theory was not common, even for articles using quantitative methods. Of the 889 studies only 39% referred to a theory (30.5% specifically mentioned and 8.7% implied). Most of these theories were cited in quantitative studies, especially surveys.

The theories most frequently mentioned were ones relating to uses and effects of media, and also that only three theories (Information Processing, Uses and Gratifications, and Media Construction of Social Reality) were cited in 10% or more of the studies.

MEDIUM

The traditional broadcast and print media were most likely to be studied in leading mass communication research journals during the last two decades. Studies on broadcast exceeded studies on print in both decades. The overall difference of 13.5% between the two areas is statistically significant.

Although we are now in the age of the Internet and the World Wide Web, this was not yet reflected in mass communication research published in major journals in the 1990s.

There was a slight increase from the 1980s to almost 7% in the late 1990s, but overall studies about the Internet constituted only 2% of all the articles we analysed. Almost all of these studies appeared in the1990s, when the Internet began to be considered a mass medium.

Broadcast research exceeded print research in all the five-year intervals studied. When broadcast research increased, print research decreased, and vice versa. Looking only at the first and last time periods, it is clear that broadcast research decreased about 10% while print research remained at the same level.

The decrease in broadcast research seemed to be due mainly to an increase in research on the Internet and other media, and non-media studies.

FUNDING

For the two decades combined, only 254 or slightly more than one-fourth (28.6%) of the published studies we analysed acknowledged receipt of financial support from an intramural or extramural source.

Weaver and Gray, studying funding between 1954 and 1978, found a similar pattern: only 26% of their studies mentioned a funding source. This funding rate is also roughly comparable to the one found by Zhu and Swiencicki who studied mass communication research funding from 1983 to 1993. Overall, 22% of their studies were funded. A clear trend can be detected from our data.

There has been a gradual decrease over the years in frequency of funding. While 36.2% of all studies were funded in 1980-1984, this decreased significantly to 23.8% in 1995-1999.

Funding in the early 1980s for published studies was nearly evenly split between university, government, and private sources with no one source dominating, similar to Weaver and Gray's findings for the 1950s, 60s and 70s. They regarded this diversity in funding sources as healthy. But toward the late 1980s and early 1990s, we found government funding decreased proportionally with a small rebound in the late 1990s.

Private funding increased slightly in the late 1980s, but decreased notably in the 1990s, especially in the last half of the decade.

University funding increased steadily during the 1980s and 1990s, becoming by far the dominant funding source in the 1990s.

The dominance in university funding can be regarded as a positive development because of the freedom of inquiry usually supported by academic institutions, but as Weaver noted, the relatively low level of funding provided by universities as compared with government and private sources also restricts the kind of research that can be done.

We found no correlation between funding and the time period covered by a study. In other words, there was no significant difference in proportion of funded studies by time span of the study (less than three months, from three months to one year, or more than one year). But there was definitely a greater tendency for quantitative studies to receive funding.

DISCUSSION

This study sought to analyse and update trends in mass communication research published in ten leading journals during the past two decades, with special attention to whether the debate over approaches has resulted in changes in methods used, which media are most and least studied, how theory-guided the research is, which theories are most often relied upon, and whether funding levels and sources have changed.

One notable finding is the lack of any increase in qualitative research articles in the journals sampled and the continued emphasis on the funding of quantitative studies.

The reasons why qualitative research is not more prominent in major journals could be further investigated. Is this due to the perceived orientation of these journals or to the actual orientation of these journals? In other words, is there a "bias" among the major journal editors in favour of quantitative research or do qualitative researchers not submit to these journals because of a perceived bias, page length restrictions, or other reasons? These questions could be further examined in surveys of journal editors and qualitative researchers.

One of the limits of our findings is that using the article as the unit of analysis does not account for the space devoted to such articles.

Qualitative research generally requires more pages to report than does quantitative. Thus we would expect journals that carry fewer articles to publish relatively more qualitative research per issue.

In the six journals with lower article frequency (they carried 12% of total articles analysed), both methods of research are represented equally, while in the four journals with higher article frequency (they accounted for 88% of the sampled articles) qualitative methods are significantly less likely to be used, confirming our expectation.

Because our sample of articles came mainly from the four journals that averaged more than three articles per issue, these articles are most likely to be shorter and thus to employ quantitative methods. These findings confirm the dominance of the quantitative social science research approach in major mass communication journals in the last two decades of the

Twentieth Century. However, these generalizations can be applied only to the ten journals studied here.

Our findings may create the impression that relatively little qualitative research is conducted in the mass communication field, but it seems likely that more qualitative research is published in other more specialized (and lower circulation) journals, book chapters, monographs, and books. Our sample of journals did not include many of the journals that qualitative researchers typically read and publish in, although it did include some, such as Critical Studies in Mass Communication and Journalism & Mass Communication Monographs.

Another major finding of this analysis is the dominance of mass communication studies focused on traditional broadcast and print media, especially television, and newspapers. Will these media continue to dominate research as we enter further into the "Internet age"?

So far there has been only a slight decrease in traditional media research and a slight increase in mass communication research about the Internet. Some of the reasons may be the difficulty of conducting Internet studies, the slow acceptance of the Internet as a mass medium, the failure of the Internet to replace traditional media, and its fairly limited reach. Yet more research on new media is expected in the coming years, at least more than was evident in our sample of articles.

One indication of this is a recent analysis by Kim and Weaver of the index of Communication Abstracts from 1995 through 1999. This abstracting service includes studies broadly related to communication from more than 200 journals, as well as reports and books.

Kim and Weaver found that Internet-related publications increased rapidly from only ten in 1995 to 188 in 1999, an increase from 0.7% to 9.5%. In addition, some new online journals have emerged, such as Convergence and the Web Journal of Mass Communication Research, and much research about the Internet is published in such journals as Journal of Computer Mediated Communication and New Media & Society.

Theoretical development is probably the main consideration in evaluating the disciplinary status of the field. As our field grows in scope and complexity, the pressure for theoretical integration increases. It seems that scholars in the field should be developing and testing theories to explain the process and effects of mass communication. However, that was not widely evident in our sample.

Overall only 39% of the studies referred to any theory, and most of these references were to previously existing theories. DeFleur's analysis of the state of theory building seems to apply to our results. Most of the articles we analysed seemed to be one-shot studies without a theoretical trail. This information is not news to mass communication researchers. A 1991 survey of major scholars in the field of communication revealed that only 37% of them thought theoretical development of the field was either good or very good.

Funding is of central importance to any field of research. However, the data we have about funding for mass communication research is limited, as few studies have empirically investigated this issue, which almost all communication scholars must face. While mass communication has been growing in terms of more and new media channels, a larger labour force, and more colleges offering mass communication education, there has been no corresponding increase in the proportion of funded research. This study finds that overall funding for mass communication remains low; there has been a steady decline in proportions of funded research from the early 1980s to the late 1990s, at least that research published in major journals analysed in this study.

In addition, a balance between university, government, and private funding sources was no longer evident in the 1990s, when the university became the main source of funding. This has one advantage: unlike government and private sectors, the university typically does not have an agenda favoring one sort of research more than another. Thus, theoretical as well as applied research can be pursued, but university funding tends to be lower in actual dollars than that from private and government sources. The decline of government support for mass communication studies may be due to government funding agencies not recognizing mass communication as an academic discipline. Mass communication scholars have a long way to go before being fully recognized by funding sources within the government. The decline in private funding is harder to explain. The increase in university funding may imply that within the university, mass communication is becoming more accepted as a legitimate field. More systematic investigation as to the cause of the changes in funding patterns would be useful.

Contrary to Berelson's 1959 declaration that the field of mass communication research was "withering away,"51 the field has actually grown and blossomed in the five decades that have followed. This is apparent from the proliferation of communication schools, doctoral programs, associations and divisions in the associations, graduate student enrollment, journals, and books.

In spite of such growth, the findings of this review of mass communication research published in ten leading journals suggest considerable stability in methods, media, and funding patterns during the 1980s and 1990s, as compared with the previous two or three decades. There were some changes in methods and in the theories most and least studied, but the general picture was one of more stability than change, at least in these major journals.

It must be remembered, however, that this observation does not include the dozens of conference papers, books, book chapters, and articles in newer, less widely circulated journals. There seems to be much change already going on in the mass communication field, but not yet in the major journals of the field.

Depending on one's view of the value of continuity and change, this can be interpreted as positive or negative. It does seem likely, however, given the dramatic changes in communication media and scholarship during the past decade, that research in the major journals in mass communication will also change in the coming decade.

This study examined one issue from each of the twenty years of investigation for each of the ten journals selected. Thus while this research of mass communication research trends is one of the most ambitious so far in terms of population studied and variables examined, we are aware that the sample may be skewed in favour of quantitative research. A larger sample that includes different journals and books (and even conference research papers) would likely yield different results. We leave that formidable task to others to explore.

Chapter 3

Explicating Web Portals for Communication Research

One of the unique features of the World Wide Web as a mass medium lies in the fact that message sources are indistinct from message receivers. The Web is literally a web woven collectively by all citizens of the Internet, resulting in massive amounts of information being disseminated by both professional gatekeepers and laypersons.

For casual users interested in efficiently obtaining news and information on the net, this proves burdensome because they now have the arduous additional task of sifting through information of unknown pedigree and determining its veridicality instead of simply attending to news of established credibility.

This might be the reason why portals, which help to make sense of information avalanches by establishing gatekeeping guidelines and streamlining information flow, are among the most popular sites on the Web, and why some scholars and practitioners believe that the portal is the key organizing unit for gaining a better understanding of the new medium.

Literature suggests that although the term "portal" is widely used, a majority of existing perspectives consider the term a "buzzword" that requires little definition or explanation. This might be one reason why the term has been under-explicated and suffers from theoretical abstraction. Indeed, little progress has been made beyond early postulations of "portals like Yahoo" or portals as sites that "consist almost exclusively of absolute links to a large number of other sites." Although such definitions serve as a rudimentary starting point, they contribute very little toward a conceptual framework that is necessary for conducting a programme of research on the topic of portals.

Even as portals are increasing in their presence as well as importance, the absence of suitable ontological definitions precludes us from not only developing a "portal typology" to facilitate better conceptual understanding but also makes empirical investigation difficult. Indeed, consistent with Strauss's opinion, portals suffer from "confusing and often contradictory definitions," which perhaps explains why, even though the "portal" has supplemented the "Web site" in Internet terminology, media researchers have devoted little attention to the topic of portals.

The primary goal of this chapter is to delineate the applicability of portals as a promising venue of research in communication technology. Specifically, it proposes a classification system for portals by performing an explication based on metaphors that are useful for describing the different kinds of portals on the Web. In accordance with the metaphorbased approach, it identifies distinguishing features of portals and outlines pertinent theoretical propositions. Finally, it examines operational considerations for studying portals and advances useful propositions aimed at building a research agenda around the concept of "portals." We first discuss the importance of metaphors in communication research before explicating the concept of portals.

METAPHORS AND COMMUNICATION

Metaphors in communication have received extensive attention, from the time Aristotle proposed that they can be seen primarily as analogies, commonly referred to as the comparison theory of metaphor. Metaphors are universally employed to illustrate something novel by orienting to something more commonly understood. Indeed, as several scholars have argued, metaphors are not just pretty linguistic artifices but critical devices when faced with the task of reducing an abstract concept to something that is easily comprehensible. As Centner and Jeziorski state, "...a faculty for analogical reasoning is an innate part of human cognition...." Recent proliferation of research on metaphors has shown that metaphors are central to communication processes, and that they can be especially useful for elucidating abstract theoretical terms or concepts.

Metaphors have also enjoyed a rich history in the formulation of several mass communication theories. Indeed, Wilbur Schramm's early postulations regarding the effects of mass media were based on metaphorical allusion when he suggested that the process and effects of mass communication was similar to that of calcareous water dripping slowly from stalagmite on a cave floor. Schramm offered this metaphorical analogy to suggest that the effects of mass communication were both gradual and incremental, and hence needed study over time. Not surprisingly, several prominent theoretical frameworks and propositions in the field have employed metaphorical devices. These include "magic bullet," "two-step flow," "diffusion," "cultivation," "agenda setting," "spiral of silence," and "sleeper effect," among others.

Metaphors are akin to heuristics because they help to ease cognitive overload by allowing users to develop their own mental shortcuts. Fundamentally, metaphors are "linguistic comparisons of the form 'A is B.'" That is, although perceptions of "A" and "B" may vary based on individual differences, they are essentially two distinct terms or conceptual realms that can be linked together by deployment of metaphors.

Consistent with Boyd's belief that metaphors are essential in the comprehension of new scientific propositions, a metaphor-based approach is particularly useful when explicating technological "buzz-words" (such as "portal") that suffer from conceptual and empirical obscurity. Boyd sees the role of "theory-constitutive" metaphors as affording "epistemic access" to "important and interesting aspects of reality." Applying this rationale to Web portals, a metaphor-based explication appears to be particularly useful because portals are both relatively novel in media research and conceptually fuzzy. By classifying portals in terms of intelligible and everyday metaphors, and also by drawing out the defining features of each metaphor, such an explication has the potential to offer "epistemic access" of portals to Web users in terms of those variables that are relevant to communication research. As an alternative to the popular technique outlined by Chaffee, the metaphor-based approach to explication has certain distinct advantages:

- It leads to conceptual clarity by examining connections in terms of familiar, intelligible analogies;
- It assists in identification of distinctive features of each metaphor; and
- It better facilitates the all-important leap from the conceptual realm to the empirical domain by exemplifying-and therefore concretizing-the concept. For these reasons, we perform a metaphor-based explication of portals.

Although there are several theoretical frameworks underlying metaphor research, our approach draws on the perspective of equating a "topic" to a "vehicle." According to metaphor scholars, the purpose of employing the "topic" and "vehicle" approach is to uncover an efficient way of allowing a concept to represent those properties and underlying characteristics that are most applicable to the concept. That is, the deployment of a metaphor allows useful bits of information to be conveyed from the topic to the vehicle.

To clarify, consider the following statement: "The United States is a melting pot." Here, "United States" is the topic and "melting pot" is the vehicle. The central idea is that most people would find the meaning of the base term ("United States") to be instigated by the ease and efficiency with which they can comprehend the meaning of the vehicle ("melting pot"). That is, individuals' assessment of the United States would be based on construing it as a melting pot enmeshing various cultures, races, and identities..

Ultimately, the effectiveness of a strong metaphor lies in its potential to represent familiar features and hence answer "how things are." Indeed, as Black pointed out, the appropriateness of representational features is what may be eventually useful to elucidate the psychological and informational facets of successful metaphors. Given what we are attempting to accomplish in this chapter, we offer five metaphorical conceptions (or vehicles) of the topic of "portals" for stimulating theoretically driven social-science research on this unique venue of online mass communication. These are the vehicles of gateways, billboards, networks, niches, and brands. These metaphors are derived by a process of meaning analysis.

The particular metaphors were selected because they are most evocative and applicable to most portals, and hence most conducive to empirical examination using the variable-centered approach recommended by Nass and Mason. Thus, we identify five distinctive variables that best represent the metaphors of gateways, billboards, networks, niches, and brands.

These variables refer to the "5Cs" of control, content, community, customization, and commerce. They accentuate each of the five metaphors by meeting the exhaustiveness and distinctiveness criteria as well as by representing prominent variables in online communication.

Portals Are Gateways. At a rudimentary level, a portal can be conceptualized as a Web site that serves as a primary starting point for users connecting to the Internet. Some of the current major portals, according to this definition, include iGoogle, Yahoo!, and Netvibes. Ruefli, Whinston, and Wiggins opine that AOL and CompuServe can also be considered portals in that they symbolize entry points for their customers to get on the Web.

Cohen equates a portal to a "point of presence" or gateway access to the Internet. According to IBM, an Internet portal is "a single integrated, ubiquitous, and useful [point of] access to information, applications, and people." Connolly states that "a portal is a gateway to the Web that allows the plethora of information available on Internet and Intranet Web sites to be organized and customized through a single entry point."

These definitions suggest that the consensus perception is one where a portal is treated as a "door" to access information on the Web or to access the Web itself.

The "portals are gateways" metaphor also points to the importance of control as a principal defining feature. Control can be examined at two levels. For instance, the "gateway" can certainly exert some semblance of control because it not only dictates what features will be offered to users but also how users will access those features. At another level, users can also exercise control over the nature of their entry into the Web by choosing specific gateways whose gatekeeping practices are in line with their interests (e.g., AOL). For users, exercising such control will likely lead to greater empowerment.

Portals Are Billboards. A portal can also play a powerful role in building consumer awareness and confidence in other portals or Web sites. This is especially true of megaportals (mammoth or extra-large portals such as Yahoo! and WebMD). When users enter such a megaportal, their eyeballs are immediately captured, and the brands they see there can make an impression and conceivably stimulate clicking behaviour. This would be especially true if the megaportal enjoys perceptions of high credibility with its users, which may then influence their perceptions of the advertised portal or Web site.

Of course, portal designers and owners are aware of this marketing function that they potentially serve, and established portals enjoy high advertising demand. For the advertising site, it is difficult to build traffic on an isolated Web site. As a result, many online sellers establish alliances with portals such as Yahoo! and MSN so that they can maximize the "billboard" potential of these portals and hence increase the likelihood of their own content enjoying high visibility.

Thus, the portal is a veritable gallery that serves as a billboard advertising a diversity of content, both informational and commercial.

From a user's perspective, both the availability of content as well as the awareness of different types of content is increased because one is exposed to a variety of content from multiple vendors and information sources.

PORTALS ARE NETWORKS

Online networks are analogous to Rheingold's conceptualization of virtual communities as "social aggregations that emerge from the Net when enough people carry on those public discussions long enough, with sufficient human feeling, to form webs of personal relationships in cyberspace."

The fundamental ways in which online networks differ from "traditional" offline networks pertain to how the former are not constrained by barriers of time and space, but formed on the basis of commonality of interests. Thus, the information-delivery capability of the Internet hasn't so much built a new business as it has created new Net-based community networks.

These networks need not be comprised entirely of known others, but from shared experiences with unknown others. For example, Paul McCartney's concert at the Cavern Club in Liverpool forty years later was not broadcast on television but on the Internet, creating a shared experience for Beatles fans who know that they are part of a specific network of similar others. Therefore, a significant feature of successful portals is that they should be able to leverage commonality of interests, or "affinity," to form a network of likeminded users who come together to serve a specific purpose or share similar interests. Such users may perceive a strong sense of membership.

Membership refers to the feeling that individuals have devoted part of themselves to becoming a member, and therefore believes they have a certain entitlement to belong. As research in community psychology has shown, factors such as membership and a sense of belonging can effectively nurture a sense of community. For example, HaReshima. com is a portal that brings together a network of Jewish users to discuss such varied issues as Jewish study, Kosher resources, Jewish culture, Israel, and so on.

Portals Are Niches. Portals also have the potential to target certain specialized consumers. Researchers have suggested that targeted information may be perceived as effective because unique advertising features have been customized to the attributes of a targeted consumer segment, and the target population will make mental connections between the presented information and themselves. Correspondingly, niche marketing concentrates on select, specialized segments that are most likely to be receptive to the products/services being advertised. That is, by focusing on a specific target or niche segment, portals can offer enhanced customer-centric services.

Depending on the degree of specialization being offered, the term "portal" assumes two meanings. In addition to traditional, general interest, horizontal portals like Yahoo!, we are witnessing a rapid proliferation of vertical or niche portals. Horizontal portals cover a wide array of topics and features, and also act as repositories for an extensive range of information. In contrast, vertical portals, or vortals, are considered to represent category leaders in a given topical group or cater to a specific segment of users.

Essentially, horizontal portals (e.g., Yahoo!, Lycos, MSN) may be considered as all-purpose portals because they cater to a wide demographic segment. On the other hand, vortals cater to a specialized demographic segment, and hence are referred to as specific-purpose portals. For example, MissionAllergy.com is a vortal because it offers a wide range of services and information pertaining to allergies.

Thus, the distinction between horizontal portals and vertical portals is largely contingent on the degree of "nicheness," which relates to the specificity with which customized value can be created and delivered to each user. The element of customization is an important distinguishing feature of niche portals, because vertical portals offer more tailoring and customization features than horizontal portals. For example, MyYahoo.com is a niche portal (compared to the more generic Yahoo!) because it offers a wide range of selections customized to the individual user.

PORTALS ARE BRANDS

Branding is an important issue when considering successful portal design. Brand loyalty in the online domain is quite different from that in the analog world. Factors that affect brand loyalty in the online environment are speed, ease of use, and the ability to deliver what a user is looking for. In fact, some findings suggest that users weigh these factors more heavily, compared to other factors such as pricing advantage. That is, brand loyalty is derived from users' experiences when using the portal or site.

In fact, the portal experience becomes one of the most important means for building and reinforcing brand identity and preferences. How well the portal performs its intended function (namely, providing a gateway to the Web as in AOL, creating a vibrant community as in BET.com, or providing up-to-date information as in CNN.com) is likely to dictate the association of a particular portal with a particular identity. In effect, a portal becomes a brand name for a given category or genre of Web-based communication. Sometimes, this branding derives from corporate identity established with older media (e.g., CNN and MSNBC), but other times, new brands emerge within the Web medium (e.g. salon.com, drudgereport.com).

Thus, we may propose that the portal is the brand. The "portals are brands" classification is especially pertinent when examined from the commercial or transactional perspective. That is, a portal acts not only as a gateway but also as a one-stop shopping complex.

Users are likely to find-and fulfill-all or a specific expected domain of their transactional needs by visiting that site.

For example, the process of purchasing a used car would include product research (e.g., make, model), product discovery (finding an appropriate used car), quality check, pricing, and extended warranty.

Thus, a portal like cars.com is a one-stop full-service operation, where a potential buyer can execute every step involved in purchasing the car.

DEFINING FEATURES OF THE "PORTAL AS METAPHOR" CLASSIFICATION

Yet another way of facilitating our theoretical understanding of portals is by examining their salient features. Searle suggests that the primary function of metaphors is to "call to mind" the mechanisms which can link a metaphorical phrase to a speaker's interpretation of the particular metaphor.48 In the human-Web site interaction context, merely identifying a portal in terms of metaphorical dimensions, while ontologically useful, would still not make explicit the underlying properties of the site suggested by the metaphor.

For that to happen, the metaphor has to be drawn out in terms that can be empirically observed. Our explication thus far of metaphors enables us to distill distinct attributes that typify portals and hence specify outcomes, i.e., we can identify certain distinctive features based on what portals can do. Although there probably are other attributes that necessitate consideration, we propose that the features of customization, content, control, community, and commerce-the 5Cs-are particularly noteworthy in developing theoretical propositions and related operationalizations. Each of these important features is discussed below.

CUSTOMIZATION

The use of terms such as "proactive," "user-centered," and "user-controlled" to describe portals is an implicit recognition of their customization potential. Portals can not only empower users by giving them the ability to customise content, but they can also anticipate a user's wants and deliver relevant content. The ability to isolate individual users and target content specifically toward them is recognized as an important attribute of portals. It is therefore not surprising that the consensus opinion seems to be that "better customization makes for a better portal."

Furthermore, the elements of control, content, community, and commerce are influenced by customization. That is, presenting users the opportunity to customise information gives them greater control over their portal experience. Moreover, the customization feature can provide individualized content, can effectively build a spirit of community, and can facilitate transaction. In order to avoid being overwhelmed by "portal glut," strategies such as customization and personalization may be adopted by portals to cultivate feelings of loyalty and desire to revisit the portal site.

CONTENT

Portals cover a wide array of topics and features, and also act as repositories for an extensive range of information. Although sometimes referred to as horizontal portals, they typically feature a search engine, a directory of Web sites, headline news, weather information, stock quotes, telephone and e-mail directories, possibly map information, chat groups, message boards or forums, and sometimes e-mail service and personal Web sites. All these different content features are available as "channels" or "windows," and users can customise the portal such that they can select and arrange only those channels that interest them.

A portal can also be likened to a catalog in that it is a compendium of stored information that is up-to-date and available in multimedia formats. In a similar vein, a portal is analogous to a collection, or "an accumulation of information resources intended for a user community or a set of communities." The underlying characteristic here is that such a collection should be user-centered and user-controlled. By selecting what information they choose to receive from portals, users perform the gate-keeping function themselves. Because users can effectively act as gate-keepers, it gives them a greater choice of content.

An implicit acknowledgement here is that offering users the ability to customise their content preferences will determine their ability to navigate through a maze of information, and help them select information that will be most useful to them. This conceptualization assumes that portals are user-centered and can empower users to construct personal information systems that are receptive to individual needs by their ability to respond in an interactive manner. Thus, by providing not only a gateway to content, but also a venue where content can be created, portals offer easy access to an immense amount of information.

CONTROL

Because of their functionality, portals have the potential to offer a high degree of user empowerment compared to ordinary Web sites. Some important elements that users desire control over are exploitation, exposure, functionality, and content. Exploitation refers to how user information is used, and by whom. Users loathe the idea of their personal information being disseminated without their permission. They also demand control over how the information is used. That is, will the information be used to offer better site experiences, or will it be used to send invasive, undifferentiated messages?

Exposure, functionality, and content all relate to the degree of control mat a portal offers. These refer to how and when the user has access to customized offers or content. Exposure and functionality include being able to view recommendations based on prior behaviour, or based on the behaviors of other users with matching profiles. The degree of control is also predicated on the portal's ability to offer customized content (such as My BBC, My Lycos, My Yahoo), a feature that many users appreciate. In addition, interface functionality allows the portal to inform a user when certain events occur (e.g., a special airfare to a particular destination), and the ability to be selective about the type of content that is displayed (e.g., to receive news about their favourite sports team).

COMMUNITY

A successful portal is one capable of leveraging "community knowledge," that is, relevant knowledge that a site acquires about users with similar tastes and values, enabling them to cater to user needs. Thus, some portals not only cater to a target network of users but they also have the capability to build an awareness of community. Portals nurture a true sense of community by allowing users access to comments and activities of likeminded others. By generating an impression of community, portals help to strengthen the sense that each member of the network has a role and stake in the portal.

Furthermore, Web 2.0 technologies have made it possible for portals to carry highly specific RSS feeds relevant to a narrowly defined community. Users can now share ideas and impressions with one another by way of blog comments and other feedback mechanisms built into portals. Several newer portals such as Netvibes let users feature their sharing (e.g., Flickr) and social networking (e.g., Facebook) sites on the main page, thus converting one's portal into a reflection of one's own community.

COMMERCE

Given the vast transactional potential of the Internet, portals can also be conceptualized in terms of commerce. In general, commercial portals are password-protected, with the underlying assumption being that a single log-in can facilitate easy navigation and accomplish a variety of transactional activities. These portals also employ encryption technologies (e.g., SSL) to ensure secure transactions. Typically, commercial portals should be able to provide customers personalized product offerings from a range of available content.

For instance, an individual interested in purchasing a computer can log into Dell Online, customise a computer based on his/her preferences, and complete the transaction. Amazon.com is a proactive interface in that it tries to influence transactions by offering individuals customized recommendations. The commerce element is also inherent in B2B portals because they cater to specific businesses by offering industry-specific information and facilitating transaction (e.g., Plastics.net).

SYNOPSIS OF THE 5CS FRAMEWORK

In summary, our postulation of the 5Cs framework

resides in charting those features of metaphors that lend themselves best to empirical investigation using the variable-centered approach. Thus, when equating the topic of "portal" to the metaphor of "gateway," the attribute or feature that is most relevant is that of control. In a similar vein, when proposing how a portal is analogous to a network, billboard, niche, and brand, the features that best exemplify each of these metaphorical mappings are those of community, content, customization, and commerce, respectively.

This does not mean that there is not-or could not be-an overlap between or among these features based on the different vehicles; rather, we suggest that each of these portal metaphors accentuates one essential element more so than any other element. That is, the feature of control would be foremost in the conceptualization of a portal as a gateway but not as much to any of the other vehicles of network, billboard, niche, and brand. If the conceptualization established a feature that could potentially be equally spread across two vehicles, then it would dispossess the metaphorical allusion of its distinctiveness and hence deprive the conceptualization of theoretical clarity.

Based on the explication, we can illustrate how each portal metaphor signifies a role served by a specific (dominant) feature. Our discussion of outcome-based specifications suggests that, although each of the 5 Cs is distinctive on its own, it also is related to one (or more) features along psychological and/or ontological dimensions. The interconnectedness between-and among-the 5Cs indicates the variable nature of portals. That is, each of the 5Cs can be present in specific types of portals, with some Cs being reflected more prominently in certain types of portals, compared to others.

PROPOSITIONS FOR EMPIRICAL RESEARCH

Our conceptual exposition of Web portals is only as valid as the empirical support for theoretical propositions generated from it. A useful starting point is to consider the focal concept and ask whether it can be thought of as a variable. A portal can be conceived as a variable to the same extent that a Web site can be regarded as a variable. That is to say, when we talk about applying operationalizations to Web sites, we do so by manipulating specific elements that are assumed to be defining characteristics of Web sites. Based on our explication, then, we forward the following propositions that would benefit from empirical investigation.

P1: Each classification of a portal according to a specific superordinate category is contingent on the portal manifesting the defining feature of that particular superordinate category.

Fundamentally, a portal is a subordinate category of one of five superordinate categories (gateways, billboards, networks, niches, and brands). A superordinate category subsumes subordinate categories by making explicit certain properties or features that should be displayed by the subordinate category for membership into the superordinate group. For a portal to be seen as being included as part of a certain superordinate class, it will have to unambiguously display a distinct feature that defines that particular class. P1, then, specifies the necessary conditions for a portal to fulfill the class inclusion property of metaphors. Thus, for a portal to be included under the (superordinate) class of gateways, it should reflect the "control" element. Similarly, for a portal to be included under the class of billboards, networks, niches, and brands, it should manifest the elements of content, community, customization, and commerce, respectively.

P2: For effective portal comprehension, each of the five categorizations of portals should reflect the defining feature most closely associated with the specific superordinate classification, more so than any other feature(s).

This proposition underlines the importance of what Schon referred to as "frame conflict" and "frame restructuring" in metaphor research. That is, frame conflict arises when several different meanings of a frame are created and each meaning, while convincing and persuasive in its own right, also singularly differs from other meanings or mappings. One strategy for resolving this conflict is by identifying new features that may serve to connect the frame with its corresponding metaphor.

A frame is likely to be perceived as belonging to a unique category if it affords the distillation of a particular feature, while subsuming other features. In the context of portals, the isomorphism between a particular conceptualization and a valid operationalization is likely to be realized most effectively if users are able to pinpoint the particular (variable-based) feature that is most closely associated with that specific conceptualization.

Like P1, this proposition can also be tested empirically. Applied to our explication, then, exposure to a "niche" portal should evoke (from users) perceptions of customization to a significantly greater extent than perceptions of control, content, community, and commerce. Similarly, perceptions of control, content, community, and commerce should predominate when users are exposed to portals that are conceptualized as "gateways," "billboards," "networks," and "brands," respectively.

It should be noted that users may perceive more than one dominant feature upon exposure to a specific portal (e.g., they may rate a "niche" portal as possessing both the features of customization and commerce).

Under such circumstances, a possible "frame conflict" could lead to ambiguity regarding portal nomenclature (e.g., whether the conceptualization of the "niche" portal needs to be re-thought, depending on the primary objective of the portal). In reality, though, portal designers and producers may wish to offer combinations of elements to users (e.g., a niche shopping portal that accentuates both the features of customization and commerce to an equal degree). Such a decision may divest the portal of its uniqueness (e.g., inability to categorize the portal as either a "niche" or "brand," especially if both customization and commerce are perceived to be present equally), but ultimately, the cost-benefit tradeoff can be tested empirically.

P3: The defining feature of a given categorization of a portal should influence subsequent information processing in terms of attitudes, cognition, and behaviors. One of the aims of employing metaphors to represent a term or phrase that is not readily comprehensible is to provide a meaning analysis. Empirically, the extraction of meaning can be accomplished by measures of attitude, cognition, and behaviour (or behavioral intention).

Based on our explication, user responses to portals should eventually be contingent on the strength of the specific feature that the portal offers (or is supposed to offer). So, user perceptions of a portal in terms of attitudes, cognitions, and behaviors will be influenced by discerning the defining feature of that particular portal.

For users exposed to a "niche" portal, their attitudes toward the portal would be informed by their ability to perceive the degree of customization that is offered by the portal. Additionally, their memory for information featured on the portal site as well as their navigational behaviors (such as hyperlinks clicked on) would also be dictated by their perception of customization on the portal site.

In a similar vein, user attitudes, cognitions, and behaviors upon exposure to portals labeled as "gateways," "billboards," "networks," and "brands" should be motivated by perceptions of control, content, community, and commerce, respectively.

Although we submit these propositions based on our explication and in the hope of advancing an empirical programme of research on portals, emerging scholarship on portals has begun to examine some of these predictions. In one of the first experimental studies of portals, Kalyanaraman and Sundar operationalized a "niche" portal based on the degree of customization. Consistent with P1, they found that participants exposed to different versions of customized portals (low, medium, high) were able to recognize the degree of customized information that the portal offered, with the highly customized version evoking perceptions of the portal as a "niche" site.

In addition, participants rated customization as being the most salient feature of the portal. In accordance with P2, even though participants reported that the portal had elements of community, this feature was not rated to be a defining element of the portal compared to the customization feature. Finally, as predicted by P3, participants' attitudes and navigational behaviors were dictated by the customization feature.

That is, higher levels of customization resulted in significantly more positive attitudes toward the niche portal. Also, participants' navigational activity (such as number of links clicked on, use of search function, time spent on each site) was a direct function of customization. A similar pattern of findings was observed in another recent study. Beier examined user perceptions of online news portals by varying levels of customization and found results consistent with Kalyanaraman and Sundar.

As for P3, Beier also showed that the customization feature can influence cognition-participants' score on memory for news stories was significantly higher when the news stories were customized than when they were not. Although these findings are restricted to one of the five types of portals that have been explicated in this chapter (niche portals), they provide preliminary empirical validation to the propositions and suggest a promising programme of research for mass communication scholars interested in uses and effects of Web portals.

Although the term "portal" enjoys ubiquitous presence in current new media terminology, it has attracted surprisingly little empirical attention from communication scholars. The lack of a cohesive conceptual framework has meant that the role and meaning of "portal" has been in a state of flux. Such concerns motivated us to develop a framework for understanding portals and subjecting them to empirical research.

The methodological importance of this chapter lies in its metaphor-based approach to concept explication. This approach is particularly constructive for explicating those concepts that have not been subjected to extensive academic research but have gained the status of well-accepted buzzwords. In that sense, the explication outlined in this chapter adds to Chaffee's popular method of explication by showing how to perform a meaning analysis with metaphorical conceptions rather than theoretical-operational conceptualizations that are subject to reification. In this chapter, we have restricted our focus to "vital" metaphors-consistent with Black's contention that identification of metaphors should be conceptually interesting. Thus, while there may certainly be many other instances of the "portal as metaphor" criterion, we have sought to confine our attention to those metaphors that we believe provide not just a framework for empirical research but which also help advance theoretical understanding of both the base concept (portal) as well as the variables that emphasize the concept.

Based on our explication, then, we recommend that portals be conceptualized by drawing on the defining features of each metaphor. Rather than using popular catch-all terms such as "user-centered" or "proactive" that tend to be empirically ineffectual, we suggest that a portal be conceptualized in terms of a Web interface that takes into account the elements of customization, control, content, community, and commerce. By referring to portals in terms of one or more of these elements (by employing adjectival modifiers, as needed), we not only lessen the probability of misunderstanding or misinterpreting "hazy" terminology, but also offer a variable-centered approach to facilitate empirical investigation.

The variable-centered approach affords empirical isolation of such specific variables as types of content (news versus product sales) and types of features (e.g., customization) aimed at specific outcomes such as sense of community, with consequences not only for theory development but also for business practices. For instance, Priceline.com was the undisputed market leader in its niche area (airline tickets). However, its subsequent foray into other domains (e.g., grocery shopping) eroded the site's market value even in its niche domain.

Applying the metaphors we identified earlier, the Priceline business strategy signifies a "metaphorical shift" from "niche portals" to "brand portals." This leads to some important questions, namely, the perceived trade-off between customization and commerce as well as the relative psychological importance of each of the 5Cs, providing fertile ground for empirical research.

In conclusion, and in the spirit of the metaphorical approach that stimulated this chapter, we hope to have cut the Gordian knot on portals. To that extent, this chapter is a starting point for communication research on portals and will hopefully stimulate empirical research on the emergent concept. A systematic programme of research in this direction will provide a nuanced understanding of portals in particular and the online medium in general.

Chapter 4

Communication Research: The Rhetorical Environment

No informed person questions... the indispensability of objective data-gathering and of the exhaustive statistical analysis of those data for all they are worth. The only question... raised here concerns the need to ask, "What are they worth for what?"

A few sentences later, Lynd wondered whether, in many instances, the answer to this question is "to give more lectures and to supervise the writing of more dissertations". (Should anyone, by the way, read between the lines and guess that this chapter will make the claim that the only good communication research is that which seeks to offer practical guidance in solving a real-life problem, let me be unequivocal: such a guess is way off the mark.)

Lynd's doubts about the usefulness of social scientific research in the late 1930s are essentially the same as many of those voiced by critics in the 1970s, 1980s, and 1990s. For example, the social psychologist Kenneth Gergen, in a wide-ranging critique of the social sciences as he viewed them in the early 1980s, lamented that the number of research publications in the sociobehavioral sciences has multiplied exponentially over the past three decades. Yet one is hard pressed to locate substantial gains in knowledge.

After noting the daily occurrence of major crises, both in society at large and in people's personal lives, he posed this double-barreled question:

Is it just a matter of "more hard work" before the [social]

sciences will begin to discern the constancies, the enduring principles beneath the vicissitudes of common experience? Will more time, more funding, more research, and greater theoretical effort finally allow the behavioral scientist to answer the rudiments of human conduct, and to return manifold to society its investments to date? [His laconic answer:] There is room for suspicion.

We should take careful note of the phrase, "to return manifold to society its investments." In my view, Gergen is reminding us that there may come a time when society will question whether it should continue to provide financial and other resources to support social scientific research that appears to contribute very little to enriching the quality of human life on this planet.

The distinguished psychologist Seymour Sarason, in his recent autobiography, provides a thoughtful assessment of the state of the psychological sciences. Admitting that many of his colleagues will register vigorous dissent, he deliberately walks out to the end of a limb when he declares that any field like psychology should be judged by the degree to which it understands, anticipates, and takes action in regard to changes in society.

And, more recently, in their comprehensive critique of contemporary America, The Good Society, Bellah and his associates take it as a matter of self-evident truth that "All social science is implicitly normative as well as descriptive". I refrain from piling up more quotations from credible observers.

The central issue that these and a host of other critics are addressing, epitomized in Lynd's "knowledge for what," I shall hereafter, for the-sake of convenience, designate by the shorthand term, the social relevance issue. Two cautionary notes: I am not urging that everyone is obligated to agree with the specific opinions of anyone I have cited. It is enough that we remind ourselves that such opinions have been voiced by responsible social scientists. My point is that the social relevance issue exists, and every researcher needs to give it careful thought.

Social relevance must be sharply differentiated from direct application of research results to specific problems in society. By social relevance I mean only the degree to which informed observers could say of a given example of research that it gives fair promise of casting light, now or in the future, on matters related to the quality of human life.

A theory may be highly abstract, or a set of empirical findings may make no specific reference to any real-life problem. However, such a study could still be said to have social relevance if an informed observer could perceive that it deals with concepts that constitute stepping stones toward an understanding of at least one important area of human existence.

So far I've been talking about social science in general. Since, wisely or unwisely, communication researchers commonly describe themselves as social scientists, I shall be devoting the remainder of this chapter to that area of social science we call (again, wisely or unwisely) the "discipline" of human communication studies.

More specifically, I shall be introducing and explicating the key concept, rhetorical environment, as the centre piece of a strategy-one strategy-that should make it difficult for "outsiders" to overlook the contributions of communication researchers, whether to socially relevant concerns or to significant conceptual advances. The Summer 1993 issue of the Journal of Communication, a sequel to the famous "Ferment in the Field" issue of ten years ago, is devoted entirely to the theme, "The Future of the Field."

Its pages reflect the continuing struggles of communication specialists to define exactly what it is that we do; and to convince ourselves that, whatever we are doing, it is right and proper that--at least after some repair work-we should continue doing it. There are critics who argue that we are squandering our energies on interminable controversies about the identity of our field; we should instead devote ourselves to the formidable task of producing research of uncontestably high quality. If we succeed in doing this, the argument goes, recognition of our worth will be automatic.

Colleagues in the social sciences and the humanities (and practitioners in the "real world"?) will be pounding on our doors to gain access to our warehouse of intellectual treasures. While I concede that these arguments are not without merit, a perusal of the Journal is sufficient to confirm me in the conviction that continuing the dialogue of self-criticism within our field is not only an encouraging sign of intellectual vigour, but is downright essential. Professor Beniger offers an arresting metaphor, but one that is, in my judgment, only a half-truth, when he declares:

Bibliometric studies over the past 15 years depict the field of communication as an intellectual ghetto, one that rarely cites outside itself and is even more rarely cited by other disciplines. I would agree that the great majority of scholars affiliated with the academic field of communication are cited only infrequently by authors in other fields. However, I would disagree with Beniger when he says our field is one that "rarely cites outside itself." Indeed, in my judgment, one of the indicators of our disciplinary weakness is that a very large proportion of the published research of communication scholars is top heavy with citations from "non-communication" sources. For years we have heard complaints that communication theorists have borrowed most of their seminal concepts and many of their theoretical models from "outsiders".

Nevertheless, Beniger is certainly right when he says:

Although no one discipline could possibly embrace the entire range of academic interest in information and communication, certainly any organized field that calls itself communication might be expected to play a central role. Alas, just the opposite has been true.

Assuming this state of affairs to be the case--and it is hard to deny--we now face the really gut-level question: Why? Two possible answers have been suggested: First, too much of our research, it is said, is simply second-rate work. Too much of it is trivial, or derivative, or unimaginative, or biased, or downright incompetent. It is also charged that too many of our studies are conducted in a vacuum, ignoring possible relationships with other studies or other "variables." Indeed, I myself have long criticized a goodly portion of communication research on these grounds. This, as you might guess, has been particularly true in my own specialty, organizational communication. (For example, it has suffered from its historic bias, corrected only very recently, in favour of investigating almost exclusively problems originated by management.)

But this whole argument fails to take into account that the other social sciences have been found guilty of the same crimes as those charged against the communication discipline. And yet the other social sciences enjoy, by common consent, a much higher place in the academic pecking order than do we.

The second suggested answer to the "why" question is that we have done a poor job of communication: we have failed to let the rest of the academic, not to mention the non-academic, world know of our work, even when that work is of the highest quality and when that work is clearly relevant to an understanding of high-profile social problems.

For example, your dean, Professor Wartella, delivered an address last year in Wichita that has sometimes been referred to as a "call to arms." Professor Wartella's central argument was that "communication research and scholarship can make a difference in children's media, but... they usually do not". She urged communication researchers to "put aside our paradigm debates and focus instead on the public nature of our enterprise".

She pointed to three specific examples of important public policy issues: the Children's Television Act of 1990, the development of Whittle Communications's "Channel One," and the 1992 congressional debate over the funding of public broadcasting. Then she laid it on the line:

These are but a few of the current public issues which cry out for reasoned discussions and informed communication scholarship. Yet too often communication research is either not mentioned in the discussion, is irrelevant, or uninformative, or all three.

If only I had the courage to be a plagiarist, I would be claiming authorship of those words. That the field of communication study, then, falls short of the potential it ought to enjoy, both in academe and in the larger society, seems to be an indisputable conclusion. We are on thin ice, for example, when many large foundations do not even list "communication" among the specialties available for financial support. We are on thin ice when the administrations of major universities propose abolishing departments of communication-and on several campuses in recent years, such efforts have been successful. (Do administrations consider wiping out departments of English, or psychology, or history?) We are on thin ice when, in a major university with a prestigious department of speech communication on campus, the department of political science is awarded-competitively-a grant to support a study explicitly devoted to an analysis of the rhetoric of presidential campaign speeches.

The president of the Speech Communication Association, the president of the Central States Speech Communication Association, and a candidate for the presidency of the International Communication Association, all have issued written statements in 1993 sounding the alarm bell. In the words of one of them, "Our discipline is currently under siege on campuses across the U. S. I am not so presumptuous as to offer myself as the savior of the discipline. But I will hazard a few recommendations:

- I know this is obvious, but we simply must find ways to reduce the proportion of publish-or-perish potboilers that appear in journals under our control. Simultaneously, perhaps enhancing our efforts by creating more awards for outstanding scholarship, we must find ways to stimulate the production of superior studies. This will mean, in many cases, encouraging researchers to explore innovative, non-traditional methods. (I shall come back to this later, with special reference to the concept of rhetorical environment.)

- No doubt about it, we must indeed find ways to spread the word, in both academic and non-academic circles, when we feel confident that a given study will almost certainly meet with the acclaim of sophisticated critics, both "insiders" and "outsiders."
- We must engage in a concerted effort of "consciousness raising" among all our researchers about the social significance issue. I do not mean that every study we produce must be saturated with social significance. What I do mean is that, everytime-I repeat, every time-we select a problem for investigation, we force ourselves to confront the question: What are the probabilities that this study will emerge with findings that, directly or indirectly, now or in the foreseeable future, will contribute to our understanding of at least one important problem facing human beings in their everyday lives?
- Then, should our study yield such findings, we must not be content to let those findings lie interred forever in the pages of an academic journal. We must initiate efforts to publicize the study, either among other academic disciplines, or in the mass media-preferably both. For decades, the traditional attitude among social scientists could be described in such terms as these: "I am the theoretician; I am the scientist. When I have completed a study, my obligation ends there. It is up to others (creatures of lesser talents, no doubt) to do what they will with the findings." This attitude is still widespread. But, in my judgment, it is one of the most vicious and irresponsible tenets ever put forth in supposedly intelligent circles. I would hope that, at least among communication researchers, it can be stamped out. (For an encouraging counterexample, we can take note of the Association of Atomic Scientists, a group of natural scientists who have striven, vigorously and unceasingly, to inform the general public about the consequences of splitting the atom.)

- Finally I am about to make a suggestion that, I am sure, will strike many of you--perhaps even all of you-as inexcusably romantic. I am going to talk about passion. That's right-passion. Suppose a researcher happens to find a subject, especially if it derives from an urgent social malaise, that arouses strong feelings. The feelings, shall we say, are unusually powerful: the researcher's inner voice cries, "This is outrageous. Something has to be done, and I must be involved in whatever that something is." This is an example of passion. Be assured: I do not for a moment propose that every researcher must be fired up with an all-consuming passion about any research problem. But, occasions do arise when a researcher is really turned on by a problem--whether it be a disastrous social condition, or a cruel life style of an oppressed group, or a source of widespread interpersonal distress. When this happens, the researcher may decide to devote most, or even all, of his or her research labors to investigating topics (within his or her area of expertise, of course) that show promise of contributing to an understanding of the problem.

Does this mean the abandonment of true research for impassioned advocacy? Not at all. To be sure, there is always this danger. The researcher may indeed, as a citizen, assume the role of advocate, but the roles of public advocate and nonpartisan scholar must at all times be separated. Let me tell you now about the case of Professor Charles Perrow.

Perrow, of Yale University, has long been recognized as one of the most distinguished organizational sociologists in the English-speaking world. He is the author of numerous studies dealing with a wide range of organizational phenomena-including the classic Complex Organizations-A Critical Essay.

Hence, the Speech Communication Association was indeed fortunate to have Perrow as a speaker at its 1988 convention in New Orleans. In a wrap-up session of a preconvention conference, he was asked by an audience member to tell us about his research plans for the near future. I can still vividly recall the substance of his response, for he spoke passionately of his conviction that the worldwide epidemic of AIDS will become, in the next century, one of the most catastrophic scourges ever visited upon humankind. He told us he was so depressed and so alarmed that he would devote all his future organizational studies to the investigation of topics related to combatting the AIDS epidemic.

This meant, he confessed, the abandonment of his current programme of research. Now that is real passion. And I have not the slightest doubt that Charles Perrow's scientific research of the future will be just as brilliant as it always has been-possibly the most brilliant of his entire career. I must now tell you that/feel almost as passionate as Perrow, when I contemplate the deplorable state of many rhetorical environments in late twentieth-century America.

But before explaining why I feel that way, I must, of course, tell you what I mean by "rhetorical environment." I use the term in the following sense: For a specified group, organization, community, or public; and at a specified time, it is frequently possible to identify a cluster of attributes that characterize most of the persuasive or argumentative discourse--that is, the rhetoric--that takes place. This identifiable cluster of attributes is what I call the rhetorical environment. It includes linguistic styles, argumentative tactics, preferences for certain topics over others, and the like.

Researchers who are interested in depicting what they believe is a specified rhetorical environment will find themselves asking a set of criterial questions. Following are examples of such questions-the list is illustrative, not exhaustive. (It will be noted that I deliberately make prominent use of examples from organizational communication.)

- What topics are most commonly at the centre of rhetorical discourse? For example, in discussing candidates for high political office, the media in recent years have engaged in feeding frenzies based on alleged sins or goofs in the candidates' private lives. In many corporations, "empowerment," "meeting global competition," "total quality," and "rightsizing" are among the current buzzwords.

- What topics, ideas, or lines of reasoning are taboo? For example, it is frequently charged that radio and television talk shows almost never feature speakers who question the basic pillars of the American system of capitalist democracy; the so-called controversies tend to focus on proposals for tinkering with the status quo. And we are all familiar with that bumper-sticker commandment: "America-love it or leave it!" In the corporate world, there are many topics for potential discussion that are off-limits to all but the very highest echelons of management. For example, even in some of the most "progressive" and "humanistic" companies, employees who are heard saying anything good about labour unions can quickly become members of an endangered species.
- What are the attitudes toward, and what are the typical ways of conducting, controversy? Is it the practice, for example, to avoid open debate about major issues, to sweep troublesome problems under the rug? If serious issues are given exposure at all, is such exposure presented in such a manner as to facilitate thoughtful analysis? We are all familiar with the two-minute, the one-minute, the thirty-second, or even the ten-second sound bite as examples of what all too often passes for serious argumentation on television. And, of course, in the organizational world, only a handful of companies or government agencies go so far as to permit-not to mention encourage-open debate on the pro's and con's of corporate policies or actions. Moreover, the suppression of dissent in many unions has been a serious blot upon the labour movement.
- To what degree is most of the rhetoric honest, fair-minded, rational?--or is most of it deceptive, manipulative, demagogic? Are opponents respected

in their rights to speak out, or are they subjected to insults or intimidation? When we apply this question to the organizational world, we find ourselves investigating the attitudes of management--whether in a government agency, in a corporation, or in a labour union--toward those organizational members who openly express dissent (the extreme case being the whistle-blower). Some years ago an organizational critic hypothesized a four-stage model representing the most typical ways in which organizations deal with dissenters.

Although not yet put to rigorous empirical test, the model is supported by much anecdotal evidence. Briefly stated, O'Day posits two phases in the handling of dissenters; and each phase contains two "rituals." Phase One he calls "indirect intimidation." Here the dissenter is subjected first to the ritual of "nullification," in which his or her statements are regarded simply as errors.

But if the dissenter persists, then the ritual of "isolation" is brought into play. This consists of cutting the culprit off from communication with other organizational members, and from various kinds of resources. If the dissenter's voice has still not been silenced, Phase Two, "Direct Intimidation" follows. The first ritual here is "defamation," featuring charges of subversion, evil purposes, psychopathology, or gross incompetence. Finally, if defamation fails to squelch the culprit, the last ritual-expulsion--is enacted; in other words, the dissenter is fired.

More questions--many more questions--remain to be asked by any researcher desiring to create a valid description of a selected rhetorical environment. But I hope enough has been said to convey a reasonably clear idea of the sort of entities I have in mind when I speak of rhetorical environments. Incidentally, those who are familiar with the exciting work of Irving Janis and his associates in developing the concept they call groupthink, will quickly recognize the groupthink experience as an example of one particular rhetorical environment.

Earlier in the chapter I confessed to feeling real passion upon contemplating what I described as "the deplorable state of many rhetorical environments in late twentiethcentury America." The logical corollary is obvious: Were I in the early years of my academic career, I know I would be passionate about devoting most of my research labors to studies that promise a high probability of improving our understanding of rhetorical environments-especially, of course, in organizations.

Why such strong feelings about this particular topic? One reason is attributable to the simple fact that, day in and day out, I am an observer--or "consumer," if you will--of a constant barrage of debased rhetoric emanating from the print and electronic media, especially television. One day a year or so ago it struck me that we are all immersed in a polluted "environment of the word," and that the most polluted area of all lies in the domain of rhetorical discourse.

It is rhetorical discourse that makes possible public policy debate, that makes possible campaigns for public office, and that makes possible virtually all organizational decision making.

Bellah and his associates, authors of The Good Society articulated my feelings with remarkable precision when they wrote of "the debasement of public discourse," declaring that "debate has degenerated into... media mass with little sustained intellectual content". I shall have a bit more to say about this later. But, at this point I think it appropriate to focus upon my area of special study, organizational communication, to identify the most influential source of my distress about rhetorical environments.

Over a period of many years (more than I like to contemplate!) I have observed hundreds of employees, including managers, in dozens of organizations. I have observed, first-hand and close-up, how human beings spend big chunks of their everyday workplace lives.

A lengthy convalescence this year gave me an opportunity to look back upon all those years of observation, to see if I could distill from them a single Grand Conclusion.

Whether or not it is a Grand Conclusion, what I came up with was this: Millions of people in twentieth-century America are experiencing innumerable miseries on the job; and, in my judgment, many of these miseries could be alleviated were it possible to modify the rhetorical environments of innumerable organizations.

Let me be more specific by recounting for you a vivid first-hand experience with two sharply contrasting rhetorical environments within the same corporation. What I shall call Division A of Company X was a large manufacturer of heavy industrial equipment, with a workforce of more than 20,000 employees.

After only a few hours in Division A I came to realise that the place was a human jungle. No one seemed to trust anyone else, and the prevailing mode of decision making featured personal insults, withholding of valuable information, and the prompt shooting down of everyone else's ideas. One index of the rhetorical environment was that many managers found it prudent to maintain "JIC" files ("Just in Case"-sometimes rendered by the less elegant "CMA"-"Cover My Ass"), to be used in self-defence. The ultimate disease symptom was the "bugging" of several lower-level managers' offices by top executives.

Division B, with about 6,000 employees, presented a starting contrast. In spite of the need for security clearance in many areas of the plant, management invited honest participation in many (admittedly, not all) decisions. Dissent, albeit within limits, was actually encouraged.

And the office walls displayed satiric cartoons lampooning managers. Most amazing of all, management even, from time to time, publicized (on bulletin boards) confessions of selected mistakes it had made. I regret to report that I have never encountered another organization with the kind of rhetorical environment that prevailed in Division B of Company X.

In recent years a small but highly respected group of organizational specialists have produced a body of writings dealing with various aspects of what I would call rhetorical environments in contemporary organizations. A good example is a book published back in 1977, Freedom Inside the Organization. It is significant to note that the author, David Ewing, was at one time an executive editor of the Harvard Business Review.

Basing much of his information on first-hand observations in many different organizations, Ewing reported in vivid detail the ubiquity of restrictions on employees' freedom of speech. He concluded that "the evidence leaves no doubt whatever that tyranny at work is an important fact of life. And in much of the workplace despotism flourishes". It is worth noting, by the way, that Ewing is no advocate of complete "democracy" as a practical mode of governance in the average organization:

There must be discipline. There must be control. There must be scope for quick and arbitrary judgments by decision makers.

Whether or not we agree with Ewing's philosophy of governance, we must concur with him--and many other organizational experts--that making employees afraid to speak up can be a formula for organizational disaster. Ah, some will object, "Ewing was writing in 1977.

This is 1993. Surely the intervening sixteen years have witnessed radical changes in management methods and organizational structures." To be sure, especially during the 1980s there occurred what can only be called revolutions in the theories and practices of organizational management. In recent years it has become almost obligatory for managements to demonstrate that they have "empowered" their employees.

The trouble is that there exists a great mass of evidence to suggest that these Glorious Revolutions have not greatly changed things in thousands of organizations. Indeed, as recently as 1988 Levering himself, coauthor of The 100 Best Companies, wrote a book called A Great Place to Work. But we need to pay close attention to the subtitle; it reads: What Makes Some Employers So Good (And Most So Bad).

How about employees fearing to speak up? Well, in 1991 a book came out under the title Driving Fear Out of the

Workplace. It reported a survey in which 70 per cent of 260 interviewees (employees working in a variety of companies) testified that they were indeed afraid to "speak up" in the workplace.

As recently as a couple of weeks ago, the Chicago Tribune provided an account of what it is like to work in many of the companies that sort mail for the U. S. Postal Service (the Postal Service is in the middle of a major policy shift, contracting out its mail sorting to private employers).

Both union officials and nonpartisan technology experts charge, according to the Tribune, that the Postal Service's new programme has resulted in creating "low-wage jobs in 20th Century sweatshops." And employees of a large California facility--which is recording a 50 per cent turnover rate in a state with high unemployment--complain of a "strict, military-style approach" toward employees.

A rich storehouse of horror stories about deplorable rhetorical environments--featuring lies, broken promises, deceptive messages, and so on--is to be found in the recent best-seller by two investigative reporters for the Philadelphia Inquirer: America--What Went Wrong?. But time does not permit the further accumulation of evidence demonstrating that the conditions Ewing observed in the 1970s can be found throughout much of the organizational world in the 1990s.

It shall suffice to quote the words of Barbara Garson, author of The Electronic Sweatshop. Speaking of the exponential growth in recent years of devices for facilitating constant (and frequently unobtrusive) surveillance of workers every moment they are on the job, Garson arrived at the following conclusion:

Among stockbrokers and middle managers, [electronic] monitoring entailed subtle loss of autonomy and signaled a decline in prestige. For clerical workers whose keystrokes are counted by the minute or airline clerks whose "stats" axe posted daily, electronic monitoring has been linked to pain, stress and serious disease.

Each of the white-collar labour-controlling devices we've so far encountered has been essentially an extension of nineteenth-century management practices. It should be obvious that an atmosphere of close surveillance is unlikely to foster a healthy rhetorical environment.

As some of you may have noted, much of what I have been talking about is commonly categorized under such headings as "organizational culture" or "communication climate."

What advantage accrues, it may be asked, in adding the concept "rhetorical environment" to these already-available designations? I concede at once that rhetorical environment can plausibly be treated as a component of either "culture" or "climate." But, as one of almost innumerable components, the strictly rhetorical aspects of culture or climate are usually given only cursory treatment--if they are mentioned at all.

Should anyone ask, "So what?" let me make explicit a basic premise that has probably been only implicit up to this point: In my judgment, the rhetorical are the most crucial of all the innumerable communication acts that take place every hour of every day in every organization. It is primarily through the exercise of rhetoric that decisions are made and actions are implemented. Hence, I am urging that the rhetorical environment be singled out for special attention, and that it be known by its own special label.

This position, I must make clear, by no means implies that rhetorical phenomena be studied in isolation from other components of cultures and climates, or that the researcher can ignore such forces as the political and economic environments in which all organizations are immersed. I shall go no further in recounting the organizational-communication origins of my passionate concern with rhetorical environments.

I propose now to conclude by suggesting a few of the many ways in which interested researchers might incorporate the concept in their work. What I am going to propose will also serve, incidentally, to add some specifics to the recommendations I made, earlier in the chapter, for enhancing the prestige and acceptance of communication research in general.

But first, some caveats. Caveat number one. Rhetorical environments are both cause and effect. Innumerable communication acts, when aggregated over a period of time, can coalesce around a cluster of attributes, thus making it possible for an observer to claim identification of a rhetorical environment.

Once created (albeit while undergoing changes m its contents) the rhetorical environment exercises, in its mm, immense-but not deterministic--influence upon the ways in which members of a given language community typically engage in rhetorical discourse. This means that researchers can focus either upon phenomena considered to be antecedents or upon those considered to be consequents of a specified rhetorical environment.

Caveat number two. As I view the concept, a rhetorical environment can never be regarded as a neatly packaged entity, amenable to precise measurement. For one thing, researchers must decide which data sources-including both observers and documentswill be used to identify a particular cluster of attributes as constituting a specific rhetorical environment.

A moment's reflection will confirm that different observers of the same social scene may (and usually will) provide different opinions on such matters as (a) whether any rhetorical environment can be identified at all; and, if so, (b) what its attributes are.

Moreover, many rhetorical environments that appear to be obvious to the researcher or other "outsiders" are totally invisible to the participants themselves.

This is likely to be the case whenever we are dealing with "unobtrusive controls" (whether in the internal governance of an organization or in society at large). Some scholars may wish to make use here of such concepts as "hegemony" and "ideology" (in any of its various meanings). On unobtrusive control in the organizational setting, researchers should consult the definitive analysis of Tompkins & Cheney.

Caveat number three. Researchers must not fall into the trap of assuming that, for any selected social entity, only one rhetorical environment will emerge--one can recall the case of Divisions A and B of Company X. Two or more distinctly different rhetorical environments will often exist, side by side, in the same group or organizational unit.

Thus, it is now acknowledged that, in many of the fabled high-tech companies in the equally fabled Silicon Valley of California, at least two cultures--hence, rhetorical environments--co-exist.

The laid-back, non-hierarchical, free-wheeling culture of the professionals--the scientists and technologists--frequently fails to percolate down to the lower-level production and maintenance workers. At these lower levels, in fact, harsh and regimented working conditions are widespread, with greatly restricted opportunities in the workplace for informal interpersonal communication or even for relaxation.

With these caveats out of the way, let me briefly sketch just a few of the ways in which researchers, if they are so inclined, might make use of the concept of rhetorical environment.

- Investigators should keep in mind that rhetorical environments can be examined in a wide diversity of settings. Although I have (understandably) drawn examples from organizations and, to a lesser extent, from public discourse, the concept can be applied to the study of families, small groups, communities, and other social entities, as well as from the more obvious cases of political campaigns, television treatment of public issues, radio and TV talk shows, and the like-not to mention organizations.
- No researcher is obligated to make a given rhetorical environment, taken as a Gestalt, the centre piece of a particular study. Indeed, I would prefer that scholars with various interests and areas of expertise would apply their talents most of the time to selected aspects of a rhetorical environment rather than attempt to encompass the whole thing at one fell swoop.

Let me cite a single, admittedly modest, example. A

team of two researchers from a business school chose to examine just one componentadmittedly a highly influential component--of what is actually the rhetorical environment (no, the authors never used the term) within a single company, the Dana Corporation. This company gives high prominence to a basic document called "The Philosophy and Policies of Dana." A significant feature is that, unlike many official corporate documents, its authorship is identified as the "Policy Committee"--a four-member group. This fact made it possible for the researchers to seek out the real-life "rhetors" and interview them. The objective was to discover what the writers perceived as the rhetorical options available to them, and what their reasoning was in making their choices among these options. In other words, here was a magnificent opportunity to track down an official document and to find out how it was actually composed. (Most of us, I am sure, would dearly love to trace many policy statements, rules, regulations, and instructions to their original authors, asking them just how they came up with such monstrosities.)

Here, then, is an example of research featuring a close examination of a quantitatively small, but qualitatively influential, component of the rhetorical environment in a real-life company. I commend the Rogers & Swales paper to future researchers seeking ideas for selecting topics relevant to rhetorical environments.

- In addition to its other features, described above, the Rogers & Swales study illustrates the application of my next suggestion: that we should encourage research projects in which two or more academic specialties are combined for purposes of analyzing the same events, or data bases, from different perspectives. Professor Priscilla Rogers, although employed in a business school, brought to the study her expertise as a rhetorical scholar; and Professor

John Swales, employed in the same business school, was able to contribute his knowledge of linguistic analysis. The result was almost certainly a more insightful study than either investigator would have produced, working alone.

What I am urging, however, goes beyond the two-member team represented by Rogers and Swales. I have in mind what may be called integrated multi-disciplinary research teams. Such teams are not simply convenient, haphazard combinations of scholars drawn from several different disciplines or theoretical orientations. Rather, they are closely-knit, carefully constructed organic entities. They would bring to bear a synthesis of different--even sharply divergent--strategies upon a concerted, or integrated, study of a commonly shared event or data base.

To indicate what I mean, one can try imagining teams made up of three or more experts representing some or all of the following specialties (the order of items is random):

An anthropologist a communication experimentalist a rhetorical critic a social psychologist a sociologist a Critical Theorist an organizational theorist a political scientist an interpersonal-communication specialist a discourse analyst an ethicist [Hold onto your hats!] a theologian.

It is my conviction that rhetorical environments are of such a nature that they are best investigated by such integrated multi-disciplinary teams-if such teams can be created!

- A corollary of the third suggestion is that communication researchers should screw up their courage (not hard to do if they are protected by tenure) and fearlessly try out non-traditional research methods. But by non-traditional I do not mean flaky. Indeed, a number of non-traditional methodologies have been successfully applied by a small number of respected scholars. For example, there is the

Socratic-dialogue-argumentative-confrontational depth interview (vs. the bloodless, neutral survey interview) employed by Bellah and associates in their Habits of the Heart. It is a technique they say they copied from the political scientist Robert Lane, author of the classic Political Ideology: Why the American Common Man Believes What He Does.

This type of interview may easily be the most appropriate for researchers attempting (a) to ferret out the dominant premises (some of which are seldom articulated) in a given rhetorical environment; (b) to learn the reasons individuals offer for their commitment to these premises; and to find out how or why individual partisans defend their adherence to positions widely regarded as "extremist." For example, it would be enlightening to conduct Socratic interviews with respondents who are strong defenders of the following pronouncement by the Rev. Pat Robertson (who campaigned in 1988 for the Republican presidental nomination):

The Iowa ERA amendment is part of a feminist agenda... that is not about equal rights for women. It is about a socialist, anti-family political movement that encourages women to leave their husbands, kill their children, practice witchcraft, destroy capitalism, and become lesbians. [Verbatim quotation as found in several newspapers and magazines]

- All rhetorical environments have histories, some brief, some extending over many years. Hence, the craft of the historian can be highly useful in many studies of rhetorical environments. When and how did a given environment apparently get started? With what persons and what events was it dominantly associated? These are a few of the questions that historically-oriented researchers might address in efforts to identify the antecedents of a given rhetorical environment.

Let me cite an excellent example of historical method

applied to the analysis of a real-life rhetorical environment. I refer to Manchester's famous depiction of the "general atmosphere of hate" that prevailed in Dallas when President Kennedy made his ill-fated visit in November of 1963. What Manchester did was to trace the antecedents of this "atmosphere of hate" (that is, rhetorical environment) in the history and culture of Dallas.

It is worth noting that this historical approach is congruent with the position advocated some years ago by a political scientist who has specialized in the study of organizations. L. B. Mohr, in his book Explaining Organizational Behaviour (1982) challenged the value of constantly multiplying conventional studies that accomplish no more than add dozens of variables to an already huge and bewildering accumulation, from which very few really robust generalizations have emerged. He urged researchers to devote closer attention to the study of dependent--rather than independent--variables.

One obviously important way of doing this is the retrospective investigation of antecedents.

- One obvious implication of the foregoing suggestion is that we should explore ways of undertaking long-term studies, in which observations are made and data gathered over periods of several years. Would such an endeavor require generous funding? It most certainly would. Probably something on the order of magnitude of the $20 million grant that Walter Annenberg announced, just a few months ago, to the University of Pennsylvania, for the establishment and support of a new "Public Policy Centre." (Incidentally, the brochure describing the Centre lists, among possible research questions, a number of topics closely related to the rhetorical environment concept.)

Therefore that we must keep constantly in mind the issue of social relevance. And that, in the concept of rhetorical environment, we have a splendid opportunity to undertake research that will be fruitful in developing socially relevant findings (while at the same time, of course, providing a context for generating respectable theories). I entertain the hope that there will be others who will share my passionate determination to do something about the deplorable state of public discourse in contemporary America. Indeed, in my soberest moments, I fear that the current rhetorical environment threatens the very survival of democracy itself. Can we, in our dual roles as nonpartisan researchers and as citizen advocates, really make a difference--a difference in the desperately urgent task of combatting an abysmal rhetorical environment that trivializes (when it does not completely smother) discussion of important public issues?

Can we dream an impossible dream? How about several universities combining forces to create something like a "Consortium for the Study of Public Discourse"? Think about the possibilities. Such an entity could become one of the preferred sources of information for both academic and mass-media representatives seeking the latest research-buttressed information. It could be a powerful instrument for attracting funding to support communication research--especially expensive long-term research. It could also disseminate, from time to time, critical--but nonpartisan--appraisals of selected aspects of the general rhetorical environment. And communication scholars could finally put to rest the question, "Knowledge for What?"

Chapter 5

The Status of Internet-based Research

Although the Internet may be portrayed as a communication technology unique to the 1990s, this depiction is somewhat misleading. The Internet's origins are in fact traceable to the 1960s development of the military-funded communication network, ARPANET, with the Internet officially making its debut as a civilian tool for communication in 1983.

However, widespread public awareness of the Internet's existence did not occur within the United States until the early 1990s when it was privatized and online services such as America Online (AOL) were developed to serve the general public. Hence, there is a tendency to think of it as a turn-of-the-twenty-first-century phenomenon.

Prior to the 1990s, early public access to the Internet was limited mostly to government agencies, universities, and computer-related organizations, such as hardware and software developers. Initially, users experienced the Internet in the form of text-based communication applications such as e-mail and navigation systems such as Telnet.

In 1992, the World Wide Web (WWW) became publicly available in the United States and began to diffuse widely in 1993 with the release of the iconbased web browser Mosaic, which made web navigation more "user friendly" and visually appealing. Subsequently, use of the Web helped to popularize the Internet in general. As use of the Internet has shifted from a small community of researchers and government employees to a worldwide community, researchers recognize the Internet as an important area in need of study. The widespread diffusion and adoption of the Internet in the United States and abroad provides scholars with numerous research opportunities.

Because the Internet functions as a channel for communication, this is especially true for the field of communication. However, as with any innovation, it can be difficult at first to know how to approach the investigation of an innovation's contribution to and effects on the society into which it is introduced. With regard to the Internet, communication researchers, as well as others, must grapple with numerous decisions, such as determining how applicable existing theories and methods of inquiry are to this newest communication technology.

While the arguments for why and how to study the Internet vary, a common theme to arise within our discipline concerns the unique opportunity that today's communication scholars have to witness and record, first hand, the introduction of a major communication technology. Scholarly journals are one forum where communication researchers record the results of their research for the benefit of current and future generations of scholars.

Published articles inform other researchers of the types of approaches being used to study a wide variety of topics, including the Internet. A number of disciplines are conducting Internet research as is evident when searching electronic databases.

For example, a simple keyword search conducted in December 1999 in the Social Sciences Abstracts database on the term "Internet" yielded a return of 969 articles published across a diversity of disciplines, most notably in the areas of business, demographics, law, and policy studies.

Each discipline, including communication, typically contains a core set of journals considered to be "leaders" among all others in terms of their coverage of subject matter, length of publication, and quality of published articles. The question asked in this study concerns how leading journals in the field represent Internet-based research conducted by communication scholars, because an important goal of scholarly journals is to document a field's evolution over time.

This study examines the content, frequency, and pattern of published Internet-based research articles-studies that focus on some aspect of the Internet-in leading communication journals for the purpose of assessing how these journals are keeping pace with the Internet's influence on the communication process. It also considers how these journals represent our response to these changes to other disciplines in the social sciences.

THE IMPORTANCE OF COMMUNICATION SCHOLARS RESEARCHING THE INTERNET

Within the discipline, a handful of articles has addressed the importance of communication scholars studying the Internet. The reasons for study as well as the ways in which the Internet should be studied are varied. For example, in 1996, the Journal of Communication devoted the majority of its winter issue to "The Net." Within this issue, in a dialogue between Newhagen & Rafaeli, Rafeali pointed out that the development of the Internet, in part, is rooted in academe and, as such, "this alone behooves our involvement" in its study.

Beyond this statement Rafeali suggested that researchers focus on what he called the "five defining qualities of communication" on the Internet which, although somewhat abstract, included "multimedia, hypertextuality, packet switching, synchronicity, and interactivity." Newhagen argued that communication researchers must take a more active role in understanding the Internet by first understanding computer architecture, an area often left to engineers.

A bridge must be constructed between the worlds of communication and engineering so that communication researchers no longer find themselves in the position "where the engineers roll out a new technology, and we hold up numbers from 1 to 10, rating it."

Concerning the benefits of studying virtual reality, Biocca stated, "Communication researchers rarely have had the chance to observe the introduction, diffusion, and sociocultural presence of what may become the next dominant communication medium." However, he cautioned against viewing new communication technologies as a revolutionary by stating that many "new" technologies build upon, and borrow from, existing ones.

As such, researchers are likely to start out using existing theories and methods to study a new technology. He suggested focusing on questions such as the shape the medium is taking, and how the medium shapes and is shaped by the user-areas well suited to communication research. In a 1993 article, writing more broadly about humancomputer interface design, Biocca, as Newhagen was to do later in 1996, called for communication scholars to be more proactive in researching computer-mediated communication (CMC) by taking part in the design and development of new communication technologies.

Although, both of Biocca's articles were written just prior to the Internet's widespread public diffusion, his ideas, as if in anticipation of its introduction, are very applicable to the Internet and have been echoed in the later writing of Newhagen and Rafaeli.

Other communication scholars assuming the importance of studying the Internet have suggested additional approaches to its study. December argued for the need to define specific units of analysis for Internet research that would act as guideposts for researchers, helping to facilitate cross study comparisons.

These four units were defined as media space, media class, media object, and media instance. He also proposed a definition of Internet-based computer-mediated communication as that which involves information exchange that takes place on the global, cooperative collection of networks using the TCP/IP protocol suite and the client-server model for data communication.

Messages may undergo a range of time and distribution

manipulations and encode a variety of media types. The resulting information content exchanged can involve a wide range of symbols people use for communication.

As such, he argued that the Internet is not a single medium but is instead made up of several media. Additionally, he cautioned that researchers studying on-line services such as Prodigy or America OnLine (AOL) should be aware that they were not actually conducting Internet-based research because these access providers offer proprietary services not available on the Internet. While this caveat is technically correct, it is perhaps overly restrictive. In addition to offering proprietary services to its users, on-line vendors such as AOL also function as Internet Service Providers (ISPs), allowing for communications to be exchanged via the global network.

In contrast to December, Morris and Ogan viewed the Internet as a single flexible mass medium capable of the synchronous and asynchronous transmission of text, audio, and video communication. They argued that the Internet provides the opportunity for communication researchers to rethink rather than abandon traditional views on mass media and to adopt a more flexible perspective on communication models. Additionally, they suggested that researchers study the Internet using a variety of existing frameworks, such as network analysis, and theories, such as social presence.

In summary, these scholars essentially argue that communication in relation to other disciplines should be a leader, if not the leader, in researching the Internet because it is a communication phenomenon. Communication scholars need to be proactive and creative in their research designs in order to reach this goal. To do this, they must possess a thorough understanding of how the technology works by taking an active role in the design and evaluation of future Internet applications.

RATIONALE

Knowledge of the extent to which Internet-related topics have been addressed and what methods of inquiry have been applied can assist communication researchers in placing their work within a broader range of studies. This information also identifies over- and under-emphasized topics and methods. Lastly, knowledge of the degree to which the Internet is represented within a discipline can provide researchers with a sense of the area's development and relative importance to the field as a whole.

It is not uncommon for communication researchers to analyse articles within an individual journal or a range of journals in order to assess the status of the discipline as a whole with respect to a particular issue. Examples of these studies include analyzing the frequency with which qualitative research is published, investigating the content and quality of published content analyses, and assessing the status of published mass communication articles by women across eight journals. Continuing this type of inquiry, this study examines the publication history of Internet research among five leading journals in the field.

JOURNAL SELECTION CRITERIA

While acknowledging the presence of newer electronic Internet and new technology-specific publications such as Internet Research and Journal of Computer-Mediated Communication, this study purposely focuses on mainstream, established communication journals. The reasons for this emphasis are threefold. First, and most obvious, the Internet is a channel for communication and as such it falls within the realm for study by communication researchers and, in turn, publication in our leading, established communication journals.

Second, established journals-those in existence for a period of decades-have the distinct advantage of having built both a reputation and a following over time. These journals are widely read within the discipline, contributing to scholars' perceptions of and currency with changes in the field. A third reason, closely related to the second, is that established journals can be viewed as historical records that document the field's evolution. Ideally, these journals reflect trends in the development of a discipline and the segments of society with which it deals as accurately as possible for the benefit of current and future scholars.

Selection of the five journals examined in this study employed two criteria: previous research identifying leading journals in the field and the reputation of Social Sciences Abstracts as a valid resource for communication research. In a content analysis of women's published research in mass communication, Dupagne, Potter, and Cooper identified eight leading communication journals, defined according to high circulation counts and low acceptance rates.

The journals identified in their study included: Communication Monographs, Communication Research, Critical Studies in Mass Communication, Human Communication Research, Journal of Broadcasting and Electronic Media, Journal of Communication, Journalism Quarterly, and Quarterly Journal of Speech. These journals functioned as a starting point for this study; however, application of the second criterion, communication research indexed in Social Sciences Abstracts, resulted in the omission of four titles from the original list.

The decision to further limit the journals examined was based on a twofold rationale. First, electronic databases are increasingly used by scholars to conduct literature searches because of their ease of use and convenience in comparison to print indexes. Within the vast realm of electronic indexes available for searching, Social Sciences Abstracts is a widely used leading index published by the highly reputable indexing service, H. W. Wilson Company. Second, subject-specific indexes, such as Social Sciences Abstracts, are typically more useful to and more likely to be used by scholars than general indexes, such as Expanded Academic Index, because they cover indexed journals in more detail, are more likely to index all articles in a journal rather than a chosen few, and they provide longer, more detailed abstracts.

By restricting the focus to leading communication journals·indexed in Social Sciences Abstracts, this study attempts to take into consideration a broader view concerning how scholars in other disciplines might perceive the role of our discipline in the area of Internet research based on the presence of communication journal articles contained in the index. With the application of this second criterion, the final list of journals examined in this study include: Communication Research, Human Communication Research, Journal of Broadcasting & Electronic Media, Journal of Communication, and Journalism & Mass Communication Quarterly.

MEASURES

This study uses December's definition of Internet-based communication but with a slightly more liberal view on what constituted Internet-based communication. An article was considered Internetbased if it focused on computer-mediated communication technologies requiring access to an ISP, including services such as AOL or Prodigy, or closely simulated an Internet-based communication environment (e.g., intranets, e-mail exchange between AOL members). This definition broadly included the Internet in general, intranets, World Wide Web (WWW), e-mail, mailing lists, bulletin boards, newsgroups, chat, virtual reality games such as multi-user domains (MUDs), and video/audio/ text computer conferencing. From the interfaces specified above, it can be seen that in most instances Internet access was necessary for communication to occur.

As with any area of research, certain information is useful in providing scholars with an overall sense of an area's progress or current status. For the purpose of this study, the concept of current status is operationalized into nine measures-author name, authorship, author rank, affiliation, topic, interface, method, total number of Internet-based articles per issue, and total number of research articles per issue.

Identification of an area's primary researchers provides scholars with a sense of which perspectives may be dominant in an area of study.

While quantity of publication by an author does not

necessarily equate with quality of research, it can provide scholars, especially those new to an area, with a starting point in the literature. The same can be said for the order of authorship on an article.

Distinguishing between primary and secondary authors can indicate, but not necessarily guarantee, which researchers are initiating studies, taking primary responsibility for the studies, and acting as primary contacts or "experts" in an area. Knowledge of which universities or organizations are conducting research in a particular area is beneficial for those interested in matters such as networking, educational, and employment opportunities.

The rank (e.g., faculty, staff, student) of an author provides information on the diversity or homogeneity of the contributors to an area of research.

RESEARCH QUESTIONS

This study attempts to answer two basic questions. First, what is the frequency and pattern, if any, of published Internet-based research articles in five of the leading communication journals? Second, what do the contents of these articles reveal about the status of Internet research within and outside of the communication discipline?

METHOD

UNIT OF ANALYSIS

The unit of analysis for this study was the scholarly communication research article that focused on Internet-based communication. This included "research in brief" articles but excluded editorials, rejoinders, and book reviews. Coders primarily read titles and abstracts to determine if an article fit this study's definition of Internetbased research. In instances where article titles and abstracts did not provide sufficient information, coders skimmed the articles for details.

POPULATION DATA

All research articles were examined in four major

communication journals between the years 1994-1999. Because frequency of publication over time was one question asked by this study, population data were used instead of sample data in an effort to obtain a more accurate depiction of publishing trends across time by these journals.

The four journals selected for the main study included Communication Research, Human Communication Research, Journal of Broadcasting & Electronic Media, and Journal of Communication.

A fifth journal, Journalism fa Mass Communication Quarterly, was selected for a pilot study to test the codebook. To identify leading communication journals publishing Internet-related articles, a basic keyword search was conducted using the term "Internet" in the Social Sciences Abstracts electronic database; four journals were consistently referenced in the search results and thus selected for closer examination. One limitation of this selection process concerns the exclusion of some communication journal titles from the Social Sciences Abstracts index.

However, this limitation was considered acceptable given the broader focus of the study discussed earlier. Despite this limitation, the five journals selected for this study are examples of the mainstream publication outlets available through most of the field's major associations: the Association for Education in Journalism and Mass Communication, Broadcast Education Association, and International Communication Association.

The starting year for the study, 1994, was selected because, based on the Social Sciences Abstracts search results, in general, Internet publications did not begin to increase until that point in time. The first recorded Internet article in the database occurred in 1992; one article was referenced in 1993. However, in each year thereafter, the number of articles increased steadily. This pattern is consistent with the growing popularity of the Internet with the general public in the United States.

The communication journals selected for study during this time frame contained a total of 961 research articles (323 from the pilot study and 638 from the main study). Each article was examined to determine if it met the definition of Internet-based research. Those articles that qualified were then coded.

OPERATIONAL DEFINITIONS

To answer the questions proposed in this study, nine measures were recorded for each Internet-based research article: author name, authorship, author rank, affiliation, topic, interface, method, total number of Internet-based articles per issue, and total number of research articles per issue. For each article the last name and initials of all authors were recorded. Authorship was coded as primary (first author) or secondary (all additional authors). The rank of each author was coded as faculty, student, staff (university affiliated, nonfaculty/non-student employees), government employee, business employee, or other. Author affiliation was recorded as the name of the university or organization with which the author was identified at the time of publication.

Rather than attempt to anticipate the range in subject matter, article topic was recorded as open text by each coder and then later grouped into six broad categories: access, adoption/diffusion, policy, research/theory, social interaction, and other. Interface, the application used to communicate via a computer, was divided into eight categories: World Wide Web, e-mail, mailing lists/newsgroups/bulletin boards, chat rooms, virtual reality game sites (e.g., MUDs, MOOs), video/audio/text-based conferencing, Internet in general (no specific interface identified), and other (coders recorded the specific interface).

Method of inquiry was coded as policy study, critique/essay (non-policy studies), interview/case study, content analysis (qualitative and quantitative), experiment, survey, other (coders recorded the specific method) and combination for multiple methods used within a single study (each method was recorded and then weighted). Lastly, for each journal issue, coders recorded the total number of Internet-based articles and overall total number of research articles.

CODING PROCEDURES

The author and another communication researcher acted as coders. The codebook was created by the author and reviewed for clarity by the second coder. A pilot test to check for intercoder reliability was conducted on all issues of Journalism & Mass Communication Quarterly, 1994-1999, resulting in a 100% overlap of 323 articles.

Discrepancies in coding were discussed, and slight modifications for the purpose of clarification were made to the codebook before proceeding to the four journals selected for the main study. Reliabilities for the number of Internet-based research articles and total number of articles for the pilot test were at the acceptable levels allowing for the inclusion of these articles in the study, under separate reporting.

Intercoder reliability for the main study was calculated using a 20% overlap. Issues for the reliability check were selected using a stratified random sample. The total overlap between the coders contained 128 articles.

INTERCODER RELIABILITY

For the main study, the level of agreement concerning which articles qualified as Internet-based research was 98.4%. Percentages of agreement and Scott's pi corrections for chance (where applicable) were as follows for the measures: author name, 97.9%; authorship, 97.9%,.96; author rank, 97.9%,.97; affiliation, 97.9%; topic, 94.3%; interface, 96.9%,.96; method, 97.7%,.97; and total number of research articles per issue, 96.9%.

For the pilot study, percentage of agreement for Internet-based research articles was 84.6% and 99.7% for total number of articles per issue.

RESULTS

Frequency analyses are reported for each measure. With the exception of overall trends in publishing, all other measures report data collected from the four journals in the main study. This is because intercoder reliability for the pilot study was only reached on the two measures: Internet-based articles per issue and total articles per issue.

TRENDS IN PUBLISHING

Of the 961 research articles analysed, 37 (3.9%) were Internet-based. Among the four journals in the main study, 4.1% (26 of 638 articles) were Internet-based. Trends in the publication of Internet-based articles across the five journals revealed no distinct pattern of increase, decrease, or stabilization during the six-year time period. This finding was also the case within each of the five journals.

Overall, the Journal of Communication (32%) published Internet research articles the most frequently followed by Journalism & Mass Communication Quarterly (30%), Journal of Broadcasting & Electronic Media (24%), Human Communication Research (8%), and Communication Research (6%). The percentage of published Internet-based research articles varied widely by year; however, a trend line reflecting a moving average suggests that the number of articles has increased over time.

TOPIC, INTERFACE, AND METHOD

Social interaction (31%) was the topic most often researched. This was followed by research/theory (23%); other (15%), which included the topics of competition among local news web sites, digital art on the WWW, TV audience feedback via email, and portrayals of the Internet in magazines; access (12%) and adoption/diffusion (12%); and policy issues (7%). The interface studied most often was the Internet in general (42%) followed by mailing lists/newsgroups/bulletin boards (19%), WWW (15%), email (12%), and chat rooms (4%), video/audio/text conferencing (4%), and other (4%) which included an Internet-based interactive health programme.

The two most frequently used methods of inquiry were content analysis (27%) and critique/essay (27%). These were followed by experiment (11%) and survey (11%), and, lastly, policy study (8%), interview/case study (8%), and combination

(8%), which included groupings such as network analysis and content analysis, and surveys and content analysis.

DISCUSSION

The results of this study present a somewhat vague picture as to where this newest area of study is positioned within the selected journals. In part, this is due to the low number of Internet articles available for examination and thus discussion.

The results also indicate that scholars searching the Social Sciences Abstracts would find a scarcity of Internet-related research in our leading journals. It may be that the infrequent and uneven publication of Internet research in the journals examined is simply a typical reflection of any field's initial attempts to come to terms with a new area of study.

This finding suggests that Internet research is an area within the field that is clearly open for study. Within the four journals analysed, only two authors stood out in total number of publications potentially providing greater opportunity for other scholars to become better known through their research in comparison to more established areas in communication. Not surprisingly, faculty are the dominant group publishing Internet research articles, but, again, because of the newness of the area student authors may have more opportunities to publish than in more established areas. While certain universities are represented more than others, it remains to be seen which programs will eventually come to the fore regarding Internet-based communication research.

In the areas of topic, interface, and methods, similar opportunities for growth exist. However, as speculated by Biocca and Morris and Ogan, thus far, communication researchers primarily are using traditional methods to study the Internet (e.g., content analysis, essays/ critiques) with a few studies employing network analysis, as suggested by Morris and Ogan.

Additionally, research has tended to focus largely on the Internet in general, leaving specific interfaces such as mailing lists and e-mail in need of attention. Topics also seem to follow widely used categories (e.g., adoption/diffusion, social interaction) in communication research. This trend may be useful for making comparisons across different types of media; however, it also risks overlooking effects that may be unique to the Internet.

The low number of Internet-based research articles (3.9%) and the sporadic publication of the articles within the five communication journals examined may be attributed to several factors. To begin with, the Internet, despite nearly a three-decade history, is still a relatively new area of study. Although the World Wide Web, which helped make the Internet popular, became publicly available in 1992, it was not until 1995 that awareness of the Internet by the media and the general public began to increase. With this increased awareness among the populace, researchers are realizing the importance of researching the Internet, but this can be a slow process.

In 1995, Dennis Davis, the editor of Journal of Broadcasting & Electronic Media, wrote in his annual summary, "One of my editorial priorities is to increase the number of articles dealing with new technologies. To do this, the number of submissions will need to be increased. This past year 10 submissions (4.9%) dealt with new industries or new technologies. Three times as many manuscripts dealt with existing industries (30 papers, 14.8%). I would like to see a more even balance between submissions dealing with old and new industries."

To its credit, the Journal of Communication published a symposium on "The Net" in its 1996 winter issue. Factoring in the timeframe necessary for the review, decision, and printing process, the calls to action contained within this issue may partially explain the noticeable increase in the publication of articles during 1998. The drop off in 1999 may be a reflection of this cycle as well, or possibly a reflection of changes in editors' interests. Still, it seems clear that some of these journals are demonstrating a desire to publish Internet-based research articles; however, as Davis indicates, perhaps few studies are being submitted.

Alternatively, it may be that a number of studies are being submitted; however, because of the relative newness of Internet-based research some of these studies may lack the theoretical grounding often desired in published works by our leading journals. A review of the literature reveals that communication researchers are attempting to unveil the parallels and distinctions between new and traditional technology theories and methodologies, but the research waters are still murky in this area. Additionally, the emergence of new technology journals such as Internet Research and New Media and Society, may serve as alternative outlets for these studies, thus siphoning off submissions to the mainstream, established communication journals. As well, given the crossdisciplinary nature of the Internet (e.g., computing, communication, human factors), depending on the topic, communication researchers may be submitting their works to journals in other fields. If this is the case, then the communication journals examined might more actively solicit Internet research submissions in an attempt to better represent the amount and type of research being conducted in this area.

While this author does not advocate the lowering of acceptance standards for research articles, communication journals could potentially foster increased publication of Internet research, following the lead of the Journal of Communication, by dedicating issues to symposia on the topic. These symposia could be viewed as debuts of Internet research that, while possibly less theoretically rigorous, would be considered valuable contributors to the development of future, more theoretically based studies.

The main point to be emphasized is that the communication research community is widely dispersed across numerous universities and organizations worldwide. Scholarly journals function, in part, as a communication link between researchers. Communication scholars interested in studying the Internet benefit most by knowing who else is researching in the area and what results have been found. Leading journals play an important role in conveying this information, but only if that information is being published. If it is the case, which remains to be seen, that Internet research is not being published because of a lack of strong theoretical foundations, then an important question needs to be addressed. Namely, how are scholars to build theory if they do not have access, which these journals can provide, to studies on which to build a foundation? The answer may lie in the emergence of topic-specific journals such as New Media and Society.

In 1996, Morris and Ogan, commenting on the Internet's growth (25 million at the time), asked, "Why, then, have communication researchers, historically concerned with exploring the effects of mass media, nearly ignored the Internet?" This is a question still in need of an answer, or possibly reformulation. We might also ask why our leading journals appear to be slow on the uptake. Notably, Wartella and Reeves, in a 1985 study that examined historical trends in publishing about children and the media, observed "that the relationship between research activity and media popularity is not simultaneous." Their findings illustrated that research related to a communication technology (e.g., film, radio, television) often lags behind the diffusion rate of the technology, a pattern confirmed in this study.

Nevertheless, Internet research appears to be an area of study with which communication researchers must become more comfortable and skilled at conducting. Unlike television, radio, or print media, the computer requires certain knowledge and skills to operate-and ultimately to study. As Biocca and Newhagen and Rafaeli argue, communication scholars are being called upon to take a more active role in the understanding and design of new communication technologies. These challenges, as well as knowledge and skills requirements, may act as barriers for some researchers who are less technically oriented. This particular barrier may be offset over time as communication programs develop tracks of study in new technologies on both the graduate and undergraduate levels that emphasize familiarity with and understanding of computer communication technologies.

Additionally, the Internet can simultaneously function as an interpersonal and mass channel for communication. This hybrid nature tends to blur the traditional lines used to distinguish different types of communication from one another. Is the Internet really a form of mass communication? Questions such as this one make it difficult for communication scholars to identify perspectives from which to study the Internet.

Finally, because Internet research is more or less in its infancy and as such lacks a strong history of research on which to build, communication researchers must be especially thoughtful about and creative in their approach to its study. They must also make the effort to network, outside of journal publications, with other Internet researchers to share research strategies and results. Certainly, not every communication researcher is interested in studying the Internet nor, given the numerous areas available for study within the field, should it be the focus of every communication scholar or the sole topic of our leading publications. However, in general, to overlook the Internet as an area for study is to be remiss as a discipline.

Before concluding, two limitations must be addressed regarding the narrow focus of the research. First, the conclusions drawn from this study are primarily limited to the five journals examined. It should be noted, though, that these journals have historically attempted to keep pace with changes in the discipline so that cautious speculations of a more general nature about the discipline's response to the Internet might be made. However, additional research examining a broader range of communication journals is necessary to confirm these speculations. Second, the definition used to identify Internet-based research excluded articles examining computer-mediated communication more generally. Future studies may wish to examine this broader category of research as well.

This study makes two primary contributions to the field. First, it informs communication scholars of the content and amount of published Internet research in leading journals that represent our research efforts both within and outside of the discipline. Second, it generates discussion concerning why the numbers are relatively low in light of earlier calls to action regarding the importance of studying the Internet. Both communication journals and communication scholars play important roles in determining where Internet research will be positioned within the discipline, as well as where the discipline will be placed relative to other fields investigating the technology. Despite the small number of Internetbased articles published by five of our leading journals during the sixyear time period examined, communication scholars studying the Internet should be encouraged in that, overall, the number of articles published appears to be increasing.

However, to more accurately reflect the Internet's importance as a research topic within the discipline, it is hoped that the findings in this study will encourage communication scholars to submit more of their Internet-based research to our leading journals while current and future editors of these journals will be encouraged to include more of these articles in their publications. As a discipline we possess the potential be a leader in Internet research, and our core journals can, and should, reflect this potential not only to scholars within the field but also to the larger academic community.

Chapter 6

The Foundation of Media Effects Research

Measurement or manipulation of exposure is the foundation of research examining effects of mediated information such as news, music videos, Internet sites, and advertising. It is equally fundamental to studies of intentional influences on that environment such as behaviour change communication campaigns. Our ability to test theory and to establish media or campaign effects is a function of our ability to successfully manipulate or measure exposure to mediated communication, and to analyse effects of that exposure.

Exposure, in principle, is a straightforward concept. McGuire's information processing model, for example, distinguishes exposure as the prerequisite for subsequent attention, comprehension, and retention. Accordingly, we may define exposure as the extent to which audience members have encountered specific messages or classes of messages/ media content.

However, operationalizing such a definition is a messy business. This definition says exposure refers to a person's merely encountering the messages, whether or not they are noticed enough to be remembered.

After all, noticing the relevant messages in the communication environment is almost certainly confounded with variables that may predict attention to the content of that message, such as prior knowledge or involvement with the topic. It is also quite possible that exposure may leave an affective if not a cognitive impression of some kind, even if the messages have not been attended to well enough to be remembered. However, if messages are not processed thoroughly enough to be recalled, how can exposure be self-reported?

As a result, operations for exposure either take the conservative position of estimating exposure from the possibility of exposure, absorbing the error associated with not actually encountering the messages of interest, or use various techniques to obtain self-reports of exposure, and then use various strategies to control the effects of selective attention due to prior knowledge or involvement which would otherwise undermine causal claims.

Each available approach involves significant trade-offs and uncertainties. Some of these strategies have recently been evolved or incorporated into studies of exposure, making a critical review of methods used to study exposure effects timely.

USING SELF-REPORT MEASURES OF EXPOSURE

The most straightforward way to assess people's exposure to mediated communication is to ask them. Given the thousands of messages and other mediated content to which an individual is exposed in a month, the accuracy of such recall is often problematic. Since exposure to messages and media is, outside of the research lab, volitional and self-selected given prior knowledge, involvement, and other variables typically associated also with outcomes of interest, the direction of causality is also problematic. The task of the media effects researcher using self-report measures is to minimize these problems insofar as possible. The issues with respect to such operations are well-recognized and will therefore be only briefly reviewed here.

Global Self-report. One may simply ask respondents how often they watch the news, play "first-person shooter" video games, or listen to conservative talk-show radio programming. Perhaps the best-known, though widely criticized, example of such analysis is found in early cultivation research in which amount of television viewing was correlated with fears concerning crime and violence. Problems include the lack of specificity regarding the actual content of media exposure represented by global self-report, which would result in underestimates of effect sizes and lack of control for third-variables and reverse causality.

One strategy to address effect size problems is to increase specificity of exposure measures. Asking about frequency of watching specific crime dramas and reality cop shows is more precise than asking about overall TV viewing if one is interested in effects of violent TV content. Specificity of media exposure measures should include separate measurement of media types (such as television, radio, and newspapers) as well as of media content. Another approach to obtaining detailed information about specific media use is media diaries. Respondents are asked to record all of their use of specified media over some time frame. Problems include motivating respondents to provide complete and accurate record keeping, and the time-consuming task of coding and entering data from such diaries.

A primary weakness in the use of global self-report measures is the inevitable uncertainty concerning the exact nature of the relevant content of the media to which respondents report exposure. This uncertainty can largely be removed when content analyses of those media are conducted in conjunction with the survey of exposure self-reports. Such content analyses permit quantification of specific elements of media content, such as valence of coverage, sources used, and ethnicity of people portrayed.

This should facilitate more precise theoretical specifications of mechanisms as well as increasing predictive power. The claim that one has characterized the content of a medium is only convincing, however, insofar as one has successfully defined a corresponding population of messages and has randomly sampled or taken a census of those messages.

RECALL AND RECOGNITION

More precise than global exposure self-reports, but also

more resource-intensive, are exposure self-reports that involve the recognition or recall of specific messages. In recognition measures, messages (or sometimes verbal descriptions of specific messages) are presented to the respondent. In recall measurement, the respondent is asked to describe content of messages that he or she has seen, which then must be analysed by coders to assess the accuracy and completeness of recall. To use these methods, one must have a relatively small population of messages from which to sample test messages (for recognition measures) or against which to compare open-ended recall measures.

Such approaches, then, are typically more appropriate for the evaluation of specific media-based campaigns than for studies of the existing media environment, unless one is interested in the impact of specific programs, articles, or other messages. In general, recognition measures appear to be preferred over recall for several reasons.

Coding of free or cued recall is time-consuming, difficult, and error-prone. More important, people who process messages with relatively little attention are likely not to remember them in the context of a free recall task, but are more likely to recognize them. Therefore, recognition measures are probably less confounded with variables related to attention such as prior interest in the topic than are recall measures, and therefore are closer to the conceptual definition of exposure.

One of the principal problems of recognition measures, however, is the tendency of people to report recognizing messages that they in fact have never seen. The primary reason is probably respondent uncertainty: people are exposed to a great many messages on most topics, and it is easy to mistake a message presented in a recognition task with other rather similar messages that one may have seen. Other possible reasons include social desirability-the belief by a respondent that he or she "should" have seen the message-or simply response set when other messages in a test group are in fact recognizable.

A simple strategy for handling this problem is through

use of foils or ringers. These are messages that could plausibly have been of the type being tested, but were never shown and are different enough from messages actually shown that legitimate confusion is unlikely.

Recognition of foils can be used as a statistical control for response set and social desirable response bias; analysis of foils in a treatment/control design also suggests that simply using a "might have seen" response category, and coding it as "never seen," can reduce error due to false recognition. Analysis of foils/ringers and "maybe" responses are useful for reducing the impact of false recognition, social desirability, and response set, but they do not address underlying problems concerning direction of causation, third variable explanations, and selective exposure.

THE DOSE-RESPONSE PROBLEM AND USE OF COVARIATES

As Hornik points out, the relationship of amount of exposure to media effects is a key applied question, on which the expenditure of many millions may depend. Establishing a "dose-response" relationship between exposure and outcomes also goes a long way towards validating the effect of a class of messages.

Unfortunately, in field contexts amount of exposure is self-selected, not manipulated. Exposure is typically a mediating, rather than a truly exogenous, variable: It may be substantially influenced by both baseline scores on an outcome variable and by many possible third variables (also known as endogeneity).

Baseline scores can only be effectively controlled in longitudinal research. Use of statistical controls or covariates can manage third variable problems-to the extent that they are well-measured, that all relevant third-variables are identified and incorporated into the model, and that no variables are mistakenly included as covariates when in fact they are mediators of effects.

This ideal scenario can only be approximated, and there is always a substantial degree of uncertainty concerning the appropriateness of one's choices of control variables. Moreover, large numbers of covariates make for cumbersome models that use up degrees of freedom and statistical power (overparameterization), and can only accurately account for variables with a linear relationship to the outcome variable.

One statistical method recently applied to exposure studies in the evaluation of the National Youth Media Anti-Drug Campaign is the use of propensity scoring. This was done because this government-sponsored campaign was national in scope and begun before the evaluation began.

Absent control groups, control over exposure levels, or a baseline, evaluators were dependent on assessing dose-response effects while trying to control for all the many variables that might predict variation in exposure to campaign advertising. Propensity scoring involves building a statistical model predicting the likelihood of a given level of exposure from a variety of exogenous variables that are likely to be related to exposure.

A single vector can be calculated from this model and applied to adjusting the outcome of interest for this propensity to be exposed.

This strategy has a number of desirable statistical qualities. Analyses are not encumbered with a long series of control variables-even if hundreds of covariates are incorporated in the model used to create the propensity score, only one propensity weighting must be used in adjusting a given analysis. Moreover, propensity scores do not assume a linear relation to the outcome as covariates do, and can be balanced over levels of the outcome variable.

Propensity scoring, then, addresses the degrees of freedom and linearity problems with covariate analyses, but remains as dependent as traditional covariate analyses on identifying all key third variables and measuring them with a minimum of error. Moreover, researchers using propensity scoring may be especially prone to inadvertently using mediators as covariates, because there is no price paid in statistical power or model complexity by adding in additional variables to the propensity score model.

A critical assumption when covariates are used is that they are all exogenous-that is, none of them in fact serve as mediators of exposure effects. For example, in political communication, one might want to use political discussion as a covariate, under the assumption that it might predict exposure to political coverage in the media as one seeks out information to use in such discussions. However, if effects of political coverage are mediated by political discussions (which might, for example, encourage incorporation of new information learned from the media into knowledge structures), then its use as a covariate or as part of propensity scoring might help eliminate media effects that in fact are present.

CAUSALITY AND ENDOGENEITY

The problem of reverse or reciprocal causality (or the endogeneity of exposure) is, as noted above, a fundamental challenge in most media effects questions. Research in selectivity suggests people are likely to seek out, process attentively, and remember information that interests or is relevant to them.

These selectivity m echanisms, then, are likely to increase self-report of exposure to a given type or class of messages. For example, consumer research shows that people who have an interest in a type of product are more likely to report having seen such advertising, more aggressive youth are more likely to seek out violent media content, and more politically involved people process mediated information with more attention.

One cannot ascertain in cross-sectional data whether exposure items are measuring exposure, or salience of the type of information conveyed to people predisposed to seek out and recall such information. For example, in political communication, cross-sectional studies that link exposure to political knowledge may inflate the strength of such relationships.

People who have an interest in and are knowledgeable about politics are probably more likely to seek out and recall mediated information, as well as having such mediated information increase their knowledge. Conversely, youth exposed to an anti-drug advertising campaign may be more likely to notice and recall such messages if they are experimenting with or using drugs, which would militate against finding favorable impacts of exposure in cross-sectional data.

In fact, one might state as a general principle that cross-sectional analyses that assume unidirectionality exaggerate the relationship between exposure and outcomes when the messages are consistent with the outcome, and underestimate it when the messages-as in many health prevention contexts-are intended to decrease a behavioral or attitudinal outcome of interest that may in turn be predictive of attention to the message.

The true relationships cannot be estimated with confidence. Structural equation models or instrumental variables may be used with cross-sectional data to estimate reciprocal paths. Causal models of cross-sectional data can provide useful initial evidence regarding the relative strength of reciprocal relationships, but can hardly be regarded as providing definitive evidence.

Longitudinal Analyses, Selective Exposure, and Causality. One approach to reducing these problems is to use longitudinal data analysis. Studying longitudinal effects of exposure on change in political knowledge or marijuana use, controlling for prior levels of knowledge or use, is more convincing with respect to causal influence than are cross-sectional analyses, as one can control the time-ordering of effects and the influence of prior scores on the outcome measures; in other words, one is testing the effects of exposure on change in the outcome variable.

The simple use of lagged prediction, however, may not go far enough; the contribution of selective exposure may be to some extent controlled (insofar as it is captured by the influence of baseline scores on the outcome variable), but it is still not understood unless it is explicitly modeled. Use of longitudinal data permits comparisons, for example, of nested structural models positing selective exposure effects versus selective exposure plus media effects paths.

In such models, model fit for a stability model plus the lagged selective exposure effect can be assessed. Fit can then be reassessed with the lagged media effect path added, and a chi-square difference test computed to ascertain whether adding the media effect path or paths to the selective exposure paths resulted in a statistically significant improvement in model fit.

Cross-lagged panel regressions, however, have been criticized as being statistically inferior to growth curve models. Growth curve models focus on analyzing individual respondents' developmental trajectories in a longitudinal data set, and identify coefficients for averaged trajectories that can serve as variables in a regression or structural equation model. Multi-level growth curve models can also separate out effects of "trait" and "state" components of predictor variables, which can be important in analyzing effects of media exposure.

For example, the author and colleagues used multi-level growth curve models to test the "downward spiral" hypothesis that while aggressiveness in adolescents tends to increase use of violent media content (selective exposure), this exposure would reinforce that aggressiveness (media effects). Use of the multi-level model made it possible to look in particular at effects of variation in aggressiveness over time and not simply at aggressiveness as a trait, which is less likely to be subject to media influence.

By modeling both selectivity and media effects, using either growth curve or more familiar cross-lagged models, one can move beyond simplistic discussions of competing causal directions and specify ways selectivity and effects of exposure to media content may reinforce each other or cancel effects out.

Instrumental Variable Approaches

Still another approach to improving causal inference in pre-post and other longitudinal designs is to utilize instrumental variables, a technique widely used in econometric analyses. Instrumental variables in the present context are variables that are associated with exposure but not with the outcome of interest. A classic hypothetical example (described by Hornik) would be an international development effort in which some members of the population are blocked from receiving a radio broadcast because of a mountain blocking radio reception.

Area of residence-if not confounded with income, social status occupation, and so on in ways that might also be related to outcomes of interest-can then serve as an instrumental variable estimating relationships between exposure and outcome, and exposure-outcome relationships can be estimated using two-stage least squares methods, irrespective of possible reciprocal relationships between exposure and outcome.

The problem is that it is often difficult or impossible to identify variables strongly predictive of exposure that are conceptually and empirically independent of the outcome of interest. As a result, exposure studies using instrumental variables to control endogeneity are at best a rarity.

THE PROBLEM OF LAGGED EXPOSURE EFFECTS

There are significant challenges to analyzing exposure using lagged longitudinal analyses, besides logistical issues such as cost, confidentiality, and respondent mortality. Effects of message exposure may be short-lived. If so, longitudinal lags (typically one-half year or more) may be too long to detect lagged effects of message exposure, especially for a message processed incidentally and with little attention, such as with advertising. A more sensitive way to capture the effects of message exposure, especially regarding short-lived effects as in the case of advertising, is to use time-series analyses. Such analyses, however, are most effective when exposure measures are not dependent on self-report, and therefore are discussed later.

Exposure and Attention: Conceptual and Analytic Issues. McGuire's information-processing model of persuasion highlights exposure and attention as the two prerequisite conditions for message influence. Some media effects research treats these variables as additive, controlling for exposure before analyzing the effects of attention. Other research argues that effects of exposure should be weighted by attention.

The latter argument is attractive at first glance. Certainly, it is likely that the degree to which exposure affects an individual is a function of the amount of attention that individual pays to the message.

However, this is also methodologically problematic. Attention is inherently confounded with the prior knowledge, interest, and attitudes that give rise to attention. Such prior variables might independently be related to the outcome of interest independent of exposure.

Weighting exposure by attention might produce effects that are primarily due to attention's antecedents, not exposure. Moreover, there are serious statistical questions raised by using multiplicative terms without using the additive terms in the same model. If such an approach is to be explored, use of the main effect terms as well as the weighted term is to be recommended.

Estimating Exposure from the Possibility of Exposure

An alternative to exposure self-report measurement is to identify or manipulate the possibility of exposure to a set of messages in a given population. The classic way to do this is through experimental manipulation in a laboratory setting or in the field.

Experimental manipulation, however, is not the only way to study possible exposure. One may use instead reach and frequency, using the traditional media planning terminology.

Studies of advertising can take advantage of data concerning amount, type, and placement of advertising available (at non-trivial cost) from Nielsen and other market research firms. If one is working in cooperation with advertisers, as in the evaluation of a counter-advertising campaign, one can use media buy records to identify levels of possible exposure.

Conceptual and methodological problems with respect to using each of these methods to operationalize exposure are discussed below.

Experimental Manipulations of Exposure

Of course, the only certain way to demonstrate causal relationships between exposure to media content and subsequent effects is through experimental designs. There are good reasons, though, that such studies do not fully dominate the media effects field.

The following briefly reviews the problems and opportunities associated with experimental manipulations of exposure.

Laboratory Experiment

Experimentation is well understood by social scientists, but it may be useful to note issues that have particular impact in research on effects of exposure to mediated messages. For example, the complexities of selective exposure, information clutter and competition, the casualness with which much information is processed in real-world settings, the social contexts in which messages are received and discussed, and the cumulative effects of exposure to many hundreds or thousands of messages over a period of years cannot typically be reproduced in the laboratory.

Experiments build theory and help elucidate processes, but these theories and models must be tested in the social environment as well.

The choice and presentation of message stimuli to which research participants are exposed in particular pose difficult problems.

There has also been considerable debate over how possible it is to cleanly manipulate message variables, and the appropriate ways to analyse message differences in an experiment.

Several researchers have argued that the key distinction is between true manipulation of a message (e.g., varying the source attribution) and operationalizing a message variable by presenting participants with various exemplars of different types of messages, such as humorous versus fear-inducing advertisements.

There is some consensus that in the latter case at least random effect models are appropriate, as the message variable has been operationalized through selection of examples rather than through a crossed experimental manipulation. Use of random sampling to create a pool of experimental stimuli to be used in an experiment more closely approximates the real media environment, and results in a more ecologically valid operationalization of exposure than would otherwise be the case.

Manipulation of exposure can be made a little less artificial by providing people messages outside of a laboratory environment. For example, some market research firms maintain panels of people who have agreed to serve as research respondents.

Respondents can be sent experimental stimuli, thus providing a high degree of control over exposure outside of a lab setting. Similar methods may be possible using respondents recruited through the Internet and then randomly assigned to experimental conditions.

Field Experiments and Quasi-experiments

The gold standard for any study of media or campaign effects is the group randomized trial, in which entire communities are randomly assigned to media treatment and control conditions.

The strength of inference such studies make possible is impressive. Communication effects are studied in "real world" community settings, with all the complexities of audience selective exposure and attention, multi-step flow, and community process intact.

Communities are in many respects a natural unit of analysis for exposure to mediated communication, as broadcast areas for radio and television, and circulation areas for newspapers, largely correspond with physical communities.

Media markets typically become the necessary unit of randomization in field experiments in which broadcast media or newspapers are involved. As noted earlier, this approach assumes that research participants have been adequately exposed to the message simply because they reside in a media treatment community.

Such an assumption makes for a conservative test, given the degree to which exposure depends on access to specific forms of media and selective attention to the messages provided.

The primary difficulty, though, is that the gold standard requires lots of gold. The expense of community intervention trials, such as those using media markets as the unit of randomization, has increased tremendously with the recent expectation that community trials be analysed using clustered or nested analyses in which the primary unit of analysis is the community.

This represents a very serious challenge for researchers. Communication interventions typically have small effect sizes. Such effects are non-trivial given the ability of such campaigns to reach much or most of a population. However, an expectation that such studies should be analysed at the community level of analysis reduces power to detect effects considerably.

The costs of community-level media intervention studies precludes in most cases obtaining an adequate number of communities to assure reasonable power. For example, the author and colleagues are currently analyzing results from a field study of 16 communities to test the effects of using media in communities and schools to reduce teen substance use.

Effects on virtually all attitudinal and behavioral outcomes are significant or highly significant when analysed at the individual level (with an N over 3,000); some outcomes of interest, though, no longer remain significant analysed at the community level (N = 16), though fortunately major intention and behaviour treatment effects remain statistically significant even at the community level.

Effect sizes even for outcomes that go to non-significant,

though, are relatively robust relative to typical campaign interventions.

Group randomized trials, then, have a substantial risk of resulting in Type II error that might mitigate against socially important findings.

Sophisticated journals will accept analyses of studies where treatments are applied at the community or institutional level (e.g., schools) that do not conduct a full hierarchical analysis of the data, but normally expect that these analyses are statistically adjusted for community-level or other clustering effects using procedures such as generalized estimating equations.

Cross-over Designs

Another model-the cross-over quasi-experimental design-has the potential to permit field experimentation in which media markets are used to manipulate exposure, but at a much lower cost than community-randomized designs. Cross-over designs, in which a control group is given the intervention treatment after post-test is completed on the original treatment group in the expectation that an effective treatment should replicate effects on the control group, are commonplace in biomedical research.

Indeed, such designs are standard when withholding the treatment entirely raises ethical problems. Such cross-over designs are, unfortunately, a rarity in media effects research. One example is a recent study of anti-marijuana advertising that compared two similar communities in Kentucky and Tennessee, one community exposed to the advertising, one the control.

This would hardly have been considered a publishable design, but for the use of the cross-over procedure. Successful replication of treatment effects in the control community eliminates many alternative explanations for treatment effects, such as uncontrolled variability between communities or history effects.

It is conceivable that history effects might have generated experimental effects first in the experimental community and then in the erstwhile control community, while simultaneously lowering effects subsequent to exposure in the original experimental community-but the probability of such a pattern seems small indeed.

As noted below, the explanatory power of this cross-over design was also enhanced by the use of time-series data collection. Cross-over designs using only a few communities exposed and unexposed to a media treatment do not rise to the same unambiguous evidentiary standard as the community-randomized designs described above.

However, they provide an attractive alternative to community-randomized designs to explore important research questions that would otherwise be impossible to study rigorously in the field given resource constraints, or when ethical or political considerations require that communities receive equivalent treatment exposure.

TRACKING STUDIES AND OTHER TIME-SERIES ANALYSES

Another technique in the cross-over study of anti-marijuana advertising was the use of rolling cross-sectional data collection and interrupted time-series data analysis to assess exposure effects. Rolling cross-sections involve collection of data at regular, closely spaced time points, such as every week or every month, typically over at least or more points in time.

Interrupted time-series can be used to statistically test for the effect of an intervention in changing the slope of the outcome behaviour as plotted against time. Such analyses can also potentially be used to estimate the "half-life" of message effects and, if carried out long enough, can identify confounds such as seasonality effects that might otherwise lead to misinterpretation of longitudinal findings.

Face validity of intervention findings are much enhanced when time-series analyses show that desired effects closely follow increasing distribution of and exposure to the messages of interest, and that these effects decay predictably when message exposure is withdrawn.

Rolling cross-sectional data collections and the resulting time-series data sets are known in the advertising industry as tracking studies.

Tracking studies take advantage of a unique aspect of paid advertising campaigns: precise knowledge, on a week-to-week basis, of advertising placements and the consequent reach and frequency, or possible exposure, of the communication effort.

Typically, tracking studies have modest objectives, testing for ad and brand recall and recognition to ascertain whether expenditures are achieving expected levels of awareness. However, such studies can also be used to assess impacts on self-reports of attitudes and behaviors.

Causality in such analytic models is relatively unambiguous, as exposure can be measured exogenously, using Gross Rating Points (GRPs) or other measures of exposure inputs, and not through exposure self-report. It is also possible to use self-report measures of exposure in time-series analyses; however, assertions about causal direction are much weaker when self-report measures of exposure are used than when reach and frequency measures operationalize exposure.

The assumption that messages placed were actually seen is an uncertain one, but should lead to conservative estimates of effects free from selectivity and other confounds.

Another approach to the use of time-series analyses to investigate exposure effects has been pioneered by David Fan. Fan and others using similar techniques assume exposure, and link rolling cross-sectional outcome data with rolling cross-sectional content analyses.

The latter poses significant logistic challenges, which have been addressed through computerized content analytic strategies using key terms to identify stories on a topic and the valence of the story. AP wire stories represent the media environment. Time-series analytic techniques are applied to test the association of fluctuations in amount and valence of media coverage with fluctuations in relevant public opinion polling that is carried out in an on-going way.

Such an approach has limitations. The AP wire is an imperfect indicator of all U.S. media coverage. There is no measurement of individual-level exposure to such news as a mediator of coverage effects on attitudes or behaviour-again, this method focuses on possible versus actual or self-reported exposure. It is possible that third variables may drive both coverage and behaviour (though this possibility can be tested through examination of evidence for a slight lag in exposure effects on outcomes).

Many of these limitations, however, should increase conservativeness of findings. The more serious limitation is that these techniques can only be employed for exposure to media for which on-line sources over time are readily available, and for outcomes that are tracked regularly through on-going surveys.

When such studies are an option, however, they permit exceptionally robust inference concerning real-world effects of media exposure on national populations.

The array of designs and analytic techniques available to study effects of media exposure permits convincing inferences when results triangulate across methods. This is illustrated in particularly concise and dramatic fashion in a recent meta-analysis of media violence studies, in which studies are separated by method, variation in effect size by method indicated, and the overall convergence of effects shown.

Media effects theories are theories of process, of cause and effect. Longitudinal designs that permit modeling of process over time or field experimental designs that permit unambiguous causal tests are where maturing theories must find their supportive evidence.

Longitudinal designs also permit-indeed, they demand-explicit theorizing regarding the role both of selective exposure and media effect.

In the realm of media campaigns, rolling cross-sections and time-series analyses offer researchers the opportunity to evaluate campaign impact with a precision that has previously been unattainable, and cross-over designs may increase the viability of quasi-experimental studies. Simple cross-sectional surveys and small-scale experiments provide excellent opportunities to ascertain if theoretical propositions and hypothesized mechanisms are viable and worthy of further exploration.

They are insufficient to test whether these mechanisms operate as hypothesized in the larger social world. Expanded use of more sophisticated designs and methods is necessary if the media effects and campaigns research area is to continue to advance.

Chapter 7

Reliability in Cross-national Content Analysis

Reliability-"when repeated measurement of the same material results in similar decisions or conclusions"---is crucial to content analysis. Most content analyses assess and report inter-coder reliability, which is usually defined as "the extent of agreement between coders" and is tested by having coders independently code a randomly selected number of content units.

Testing for inter-coder reliability is easily done when all units of content are in the same language. However, in crossnational comparative content analyses, typically dealing with material from different languages, reliability testing becomes more intricate.

Inter-coder reliability assessed for coding in one particular country (i.e., intra-country-inter-coder reliability) is not comparable with inter-coder reliability assessed in another country, because reliability tests are not conducted with identical (same language) units of content, even if sampling and testing procedures are the same across countries.

It appears crucial that inter-coder reliability in cross-national content analyses be tested cross-nationally in addition to intra-country. This, however, entails at least two further problems which will be the focus of this study. First, because a cross-national inter-coder reliability test presupposes that the testing is conducted with identical material and, thus, in one language, the coding may vary by coders' language skills and influence the reliability of coding. Therefore, it seems important to investigate the potential impact of coder characteristics such as language skills on coding reliability.

Second, sufficient inter-coder reliabilities do not rule out the possibility that coders deviate from what they are supposed to code. Even if the coding protocol guides coders as clearly as possible and coders are intensively trained, the coders as a group may share particular understandings of certain categories which they subsequently build into their coding.

This problem may be less threatening in content analyses conducted in only one country. However, the problem might multiply in cross-national comparative content analyses because in such content analyses coders often code not only in various country groups but also at different locations.

Especially in cross-national reliability tests, that face a potential influence of language skills, coders may agree because of similar language skills, but might nevertheless code differently from how they are supposed to code. For example, if coders do not precisely understand a unit of content due to linguistic troubles, they may tend to code residual categories instead of more meaningful categories.

This results in satisfactory inter-coder reliabilities and yet is a deviation from the coding protocol. A pragmatic approach to this problem is to assess the reliability between each coder and the coder trainers. We will further refer to this type of reliability as coder-trainer reliability. Thus, in a cross-national reliability test, coder trainers themselves code the test material, which requires their language skills to be excellent. Their overall coding serves as the measure of how coders deviate from the coding protocol.

A few studies have assessed in a cross-national fashion whether coders agree, but those studies did not address the concerns expressed here. This lack of attention to proper assessment of reliability in crossnational comparative content analyses may have severe consequences.

If, on the one hand, conventional intra-country-inter-coder reliabilities are not logically comparable between countries and if, on the other hand, it remains possible that coding may be endangered by idiosyncratic interpretations of the coding protocol, then country differences or similarities may merely be artifacts.

Our general goal is to examine both inter-coder and coder-trainer reliability in a cross-national setting. Our specific goal is to investigate how both are influenced by coder characteristics such as language skills, knowledge, coding experience, and coding certainty. Thus, this study provides initial insights into both the methodological implications of and potential threats to cross-national assessment of reliability.

ASSESSMENT OF RELIABILITY IN CROSSNATIONAL RESEARCH

How reliability has been tested in cross-national comparative content analyses seems even more important when taking into account that cross-national comparative content analyses often lack reported reliabilities9 or reliability coefficient and test procedures are not well documented.

Generally, one can distinguish between unilingually and bilingually organized cross-national comparative content analyses. This, in turn, affects the assessment of reliability. Unilingual projects usually entail translation of the coding protocol from the project language into the language of the content units.

Coders are not required to speak more than one language (typically their mother tongue, in which training and coding are done). Therefore, a unilingual analysis almost always involves intra-country-inter-coder reliabilities. Usually, these reliabilities are reported for all countries in the study, though some studies assess and report reliabilities for only one country, attempting to infer that coding in other countries is reliable as well.

A special case of a unilingual analysis involves translation of units of content from the various languages into the project language before being coded.

Bilingually organized projects typically apply the coding

protocol written in the project language in all countries which are part of the study.

The coders are basically required to speak the project language fluently. This, in principle, enables the researcher to conduct crossnational inter-coder reliability tests in the project language. To our knowledge, however, this has only been done in a few investigations.

In a study of the newspaper coverage of news in eight developing countries, Ogan and Fair investigated reliability with a sample of English-language news items and found an average inter-coder agreement of 80 per cent in the first check and of 93 per cent in the second check. In an analysis of French, Taiwanese, and U.S.

television commercials, Zandpour, Chang, and Catalano had two bilingual French, two bilingual Chinese and one American coder code twenty English-language commercials and assessed the cross-national inter-coder percentage of agreement for each of the three possible country pairs. Overall, cross-national intercoder agreement dropped in just one case below the 80 per cent level.

Investigating coverage of social conflict in the United States, Great Britain, South Africa, Israel, and West Germany, Cohen, Adoni, and Bantz presented a "modified form of cross-national reliability checking."

The authors argue that close collaboration and agreement among (obviously bilingual) researchers who thoroughly trained the coders guaranteed inter-coder reliability, both within and between countries.

However, cross-national reliabilities were neither assessed nor reported. Other studies also chose a bilingual organization, but either failed to measure cross-national inter-coder reliability or were too vague in their description of the testing for it to be concluded which sort of reliability was assessed.

To summarize, if inter-coder reliability is assessed and reported in cross-national comparative content analyses, it mostly tends to be intracountry, which is largely due to a unilingual organization of the projects. If inter-coder reliability is assessed cross-nationally, the studies are seldom explicit about a methodological rationale or, more or less, lack awareness of the methodological implications of doing so. Though implicitly mentioned, coder-trainer reliability is seldom assessed or reported.

Most important, the potential impact of coder characteristics on reliability in cross-national comparative content analyses has not been examined. We have found no study which addresses the possibility that both cross-national inter-coder reliability and coder-trainer reliability might be sensitive to coder characteristics.

This is hardly surprising; research on coder bias is only a marginal and scattered field of research. The few studies dealing with coder characteristics (but not from a crossnational perspective) have, for example, suggested that better educated and younger coders code more reliably than less educated and older coders. Two more recent studies have demonstrated that coders' political attitudes and preferences may influence coding.

RESEARCH QUESTIONS

Relevant coder characteristics may be identified by examining what the literature advises about selection and training of coders. For example, several researchers who assessed cross-national inter-coder reliability report recruiting bilingual coders. However, it is unclear whether bilingual refers to people who are native speakers in two languages or who only speak a foreign language reasonably well. We presume that often the latter is the case. Then, however, one may assume that the language skills of coders vary and, as a result, may influence the coding of a unit of content.

RQ1: Does inter-coder reliability [codes-trainer reliability] vary by a coder's language skills?

Usually, material for a cross-national test of inter-coder and coder-- trainer reliability is in the project language. This presumably makes coding easier for people familiar with the political and cultural background of the country of the material. If units of content deal with political news (often the case in content analyses), knowledge of political facts may be particularly influential. For example, a coder who does not know the parties of a particular country and their positions may have difficulties coding a story about controversies between these parties.

RQ2: Does inter-coder reliability [coder-trainer reliability] vary by a coder's political knowledge?

Generally, reliability increases with coder familiarity with the coding protocol, which is ensured by thorough training and coding practice. However, some content analysis literature alerts researchers that coders develop, in the course of their work (i.e., with increasing coding experience), routines that are inconsistent with the protocol, change their understanding of categories, or become subject to coder fatigue.

Although the potential influence of coding experience is of a more general nature and not confined to cross-national content analyses, we include this variable because its presumed impact on reliability has yet to be investigated.

RQ3: Does inter-coder reliability [coder-trainer reliability] vary by a coder's coding experience?

METHOD

We investigated the potential influence of coder characteristics on cross-national coder reliability with two studies. Study 1 was an exploratory attempt to check whether cross-national assessment of the two types of reliability (inter-coder and coder-trainer) provides some initial directional evidence of the influence of coder characteristics. Study 2 was a more elaborate conceptual replication of Study 1 and focused in depth on the impact of coder characteristics. Both studies are part of a project on the coverage of the European Union (EU) in television news and followed the design of a bilingual project. Study 1 (conducted in June 2000) was part of a cross-national comparative content analysis of the 1999 European election campaign. Study 2 (conducted in June and July 2001) was part of a cross-national comparative content analysis of routine coverage of the EU.

The two coding protocols were comparable yet not identical. Both were pre-tested several times and revised before use.

Several category definitions were based on earlier content analyses in which the categories had proved reliable. In both studies, student coders from various countries were intensively trained in country teams and supervised. After the coder training, conventional intra-country-inter-coder reliabilities were assessed for the country teams in each of the two studies.

Coder trainers of the country teams were three bilingual senior researchers who had helped develop the protocols. The coder trainers were in daily contact with one another to coordinate the coding in the groups. Before coder training started in Study 2, we also assessed in a separate test the coding reliability among coder trainers to determine if particular coder trainers understood certain categories idiosyncratically.

STUDY 1

Twenty-two students from ten different countries coded independently of one another two randomly selected English political television stories broadcast on BBC's 9 o'clock news. Training and coding were done at the University of Amsterdam.

The cross-national test of inter-coder and coder-trainer reliability was conducted in the course of the coding phase to check for potential effects of coding experience. Coders also completed a paper-and-pencil questionnaire to measure language skills and political knowledge.

We assessed inter-coder reliability for each story as the agreement of each coder with all other coders for each category separately and then averaged, still at the story level, across all categories.

We averaged the scores for particular categories across all categories because we were not interested in the reliability of a particular category, but in a more general account of the coding of the various categories. Computation of the reliabilities at the story level implies that, for each of the two stories, each coder received a reliability score which subsequently represented the unit of analysis. This increased the number of cases from twenty-two at the coder level to forty-four at the story level (twenty-two coders coding two stories).

Reliabilities were computed at the story level for three reasons. First, when working with foreign language material it may be that a particular story is not comprehended well. This, however, would strongly influence inter-coder reliability scores computed at the coder level whereas it is taken into account at the story level.

Second, analyzing intercoder reliability at the story level preserves information which would be lost in an analysis at the coder level where a particular coder's coding of a certain category is averaged across all stories. Third, inter-coder reliability is usually assessed at the coder level when few coders code many stories. In our case, however, many coders coded few stories.

Coder-trainer reliability was, also at the story level, operationalized as agreement between the coding of a particular coder and the overall coding of the coder trainers. Coder trainers coded the stories independently of one another. The few disagreements were subsequently resolved by strict adherence to the coding protocol.

Strict adherence precluded the possibility that a potential particular understanding of categories among coder trainers would be built in their coding, which eventually could have rendered their coding unreliable. Coder-trainer reliability, too, was first assessed for each category separately and then averaged across categories.

Both inter-coder and coder-trainer reliability were measured for thirty-one categories, all of which were at a nominal level of measurement. We excluded some categories from further analysis when, in the two stories, all coders had given the same score because such categories cannot be considered "variable."

The coded categories were, for example, topic, location,

main actor, responsibility for problems and for the solution of problems, conflict, or depiction of emotions.

An additive language skills index with values ranging from 0 to 20 was created from four self-report items tapping listening and reading comprehension and speaking and writing fluency.

Admittedly, self-reported measures may be subject to distortion. However, we checked the accuracy of the coders' selfreported skills by having one coder trainer rate the language skills of each coder on a scale (0 indicates very bad, 10 was average, and 20 was very good). A comparison between coder trainer ratings and the coders' selfreports revealed strong agreement.

Ten "fill-in-the-blank" questions about British political matters were used to assess political knowledge. The questions dealt with the British head of state; the meaning of the terms "GM food," "Tories," and "SNP"; the British party system; the Commonwealth of Nations; the population of the United Kingdom; former British prime ministers; the structure of the British parliament; and the accession date of the United Kingdom to the European Union.

The political knowledge scale was constructed by summing the number of correct responses (0 to 10). Coding experience was operationalized as the total hours worked as indicated on coders' pay slips. Considering language skills, political knowledge, coding experience, and the two reliability measures as metric variables, we estimated two regression models with each of the two reliability measures as dependent variable.

Across all categories and coders,average agreement among coders was 70% and average agreement between coders and coder trainers was 72%.

Because Study 1 was an initial check for evidence of an influence of coder characteristics on reliability, we were more concerned with the overall pattern and the directional consistency of potential effects than with their size or significance (with only two stories coded by twenty-two coders, it is unlikely that any effects would have reached conventional significance levels). As the standardized multiple regression coefficients, all predictors were positively related to both inter-coder and coder-trainer reliability.

More specifically, the study suggests that coders' language skills and coding experience may influence coder--trainer reliability and, to a lesser extent, inter-coder reliability. The effect of language skills was as expected, while the positive impact of coding experience is counter to the coder fatigue notion.

However, given that the coders coded only two stories, the findings should only be regarded as illustrative. Furthermore, our language skill measure may be biased because it was self-reported and the robustness of the results should be viewed with caution.

STUDY 2

The first goal of Study 2 was to replicate conceptually Study 1 with a greater number of coded stories and a more valid measure of language skills. Study 1 yielded initial evidence language skills may influence inter-coder reliability positively because elaborate language skills increase the likelihood of identical coding.

Conversely, restricted language skills may, in the extreme, result in the equivalent of random coding. Coder-trainer reliability will be positively affected by language skills because coders with more elaborated language skills are more likely to code in line with the coder trainers than coders with restricted language skills.

H1: The better a coder's language skills, the higher his / her inter-coder reliability [coder-trainer reliability] will be.

Study 1 provided weak but directionally consistent evidence that more politically knowledgeable coders coded more reliably. Because political knowledge generally facilitates processing of political news, we expect more knowledgeable coders to display higher degrees of reliability. Both inter-coder and coder-trainer reliability will be positively affected because greater political knowledge increases likelihood of. identical coding decisions while low political knowledge may lead to more random coding decisions (particularly when material was broadcast in a foreign country).

H2: The higher a coder's political knowledge, the higher his/her inter-coder reliability [coder-trainer reliability] will be.

Contrary to intuitive notions of coder fatigue, our exploratory first study provided initial evidence that coding experience increases reliability. It is unclear whether something like a critical point might exist after which reliability decreases as coding experience increases, or where such an inflection point might occur. In order to display symptoms of coder fatigue, coders may have to work far more than those studied here. Based on the findings of our first study, however, we assume that coding experience increases the likelihood of decisions identical to those of other coders and of coder trainers.

H3: The higher a coder's coding experience, the higher his/her inter-coder reliability [coder-trainer reliability] will be.

Study 2's second goal was to investigate more carefully how effects on inter-coder and coder-trainer reliability may occur. We focused on the effects of language skills as the key independent variable in this study. Political knowledge and coding experience are of more general nature and were treated as control variables. More specifically, we examined whether language skills have a direct or indirect influence on inter-coder and coder-trainer reliability. Particularly with foreign-language material, it may be that language skills do not affect inter-coder and coder-- trainer reliability per se, but rather influence the certainty with which a coder makes a coding decision. This may in turn impact inter-coder and coder-trainer reliability.

In other words, language skills' impact on inter-coder and coder-- trainer reliability may be mediated by the certainty with which a coder makes a decision. One would expect coders to feel certain about decisions if the coding protocol offers clear rules. The coding rules thus reduce uncertainty, and proper application of the rules eventually results in high agreement among coders. However, in the case of coding foreignlanguage material, coders may encounter linguistic troubles which cannot be resolved even by the clearest protocol.

These troubles diminish story comprehension, which leads to uncertainty about the coding decision. Uncertainty about a decision mediates between the linguistic troubles and the actual coding decision, thereby affecting reliability. In the worst case, uncertainty results in random coding and eventually reduces coders' chances to agree with one another.

Baron and Kenny formulated three conditions that must be met if a particular variable (e.g., coding certainty) mediates the effect of an independent variable (e.g., language skills) on a dependent variable (e.g., inter-coder/coder-trainer reliability).

We formulate the three conditions with respect to our problem. First, language skills have to affect reliability. As specified in H1, we expect a positive impact of language skills on reliability.

Second, language skills must affect coding certainty (i.e., the presumed mediating variable). As outlined above, we expect better language skills to result in higher coding certainty.

Third, when the impact of both language skills and certainty on reliability is investigated, an effect of certainty has to be found, while there is no longer an effect of language skills (or, at least, an effect considerably weaker than when only the impact of language skills is investigated). We expect higher coding certainty to lead to higher reliability as exemplified above. For investigation of the mediating role of coding certainty, we additionally hypothesize:

H4: The better a coder's language skills, the higher his / her coding certainty will be.

H5a: The higher a coder's coding certainty, the higher his/her inter-coder reliability (coder-trainer reliability) will be.

H5b: When controlling for coding certainty, a coder's language skills will no longer affect inter-coder reliability (coder-trainer reliability).

Fourteen student coders from five different countries34

(none had participated in the first study) independently coded twelve randomly selected English political television stories broadcast on BBC's 9 o'clock news and ITN's News at 6:30. Training and coding took place at the University of Amsterdam.

Categories in the coding protocol were identical or very similar to the ones in Study 1. As in Study 1, inter-coder and coder-trainer reliability were assessed at the story level across thirty-five categories resulting in 168 cases for analysis (twelve stories coded by fourteen coders).

Beforehand, five categories had been eliminated from analysis because all coders had given the same scores for the twelve stories. Political knowledge was operationalized as in Study 1 and coding experience was again computed from coders' pay slips.

However, to measure coders' language skills we used an English listening comprehension test from a preparatory book for the Test of English as a Foreign Language (TOEFL). We focused on listening comprehension because this is the most crucial component of language skills for coding broadcast news.

As in TOEFL testing, coders first listened to four taped news reports and four informative speeches (spoken by English native speakers). After each segment, coders answered four multiple-choice questions about what they had heard. The language skills index was computed by summing the correct answers, thus ranging from 0 to 32.

Coding certainty was measured by asking coders to indicate for each coding decision on a 5-point scale how certain or uncertain they were about the decision. The anchors were 0 (very uncertain) and 4 (very certain). For 64% of all decisions, coders indicated that they were very certain about the coding decision.

As in Study 1, we estimated a series of regression models to test our hypotheses. More specifically, to analyse the three conditions for the presumed mediating effect of coding certainty on reliability, we estimated three regressions as suggested by Baron and Kenny in the first, we separately regressed inter-coder and coder-trainer reliability on language skills. In the second, coding certainty (i.e., presumably the mediator) was regressed on language skills. In the third, we regressed both inter-coder and coder-trainer reliability on language skills and certainty. Political knowledge and coding experience were included as control variables.

Although our sample was not random, we do present significance tests, interpreting the results as rough indication of the robustness of effects. However, significance levels are not used for inferential purposes. We report the results of one-tailed significance tests because we assume unidirectional causality among the various coder characteristics and the coding reliabilities as stated in the hypotheses.

Average agreement among coders was 68% and average agreement among coders and coder trainers was 72%. We found higher inter-coder reliabilities (beta =.14) and higher coder-trainer reliabilities (beta =.22) for coders with better listening comprehension skills. Thus, HI was confirmed. Politically more knowledgeable coders coded more like other coders (beta =.22) and coder trainers (3 =.27), consistent with H2. Contrary to the expectations of H3, no meaningful influence of coding experience emerged.

Our second goal was to test whether coding certainty mediates the influence of language skills on inter-coder and coder-trainer reliability. As noted, language skills influenced both inter-coder and coder-trainer reliability, satisfying the first necessary condition for such a mediating role. Language skills had a strong impact on certainty (beta =.53), consistent with the second condition and H4.39 Finally, including coding certainty in a third regression model together with language skills and the control variables elicited similar results for both inter-coder and coder-trainer reliability as dependent variables.

While certainty had a relatively strong influence (beta =.40 for inter-coder reliability, beta =.20 for coder-trainer reliability), the effect of language skills decreased from a significant beta =.14 in regression 1 to a non-significant beta= -.08 for inter-coder reliability in regression 3 and for coder-trainer reliability from a significant beta =.22 in regression 1 to a nonsignificant beta =.12 in regression 3. This confirms H5a and HSb. Thus, the third condition for mediating effects was also met. The effect of language skills on both inter-coder and coder-trainer reliability was mediated by coding certainty. Coders with better language skills were more certain about decisions which, in turn, led to higher inter-coder and coder-trainer reliabilities.

As in our first study, we found that coders with higher English language skills coded more reliably, both in terms of inter-coder and coder-trainer reliability. In both cases, this impact was mediated by coding certainty.

Given that our coders' listening comprehension skills were above average (M = 25.1, s.d. = 2.8 on a scale with a maximum of 32), this finding points to the importance of recruiting coders with very good language skills for cross-national content analyses, particularly if the study is conducted in a bilingual setting.

Lower language skills reduce coding certainty and reliability. In bilingual settings even the comprehension of the coding protocol may be severely impeded if coders do not speak a foreign language well.

The mediating role of coding certainty on reliability is interesting given that the distribution was skewed (M = 3.5, s.d. =.28). The fact that coders were very certain in 64% of coding decisions is not surprising for intensively trained coders and is generally desirable. However, a more refined measure with less extreme scale anchors may have produced different results.

Politically knowledgeable students showed higher levels of intercoder and coder-trainer reliability. This effect was consistent with the results of the first study, but more pronounced. Neither inter-coder nor coder-trainer reliability were meaningfully influenced by coding experience.

This ran counter to our expectations and may illustrate the need to investigate whether and to what extent coding experience affects reliability. In order to advance our understanding of impediments to reliable coding, the intuitively plausible notion of coding experience and coder fatigue affecting reliability will have to be conceptualized more thoroughly than in this study and the literature.

For example, it may be useful to distinguish conceptually between temporary coder fatigue (i.e., coding session-related) and chronic coder fatigue (i.e., coding period-related). Analytically, it might then be interesting to investigate at what point coders become temporarily and chronically fatigued. This would help researchers not only to clearly govern coding sessions, but also to precisely plan coder supervision in long-term projects.

To some extent, the generalizability of our findings may be hampered by the case study character of our investigation. Protocols and categories were tailored to substantive rather than methodological questions; coders were not randomly selected and we cannot argue that Study 2 coders were not systematically different from Study 1 coders.

Moreover, a larger number of coders would have been desirable. However, our coders were well-trained and familiar with the protocol so that our study is as close to "real research" conditions as possible. Apart from that, the shortcomings mentioned are currently inherent to all fundamental research on reliability of content analysis (e.g., few coders). Despite their tentative character, our findings may have implications beyond cross-national content analyses and may apply to "ordinary" content analyses in three respects.

First, the mediated influence of language skills on coding reliability calls into question (not necessarily cross-national) studies in which non-native speakers coded foreignlanguage material. It may sometimes be tempting to recruit coders who are not native speakers but who speak a language reasonably well and to have them code foreign language material.

According to our findings, this can endanger both the inter-coder and coder-trainer reliability because lower language skills reduce coding certainty. Second, researchers analyzing foreign news coverage should realise that lack of factual knowledge about a country may impede coding even if coverage is in a coder's mother tongue.

It therefore seems desirable to select coders familiar with foreign countries. Third, although our measure of coding certainty is very much linked to the peculiarities of our study, it might also be used fruitfully in "ordinary" content analyses.

That is, when different types of content are analysed, it may be used to get deeper insights into the coding process and the appropriateness of operational definitions. For example, Potter and Levine-Donnerstein have suggested three types of content: manifest, latent pattern, and projective. Given that projective content coding is difficult to operationalize, this type of content may elicit less reliable coding because coders feel less certain. Our measure may help improve operational definitions of problematic types of content by systematically integrating feedback from coders in the process of operationalization.

Theoretically, this study puts forward the argument that-due to the logical incomparability of intra-country-inter-coder reliability scoresit is necessary to assess reliability in a cross-national fashion.

Previous research has largely ignored the methodological problems involved, but it seems essential that we integrate cross-national assessment of intercoder and coder-trainer reliability in our studies to increase the quality and trustworthiness of our results. Satisfactory coder-trainer reliability should not be taken for granted even if exhausting efforts such as detailed, pre-tested category definitions, intensive coder training, and supervision were undertaken.

This is particularly true for cross-national content analyses conducted with multiple coder trainers and country groups at different locations. Given that there are cross-national content analyses which do not report reliabilities, it seems important to sharpen our awareness of the pitfalls of cross-national testing and the potential necessity of a coder-trainer test in addition to the conventional intercoder test.

Empirically, we found that a cross-national test of inter-coder and coder-trainer reliability conducted with identical material and in one language may be susceptible to coder characteristics. Although consistent with the few studies reporting that coder characteristics generally do matter, our findings may also uncover some problems of the sort of cross-national reliability test presented in this study. It might simply be that coders are overwhelmed by foreign language material.

At a practical level, we suggest an alternative procedure for a bilingual setting in which several country groups and coder trainers are involved. First, the reliability of coding among the various coder trainers has to be assessed. Assuming considerable agreement among the coder trainers, this test ensures comparability among various country groups. Second, within each country group, inter-coder reliability has to be measured with a random selection of material coded by the group, and by the coder trainer.

Third, the coder-trainer reliability of each coder in the team with the coding of the coder trainer has to be assessed. It can be assumed that reliabilities are comparable across all country groups if the following conditions are met: first, the coder trainers agree in their coding with one another; second, the coders within a country group agree with one another; and, third, the coders agree with the coding of their trainer. The problems explored here suggest it is necessary to develop clear standards for cross-national content analyses, beyond those used for non-cross-national content analysis. As long as reliabilities in crossnational content analyses are suspect, the possibility remains that reported cross-national differences or similarities of media coverage are merely artifacts.

Chapter 8

Content Analysis of the Media Effects Literature

It is essential for scholars to form communities in order to share their perspectives on the phenomena they study, develop conventions about how to study them, and share the insights they generate. Periodically, it is important for scholars in a community to take stock of what they do so they can observe patterns in the direction a community is headed and assess the pattern of findings that forms the context for their thinking. This study profiles the mass media effects literature by examining published articles in terms of media studied, type of content, use of theory, method, and type of effect.

RATIONALE

According to So, "self reflection is a mark of maturity," and a field's maturity requires periodic examinations of its scholarly activity. It is important to trace the movement of ideas through the "invisible college" to see where ideas come from and which scholars and fields are being influenced by them. Self-examination is also important from a practical perspective, so we can track patterns in our literature and make better decisions about what research needs to be designed next. Kamhawi and Weaver argue that when viewing a literature "from a distance, one can discern larger patterns and trends in mass communication research. Knowing them can help researchers and students identify areas of strength and weakness, and of abundance and scarcity, in the research."

In 1979, Lowry observed that "for the most part, communication researchers have neglected to conduct systematic studies of their own output," a serious shortcoming because such studies can draw attention to what is emphasized in a field and what is ignored. In the intervening years, researchers have addressed this shortcoming, with studies generally falling into two groups: bibliometric studies and content analysis studies of the characteristics of the published research.

Bibliometric studies examine citation patterns to determine which authors, studies, and journals rely on the ideas of other authors, studies, and journals. For example, Reeves and Borgman studied citations in nine core communication journals and found communication scholars dependent on journals outside of communication. Communication journal articles exhibited five citations of other journals for each citation they received.

Rice, Borgman, and Reeves found three clusters of journals and citations: interpersonal, mass media, and residual isolated journals. Rice et al. supported the conclusion of so in their bibliometric analysis of forty years of the Journal of Broadcasting & Electronic Media, finding a greater percentage of citations from core communication journals after 1985 compared to citations in articles before 1985.

This body of bibliometric research suggests that there is a "field identity" growing over time, with the balance shifting slowly to self-citation from out-of-field citation, and communication journal studies increasingly being cited in other social science journals. Also, authors of mass media studies published in core mass media journals are likely to cite the core journals and other social science journals, but not other communication journals.

Not all bibliometric studies conclude that the field of communication is developing its own identity. So found that "communication currently still depends heavily on psychology for its intellectual input. This situation does not differ much from that in the first half of this century, when communication research was basically a spin-off from psychology." He observed that there "are indications of gradual development in the field," but that "in comparison with other social science fields, communication is still less developed and occupies only a peripheral position in the ecology of knowledge."

Content analyses studies, on the other hand, examine characteristics of published research to determine practices common among researchers. Some analyse research in only a single journal. Others focus on only one medium. Each of these studies has contributed a valuable insight to the building of a complete picture of the nature of mass media research.

This study content analyses mass media effects studies published in scholarly journals in order to construct a profile of the recent mass media effects literature so we can compare the more recent pattern to older patterns. Also, we will contextualize the patterns we find in terms of how those salient characteristics of the mass media effects literature are likely affecting the development of the research field.

MEDIUM

Research activity seems to have followed development of the different media. In an early analysis of published content, Schramm analysed articles in Public Opinion Quarterly from 1937 to 1956 and found print media dominated, with 486 articles. Perloff analysed 1,490 articles in Journalism Quarterly from 1955 to 1974, finding that among those articles concerned with a specific medium, 67% involved print media, compared to 6% about electronic media, and 26% related to both. Weaver and Gray found 56% of articles in Quarterly between 1955 and 1974 dealt with print.

Electronic media grew in research importance beginning in the early 1970s. In their analysis of research in Quarterly from 1971 to 1995, Riffe and Freitag found that newspaper content accounted for 46.7% of all content analyses, followed by television (24.3%), magazines (13.6%), and other (15.4%). They do not provide trend analyses but it is likely that the percentage of articles dealing with newspaper content decreased while the number of articles dealing with television increased over that twenty-five-year period. Such a trend was indeed reported by Kamhawi and Weaver, who found that broadcast media grew in importance to researchers through the 1980s and 1990s, accounting for 42.2% of all media studies at the expense of print, which accounted for 28.7%.

They concluded that traditional broadcast and print continued to dominate mass media research, but asked, "Will these media continue to dominate research as we enter further into the 'Internet Age?'" In an analysis of the 961 articles published in five leading communication journals from 1994 to 1999, Tomasello found that only 4% of those articles dealt with the Internet.

TYPE OF CONTENT

While published analyses focus on studied medium, few summarize type of content areas typically studied. One exception is the study by Riffe and Freitag, which found that in published content analyses, 71.0% focused on news/ editorial, compared to 10.1% advertising, 7.2% entertainment, and 11.7% visual/graphics/ other.

THEORY

Scholars who examine our literatures frequently observe that the use of theory is at a low level and that there needs to be a more explicit use of theory both in the generation of empirical research studies and in the interpretation of results. In an analysis of eight journals from 1965 to 1989, Potter, Cooper, and Dupagne found that only 8.1% of 1,326 articles were guided by a theory and provided a test of that theory; another 19.5% were tests of hypotheses but these hypotheses were not derived from a theory. Kamhawi and Weaver reported that only 30.5% of articles in ten communication journals from 1980 to 1999 specifically mentioned a theory, which led them to argue that "theoretical development is probably the main consideration in evaluating the disciplinary status of the field.

As our field grows in scope and complexity the pressure for theoretical integration increases. It seems that scholars in the field should be developing and testing theories to explain the process and effects of mass communication. However, that was not widely evident in our sample."

METHOD

Exploration of which methods are used most has been a popular topic. A few content analyses of the published literature have focused on whether a study employed a qualitative or quantitative method. For example, Schramm's 1937-1956 Public Opinion Quarterly study found the percentage of articles using quantitative methods growing. Perloff's 1955-1974 Journalism Quarterly study found that 56% used quantitative methods.

Some examinations of the literature simply count frequency of a method, such as content analysis. Riffe and Freitag focused on methods in twenty-five years of Journalism & Mass Communication Quarterly, reporting that of the 1,977 articles appearing during that period, 486 (24.6% of the total) used content analysis.

Other studies compared method used. Lowry analysed empirical articles published from 1970 through 1976 in seven journals and found 30% used survey, 19% used experiments, and 13% used content analysis. Also, 42% used subjective reports from respondents, while 21% used observations of behaviour, and 12% used archival records. Kamhawi and Weaver examined articles published from 1980 to 1999 in ten communication journals, finding that 33.3% used survey method; 30.0% used content analysis; 13.3% were experiments; 4.7% used historical method; 10.3% used other qualitative methods; and the remaining 8.4% used a combination of methods.

TYPE OF EFFECT

Despite the popularity of books and university courses on media effects, it seems only one content analysis of the media literature has looked for the prevalence of different kinds of effects. Cooper, Potter, and Dupagne analysed 1,326 articles published in eight U.S.-based internationally distributed peer-reviewed journals from 1965 to 1989. About one quarter of them were effects studies-22.4% of them dealt with effects on individuals and 2.5% dealt with effects on society.

METHOD

Providing a picture of the patterns in mass media effects thinking and research is a very large task. To be conducted in full, it would of course require examination of published journal articles, books, government reports, industry reports, instructional materials from consumer activist groups, theses, and dissertations.

Among periodicals, there are likely hundreds carrying mass media effects articles. Nonetheless, we hope to provide a reasonable start based on a counting of published studies in mainstream or "core" scholarly journals, because research journals have been called the "nerves of the discipline" and "the barometer of the substantive focus of scholarship and research methods most important to the discipline."

We began by selecting the five journals that have generally been considered the core journals of mass media research by scholars who have conducted content analyses of the research literature and scholars. We examined all issues of sixteen journals published in the odd years between 1993 and 2005.

This included 109 journal/years. Within each issue, all articles were coded if they involved mass media effects as defined below. We did not code editorials, book reviews, introductions to symposia, or editors' reports, but we did include articles labeled as "Research in Brief" or given similar designations.

In order to be coded for this study, an article first had to deal with a mass media effect. Mass media are defined as the channels of transmitting messages to particular audiences in a way to attract and condition their attention for repeat exposures. Thus, traditional mass media were included-television, radio, film, newspapers, magazines, mass market books, recordings, and the Internet-while telephone conversations, use of computers for e-mail, and the like were excluded.

Second, the authors needed to make some claim or provide some evidence that the mass medium in question exerted some influence or a recognizable effect, whether at a macro (such as an institution, the public, society, the economy) or individual level.

Each article was coded for identifying information: journal, year, issue, beginning page, and authors' names. In addition, we coded for five key variables: medium, type of content, theory prominent, method, and type of effect. For each of these variables we began with a list of coding values but during the coding procedure, the coders added values to the list when they felt the beginning lists did not include codes to capture the essence of an article.

MEDIUM

Initial codes included all media, television, radio, newspapers, magazines, books, recordings, film, Internet, new media, and other. If an article seemed to deal with all media without specifying any one in particular, it was coded as "all." If an article mentioned more than one medium specifically, those mentioned media were all coded. For example, a study might be an experiment that compares learning from television vs. newspaper; in this case the study would be coded for both television and newspaper.

TYPE OF CONTENT

We began with three categories of content: news/information, advertising, and entertainment. As coding progressed, several sub-categories were added. During the analysis, however, the sub-categories were too scattered to report frequencies beyond the three categories.

THEORY PROMINENT

This variable essentially had two values: yes and no. In order to be coded yes, the article needed to feature a theory prominently; i.e., if the name of the theory appeared in the article's title, the abstract, or in a heading or sub-heading of the article. The coder also recorded the name of the theory.

METHOD

Values included experiment, survey, focus group, ethnography, history, secondary analysis, meta-analysis, review, and theory piece. During the coding we added values for critical analysis, discourse analysis, textual analysis, and several other qualitative methods. If a study used more than one method, all were recorded.

We also added a code for content analysis. Although content analysis is not a method to generate data for effects directly, there are times when authors use data generated through a content analysis to develop a substantial argument for effects. For example, tests of the cultivation hypothesis require content analyses of patterns in the television world.

Some studies conducted content analyses that focused attention more on the presumed effects of content patterns than on the content patterns themselves; however, these studies were atypical. Another example is a study using a content analysis of newspapers that coded for story topic, use of sources, story tone, and gender of reporter. This at first appeared to be a content study, but the authors' focus was on looking for patterns in the news across gender of reporter in order to make attributions about differential socialization of reporters-thus making it an effects study; that is, how reporters were affected by their news organizations.

EFFECTS

We began with the consideration of whether the unit of analysis for the effect was at the individual or macro level. Individual level codes included attitude, belief, affect, cognition, physiology, and behaviour. Attitudes were defined as evaluations where research participants were asked for evaluations of something, such as political candidates, advertised products, elements in media content, etc. Beliefs were perceptions about the reality of something, such as how many people worked in law enforcement, etc. An affective effect is one that shows up as an emotional reaction in the participants; mood states were also included. Cognitive effects are those that focus on changes to a person's factual knowledge or the processing of information. Physiological effects are those automatic changes stimulated in the body, such as heart rate, galvanic skin response, etc. Behavioral effects focus on observable actions of the participants. Macro level codes included effects on the public, effects on an institution, and effects on the media themselves. During the coding, sub-categories were developed to capture the essence of the effects in more detail.

TESTING RELIABILITY

Approximately 10% of the sample was coded by both coders (the two authors of this study) to create an overlap that could be used to test reliability. First the unitizing was tested and it was found that there was agreement 92% of the time with the yes-no decision of whether to include the article (this was essentially a decision about whether the article dealt with a media effect). second, we tested for the percentage of agreement on the codes assigned to the variables for the part of the sample selected by both coders. We used the initial values in the design and not the elaborations to the codebook during the coding process. Percentages of agreement were as follows: medium, 92%; type of content, 91%; method, 91%; type of effect, 88%; and use of theory, 78%.

RESULTS

We identified 962 articles published in the sixteen journals in the seven years examined from the twelve-year period of 1993 to 2005. The journal presenting the greatest number of media effects articles was the Journal of Broadcasting & Electronic Media, which published an average of 18.4 effects articles per year. Eight other journals publish an average of more than 8 effects articles a year. This set of nine journals can be considered core to mass media effects scholarship-accounting for 87.9% of all mass media effects studies we found in our analysis. While the other seven journals published a substantial number of mass media effects studies (n = 116) and should not be ignored, the primary focus of those journals lies outside of mass media effects research. While Public Opinion Quarterly had been included in samples of many studies of communication literature in the past, it presented only 21 articles dealing with mass media effects over the seven years examined. Media effects researchers are now more likely to publish their research in newer journals (such as Media Psychology or Critical Studies in Media Communication) where mass media effects research is central to the editorial focus.

MEDIUM

Television is the most prevalent single medium examined, accounting for almost 41% of all coded articles. Also, electronic media appear to be more than twice as likely to show up in the mass media effects literature compared to print media.

The Internet is becoming more popular as a medium for mass media scholars to examine (12.5%). Tomasello had reported that only 4% of articles published in five leading communication journals from 1994 to 1999 dealt with the Internet.

TYPE OF CONTENT

We grouped content into three types: news and information, advertising, and entertainment. The most common type of content in the recent media effects literature was news and information, representing 33% of studies coded. Studies exploring the effects of advertising content represented 17.8% of the articles coded, and studies exploring the effects of general entertainment content represented 16.4% of all articles. Some studies (n = 100,10.4%) did not focus on a specific type of content. Another subset of studies (n = 208,21.7%) that largely ignored content included studies where researchers asked respondents about reactions to the media in general or their usage patterns by medium instead of content.

METHODS

Quantitative methods dominated in this sample with survey, experiment, secondary analysis, and content analysis accounting for 71.4% of all articles. The single most-used method was the laboratory experiment followed by the in-class survey.

THEORY

Thirty-five per cent of coded articles featured a theory prominently. This figure is higher than found previously. Potter, Cooper, and Dupagne found only 8.1% of their articles were guided by theory, and Riffe and Freitag reported only 27.6% of JMCQ content analysis studies used a theory. Kamhawi and Weaver found theory in only 30.5% of articles they analysed from 1980 to 1999.

We found a total of 144 different theories named in the 336 articles that featured a theory prominently. The theories cited most often were cultivation (representing 8% of the 336 articles that featured a theory prominently), the third-person effect (7.4%), agenda setting (7.1%), and uses and gratifications (5.7%). Only twelve of the theories were mentioned in more than 5 articles; the remaining 132 theories were spread out over the remaining 168 articles that featured a theory prominently.

This indicates a pattern of rather thin theory development. Kamhawi and Weaver40 found that only three theories (information processing, uses and gratifications, and media construction of social reality) were mentioned in as many as 10% of their analysed articles. Of these, only uses and gratifications showed up as a frequent theory in our study.

TYPE OF EFFECT

Published articles were found in all seven categories of effects. Cognitive effects were the most prevalent, followed closely by behavioral, attitudinal, and macro categories. The cognitive category was dominated by studies that examined the acquisition of factual material during a study, while the attitudinal category was dominated by studies that looked at what attitudes were formed during a study. Both of these two sub-categories of studies are characterized by experiments where the designs focused on the conditions (by medium or by content type) under which people are affected more by the media.

The behavioral category was dominated by studies that focused on patterns of media use. This literature was less likely to include studies that observed behaviour triggered during the study compared to studies that asked participants to indicate their intentions for later behaviour.

The macro effects category was composed primarily of studies that either looked at how the public (public opinion, public knowledge, or public behaviour) or the mass media themselves were affected. The belief category was composed mainly of studies that measured the beliefs participants had prior to the beginning of their study. Studies that triggered emotions dominated the affect category. Finally, there were very few studies in the physiological category.

DISCUSSION

Some early content analyses as well as bibliometric studies provided a picture of mass media research, as well as communications research, as often importing ideas and methods from other fields of study.

There are indications, however, that mass media research is "breaking away" from those "parent" fields. Bibliometric studies reviewed above, for example, show a trend toward more citation of communication research compared to research from other scholarly fields. These studies identify a core set of journals for communication and especially mass media research.

This was evident in the present study as well. Nine of ten mass media effects articles were concentrated in half of the sixteen journals analysed. It also appears that mass media research is breaking away from the traditional methods used in psychology, a departure from So's41 conclusion, based on analysis of the communication field from its early days until the 1980s, that psychology remained a strong influence over communication research.

In psychology, researchers typically start with a mid-level theory, operationalize a test using a mass media message as a treatment, then run an experiment to test the hypothesized influence. Our findings show that this is seldom the pattern with mass media effects research published in the core communication journals. Almost two-thirds of our sample mentioned no theory, and fewer than three in ten used an experimental method.

The bibliometric literature argues that it is good for communication researchers to establish a unique identity and a community of scholars who can more powerfully and efficiently focus on communication phenomena. However, it appears from our results that any move away from theories and methods that structure parent fields has not been followed by mass media researchers constructing a unique identity.

Instead, it appears that the focus of researchers has become more specialized or even fragmented. Media scholars are producing an amorphous mass of individual studies rather than constructing a field with unifying theories and methods that focus scholars' attention.

There is no dominant method used by mass media effects researchers; instead there is a wide range of methods that cover just about every social science method as well as most humanistic research methods. Also, there is a wide range of effects being explored.

Taken together, these two findings could be viewed positively, as an indication of a dynamic field, one with a willingness and ability to use many different tools to address a wide range of effects.

However, it could arguably be an indication the field is stretched thin; a wide range of effects being studied and a wide range of methods among a small number of researchers may mean fragmentation of effort, little overlap in research work, and limited programmatic study.

This could make it difficult for scholars to share

definitions of key terms and a "big picture" understanding of the overall field.

Perhaps most indicative of the fragmentary nature of the mass media effects scholarship is the low level of theory use. Theories guide research by directing attention to certain systems of explanation that need testing; they provide consistent definitions for key ideas; they gather research findings relevant to their explanations and interpret those findings in an integrated manner. Thus theories provide an important evaluative function of calibrating which findings are valid and important, and provide an important synthesis function by integrating findings into systems of explanation. To the extent that researchers cluster around a few theories, a field shares a common focus and the results of the empirical work can be more easily integrated into larger knowledge structures and more easily shared.

To the extent that theories are ignored, researchers lose considerable efficiencies in the design of studies, incorporation of their findings into a body of knowledge, and achievement of conceptual leverage for their work. The low level of theory use also makes it considerably more difficult to educate new generations of scholars. New students who expend the significant effort needed to learn the top dozen theories we found in our study would find that this learning would prepare them for less than 18% of the recently published mass media effects literature.

This study extends existing bibliometric and content analysis studies. Some of the findings of the present study give reason to celebrate, for example, the finding of a core set of common journals to publish media effects research. At the same time, some of the findings of the present study give cause for concern. The low level of theory use and the fragmentation of methods and focus, for instance, suggest a lack of cohesion and integration among effects scholars.

Communication scholars must make a better effort to consistently employ and test theories in their research. However, we stop short of arguing that media effects scholars as a group need to be less diffuse in their methods of study and exploration of specific effects. After all, one appeal of studying mass media is the number of interesting content areas (such as politics, sports, news, violence, or sex) and possible effects (attitudes, behaviour, emotions, and so on). Furthermore, the use of multiple methods may be the best way to provide the richest understanding of mass media phenomena. Therefore, scholars should continue their exploration of a variety of effects under a variety of mass media content scenarios, employing the multitude of research methods that are at their disposal.

Chapter 9

The Challenge of Applying Content Analysis to the WWW

Content analysis has been used for decades as a microscope that brings communication messages into focus. The World Wide Web has grown rapidly since the technology that made it possible was introduced in 1991 and the first Web browsers became available in 1993.

The Commerce Department estimates that one billion users may be online by 2005, and the growth in users has mirrored growth in content. More than 320 million home pages can be accessed on the Web and some Web sites are updated almost constantly. This growth and change makes the Web a moving target for communication research. Can the microscope of content analysis be applied to this moving target?

The purpose of this chapter is to examine ways that researchers have begun to apply content analysis to the World Wide Web. How are they adapting the principles of content analysis to this evolving form of computermediated communication? What are the unique challenges of content analysis in this environment? This review of pioneering work in Web-based content analysis may provide researchers with insights into ways to adapt a stable research technique to a dynamic communication environment.

Krippendorff found empirical inquiry into communication content dates at least to the late 1600s when newspapers were examined by the Church because of its concern of the spread of nonreligious matters. The first well-documented case of quantitative analysis of content occurred in eighteenth-century Sweden. That study also involved conflict between the church and scholars. With the advent of popular newspaper publishing at the turn of the twentieth century, content analysis came to be more widely used. It was with the work of Berelson and Lazarsfeld in the 1940s and Berelson in the 1950s that content analysis came to be a widely recognized research tool that was used in a variety of research disciplines.

Berelson's definition of content analysis as "a research technique for the objective, systematic and quantitative description of the manifest content of communication"8 underlies much content analysis work. Budd, Thorp, and Donohew built on Berelson's definition defining content analysis as "a systematic technique for analyzing message content and message handling." Krippendorff defined content analysis as "a research technique for making replicable and valid inferences from data to their context."

Krippendorff identified four primary advantages of content analysis: it is unobtrusive, it accepts unstructured material, it is context sensitive and thereby able to process symbolic forms, and it can cope with large volumes of data. All of these advantages seem to apply equally to the Web as to media such as newspapers and television. The capability of coping with large volumes of data is a distinct advantage in terms of Web analysis.

Holsti identified three primary purposes for content analysis: to describe the characteristics of communication, to make inferences as to the antecedents of communication, and to make inferences as to the effects of communication. Both descriptive and inferential research focused on Web-based content could add value to our understanding of this evolving communication environment.

How-to guides for conducting content analysis suggest five primary steps that are involved in the process of conducting content analysis research. Those steps are briefly enumerated below with consideration for application to the Web.

First, the investigator formulates a research question and/or hypotheses. The advent of the Web has opened the door for many new research questions. The challenge for researchers who apply content analysis to the Web is not to identify questions, but rather to narrow those questions and seek to find a context for them either in existing or emerging communication theory. The temptation for researchers who are examining a "new" form of communication is to simply describe the content rather than to place it in the context of theory and/or to test hypotheses.

Second, the researcher selects a sample. The size of the sample depends on factors such as the goals of the study. Multiple methods can be used for drawing the sample. But Krippendorff noted that a sampling plan must "assure that, within the constraints imposed by available knowledge about the phenomena, each unit has the same chance of being represented in the collection of sampling units." This requirement for rigor in drawing a sample may be one of the most difficult aspects of content analysis on the Web. Bates and Lu pointed out that "with the number of available

Web sites growing explosively, and available directories always incomplete and overlapping, selecting a true random sample may be next to impossible." Not only do new Web sites come online frequently, but old ones are also removed or changed. McMillan found that in one year 15.4 per cent of a sample of health-related Web sites had ceased to exist.16 Koehler found that 25.3 per cent of a randomly selected group of Web sites had gone off-line in one year. However, he also found that among those sites that remained functioning after one year, the average size of the Web site (in bytes) more than doubled.

The third step in the content analysis process is defining categories. Budd, Thorp, and Donohew identified two primary units of measurements: coding units and context units. Coding units are the smallest segment of content counted and scored in the content analysis. The context unit is the body of material surrounding the coding unit. For example, if the coding unit is a word, the context unit might be the sentence in which the word appears or the paragraph or the entire article. Many researchers use the term "unit of analysis" to refer to the context from which coding units are drawn.

Defining the context unit/unit of analysis is a unique challenge on the World Wide Web. Ha and James argued that the home page is an ideal unit of analysis because many visitors to a Web site decide whether they will continue to browse the site on the basis of their first impression of the home page. They also argued that coding an entire site could be extremely timeconsuming and introduce biases based on Web-site size. Web Techniques estimated that Web sites range from one page to 50,000 pages. Other researchers have attempted to take a more comprehensive approach to defining the unit of analysis. For example, in a study of library Web sites Clyde coded all pages mounted by a library on its server.

Fourth, coders are trained, they code the content, and reliability of their coding is checked. Each step of this coding process is impacted by Web technology. The Web can facilitate training and coding. For example, McMillan trained two coders who were living in different parts of the country to assist in coding Web sites. Instructions and coding sheets were delivered by e-mail and coders were given URLs for sites to be coded.

The coding process was carried out remotely and without paper. Wassmuth and Thompson noted potential problems in checking intercoder reliability for changing content. They controlled for possible changes in content by having sites that were being coded by multiple coders viewed at the same day and time by all coders. Massey and Levy addressed the problem of changing content by having all sites evaluated twice with the second visit made twentyfour hours after the initial visit to the site.

Fifth, the data collected during the coding process is analysed and interpreted. The statistical tools used to analyse the data will depend on the type of data collected and on the questions that are addressed by the research. Similarly, the interpretation will grow out of the data analysis as well as the researcher's perspective. The fact that the content that has been analysed is Web-based is not expected to change the basic procedures of analysis and interpretation used in content analysis.

METHODOLOGY

The author took several steps to identify both published and unpublished studies that have applied content analysis to the Web. First, a search of the electronic Social Sciences Citation Index was conducted searching for key words "Web" and "content analysis."

The SSCI was also searched for "Internet" and "content analysis."

Selected communication journals were also reviewed for any articles that applied content analysis to the Web. The author also sought out papers from communication conferences that applied content analysis to the Web. Finally, bibliographies were checked for all studies that were identified using the above techniques. Any cited study that seemed to apply content analysis to the Web was examined.

Eleven studies were identified that applied content analysis to computer-mediated communication technologies other than the Web.

Three studies analysed content of listservs designed for academicians and practiboners of public relations and advertising. Two studies analysed newsgroups that served as online support/information groups on the topics of abortion and eating disorders.

Two studies analysed pornographic materials found on Usenet. Two studies focused on e-mail and electronic bulletin board postings related to public affairs: Newhagen, Cordes, and Levy examined e-mail sent to NBC Nightly News and Ogan examined content of an electronic bulletin board during the Gulf War.

The final two studies focused on organizational communication issues with analysis of email messages related to an online training programme and an Internet discussion group established in conjunction with a conference.'

In addition to the studies that examined computer-mediated communication forms such as e-mail and listservs, nineteen studies were found that focused specifically on content analysis of the World Wide Web. The five steps in content analysis identified in the literature are the basis for examination of how these nineteen studies applied the microscope of content analysis to the moving target of the World Wide Web.

FINDINGS

The first step in content analysis is to formulate research questions and/or hypotheses. The majority of these studies were descriptive in nature. However, a few of these studies do seem to be moving more toward hypothesis testing and theory development. For example, McMillan proposed four models of funding for Web content based in part on level of interactivity that was determined by analysis of Web site features. Wassmuth and Thompson suggested that their study might be a first step in developing a theory that explains relationships between specificity of banner ad messages and the goal of information tasks.

The second step in conducting a content analysis is to select a sample. The sampling frame from which sites were drawn varied widely. One common way of defining a sampling frame was to use an online list of sites in a given category. A second popular technique was to use search engines) to identify sites that met criteria related to the purpose of the study. Two studies used off-line sources to identify Web sites and two studies combined online and off-line listings of Web sites. Finally, one site analysed three newspaper Web sites with no discussion of the sampling frame.

After defining the sampling frame, researchers typically draw a sample for analysis. Nine of the nineteen studies did not sample; instead they analysed all sites in the sampling frame. The goals of these studies were typically to describe and/or set a benchmark for analysis of a given type of Web sites.

Among studies that used sampling, use of a table of random numbers was the most common sampling technique. McMillan pointed out challenges of applying a table of random numbers to an online listing or search engine results.

Most lists generated in this way are not numbered leaving the researcher a tedious hand-counting task. Search engine listings may be presented in multiple hypertext sub-menus that further complicate the task of assigning random numbers. Howeverz, few of the studies cited here provided much, if any discussion, of how to address sampling difficulties that arise from using online sources to identify the sampling frame. The sample size for these nineteen studies varied dramatically from three to 2,865. The majority of the studies (fourteen) analysed between fifty and 500 sites.

The third step in content analysis is defining categories. In content analysis of traditional media, one of the first steps is to define the time period of the study (e.g., a constructed week of newspaper issues). But, in analysis of Web sites, study authors placed emphasis on the time frame (e.g., April 1997) of the study. As noted earlier, changes in the content of Web sites necessitates rapid collection of data. The most rapid data collection reported was two days and the longest was five months. Most studies collected data in one to two months.

After identifying the time frame of the study, researchers need to identify context units for coding. The most common context unit used for these studies was the "Web site." Many of the studies did not specify what was meant by the Web site. However some did limit analysis to the "home page" or initial screen seen upon entering the site while others specified examination of all pages that could be found at a given site and others indicated that they had searched sites in "sufficient detail" to identify key features.

Given the magnitude and changing nature of sites, some creativity would seem to be needed in defining the context unit. Wassmuth and Thompson devised one creative approach in their analysis of banner ads that were encountered when the coder performed a specific task at a newspaper Web site (find a classified ad for a BMW). Another approach was to have coders analyse all sites for a specific length of time-about ten minutes.

This helps to reduce bias that might be involved in coding sites of varying lengths. However, it might introduce "error" in that different coders may choose to examine different parts of a Web site during the ten-minute examination period.

These nineteen studies varied widely in terms of coding units used by the researchers. The most common coding unit was "content categories." However, no standard list of categories emerges from these studies. Nor do they rely on established lists such as the fifty categories identified by Bush. Instead, content categories seem to be specifically related to the goals of the given study. For example, Bar-Ilan developed content categories related to a specific historical figure, and McMillan and Campbell developed content categories related to the community-building features of city-based Web sites.

Another common coding unit is structural features of the Web site (e.g., links, animation, video, sound, etc.). Two studies used Heeter's conceptual definition of interactivity as a frame for organizing analysis of Web site features.

One study conducted an in-depth analysis of e-mail links. Many of the other sites also coded e-mail links as a structural element. Tannery and Wessel developed a three-level categorization system for evaluating overall sophistication of Web sites based on both content categories and structural features, Some studies also reported on "demographic" characteristics of sites such as country of origin and type of institution that created the site while others explored the nature and/or purpose of the sponsoring organization in more detail. The Wassmuth and Thompson study is unique in its analysis of banner advertisements in Web sites.

The fourth step in content analysis is training coders and checking the reliability of their coding skills. One of the primary reasons for this attention to training and checking coders is that, as Budd, Thorp, and Donohew noted, an important requirement for any social-science based research is that it be carried out in such a way that its results can be verified by other investigators who follow the same steps as the original researcher. Krippendorff wrote that at least two coders must be used in content analysis to determine reliability of the coding scheme by independently analyzing content.

Eight of the nineteen studies did not report any information about coders. Of those that did report on coders, the number of coders used ranged from two to twelve with an average of about five coders. Only seven studies reported on training of coders and most said little about how training was done.

Eleven studies reported cross-coding techniques. Most cross-coded a percentage (10 to 20%) of all sampled sites. Elliott had all sites cross-checked by two coders while Li had two coders cross-check all the data collected in the first three days ofa ten-day sample. Ha and James used a pre-test/ posttest design that enabled them to correct coding problems prior to the start of data collection as well as to check reliability of collected data.

Ten studies reported reliability of the coding. Formulas used for testing reliability included Holsti's reliability formula, Perreault and Leigh's reliability index, Spearman-Brown Prophesy Formula, and Scott's Pi. Bar-Ilan did not indicate what type of test was used to generate a 92% reliability score for her study. Reliability scores ranged from.62 to 1.00.

The fifth stage of content analysis is to analyse and interpret data. As noted earlier, the purpose of most of these studies was descriptive in nature. Therefore, it is not surprising that key findings are also descriptive in nature. One theme that emerged from several of these studies was the diversity found at Web sites. For example, Bates and Lu found that the "personal home page" is an evolving communication form, Clyde found variety in the structure and function of library Web sites, and McMillan concluded that the Web has diversity of content, funding sources, and communication models.

A second theme found in these studies is commercialization of the Web. Some studies view commercialization as positive for marketers and/ or consumers while others express concern about impacts of commercialization on public life and/or academic expression. As a counterpoint to these concerns, Gibson and Ward found the Web offered a forum for minor political parties to have a voice.

A third major theme was the fact that many site developers are not using the Web to its full potential as a multi-media interactive environment. Researchers found many sites made limited use of interactivity, graphics and motion video, and search functions. And Elliott's study suggested that there is still significant room for development of new content in important areas such as family life education.

RECOMMENDATIONS FOR FUTURE RESEARCHERS

The studies reviewed above found that the stable research technique of content analysis can be applied in the dynamic communication environment of the Web. But using content analysis in this environment does raise potential problems for the researcher. Some of these studies exhibit creative ways of addressing these problems. Unfortunately, others seem to have failed to build rigor into their research designs in their haste to analyse a new medium. Future studies that apply content analysis techniques to the Web need to consider carefully each of the primary research steps identified in the literature: formulating research questions and/or hypotheses, sampling, data collection and coding, training coders and checking the reliability of their work, and analyzing and interpreting data.

For the first step, formulating the research questions and/or hypotheses, content analysis of the Web is both similar to and different from traditional media. Content analysis of traditional media, such as newspapers and broadcast, assume some linearity or at least commonly accepted sequencing of messages. Hypertext, a defining characteristic of the Web, defies this assumption. Each individual may interact with content of a Web site in different ways. Furthermore, the Web is both "like" and "unlike" print and broadcast as it combines text, audio, still images, animation, and video. These unique characteristics of the medium may suggest unique research questions. However, in some fundamental ways, the first step in the research process remains similar. Researchers should build on earlier theoretical and empirical work in defining their Web-based research.

Approaches taken by the authors cited above tend to be consistent with Holsti's first purpose of content analysis: describing the characteristics of communication. This is appropriate for early studies of an emerging medium. However, researchers also need to move on to the other two purposes identified by Holsti: making inferences as to antecedents of communication and making inferences as to the effects of communication.

The second step in content analysis research, sampling, presents some unique challenges for Web-based content analysis. As noted earlier, a key concern in sampling is that each unit must have the same chance as all other units of being represented.

The first challenge for the researcher is to identify the units to be sampled. This will be driven by the research question.

For example, if the researcher wants to examine a sample of Web sites for Fortune 500 companies, it may be fairly simple to obtain a list of these sites and apply a traditional sampling method (e.g., a table of random numbers, every nth item on the list, etc.) But, if one seeks a different kind of sample (e.g., all business Web sites) the task may become more difficult. Essentially, the researcher has two primary sources from which to develop a sampling frame: offline sources and online sources.

If the researcher draws a sample from offline sources (e.g., directories, lists maintained by industry groups, etc.), then drawing a random sample is fairly nonproblematic. Because the sample universe exists in a "set" medium, traditional methods of sampling can be used. However, a major problem with offline sources is that they are almost certainly out of date. Given the rapid growth and change of the Web, new sites have probably been added since the printed list was created while others have moved or been removed. Online sources can be updated more frequently, and thus help to eliminate some of the problems associated with offline sources. And, in many cases (e.g., directories, lists maintained by industry groups, etc.), the list can appear in the same kind of format that is found in an offline source making sampling fairly straightforward.

But, human list-compilers are less efficient than search engines for identifying all potential Web sites that meet specific criteria. And in some cases no compiled list may exist that directly reflects the criteria of a study. In these cases, search engines may be the best way of generating a sample frame.

However, care must be taken in using search engine results. First, authors must make sure that they have defined appropriate key words and that they understand search techniques for the search engine that they are using.

If they do not, they run the risk of either over registration or under registration. Human intervention may be needed to insure that the computer-generated list does not include any spurious and/ or duplicate items.

Once a list has been generated, the researcher needs to determine the best way to draw a random sample. One way to ease the problem of random assignment may be to generate a hardcopy of the list, Then the researcher can assign random numbers to the list and/or more easily select every nth item. However, if a hierarchical search engine (such as Yahoo!) is used, special care must be taken to ensure that all items in subcategories have equal chance of being represented in the sample. In some cases, stratified sampling may be required.

Research needs to be done to test the validity of multiple sampling methods. For example, does the use of different search engines result in empirically different findings? What sample size is adequate? How can sample techniques from traditional media (e.g., selection of "representative" newspapers or broadcast stations be applied to the Web? A key concern is that sampling methods for the Web not be held to either higher or lower standards than have been accepted for traditional media. The rapid growth and change of the Web also leads to potential problems in the third stage of content analysis: data collection and coding. The fast-paced Web almost demands that data be collected in a short time frame so that all coders are analyzing the same content.

Koehler has suggested some tools that researchers can use to download Web sites to capture a "snapshot" of content. However, as Clyde noted, copyright laws of some countries prohibit, among other things, the storage of copyrighted text in a database system.

Whether or not the site was downloaded prior to analysis, researchers must specify when they examined a site. Just as newspaper-based research must indicate the date of publication, and broadcast-based research must indicate which newscast is analysed, so Web-based content analysis must specify the timeframe of the analysis. For sites that change rapidly, exact timing may become important.

Researchers must also take care in defining units of analysis. The coding unit can be expected to vary depending on the theory upon which the study is based, the research questions explored, and the hypotheses tested. However, some standardization is needed for context units. For example, analyses of traditional media have developed traditional context units (e.g., the column-inch and/or a word count for newspapers, time measured in seconds for broadcast), but no such standard seems to have yet emerged for the Web. The fact that multiple media forms are combined on the Web may be one of the reasons for this lack of a clear unit of measurement.

The majority of the studies reviewed above simply defined the context unit as the "Web site." Future studies should specify how much of the Web site was reviewed (e.g., "home page" only, first three levels in the site hierarchy, etc.). But as analysis of the Web matures, entirely new context units may need to be developed to address phenomena that are completely nonexistent in traditional media.

For example, Wassmuth and Thompson measured the ways in which the content of the Web was "adapted" in real-time to become more responsive to site visitors' needs. The fourth step in content analysis, training coders and checking the reliability of their work, involves both old and new challenges on the Web. Given the evolving nature of data coding described above, training may involve "learning together" with coders how to develop appropriate context and coding units.

But the rapid change that characterizes the Web may introduce some new problems in checking intercoder reliability. This does not mean that well-developed tools for checking reliability should be abandoned. Rather, the primary challenge is to make sure that coders are actually cross-coding identical data. If Web sites are checked at different times by different coders and/or if the context unit is not clearly defined, false error could be introduced.

The coders might not look at the same segment of the site, or data coded by the first coder might be changed or removed before the second coder examines the site. Only one of the studies reviewed above directly addressed this issue. Wassmuth and Thompson carefully defined a task to be preformed at a site and had two coders perform that identical task at exactly the same date and time.

This is one viable alternative. However, if the content of the site is changing rapidly, this control may not be sufficient. Another alternative is to have coders evaluate sites that have been downloaded. These downloaded sites are "frozen in time" and will not change between the coding times. However, as noted earlier, there may be some legal problems with such downloaded sites. Furthermore, depending on the number of sites being examined, the time and disk-space requirements for downloading all of the studied sites may be prohibitive.

The Web does not seem to pose any truly new challenges in the final step in content analysis: analyzing and interpreting the data. Rather, researchers must simply remember that rigor in analyzing and interpreting the findings are needed as much in this environment as in others. For example, some of the studies reported above used statistics that assume a random sample to analyse data sets that were not randomly generated. Findings and conclusions of such studies must be viewed with caution. Such inappropriate use of analytical tools would probably not be tolerated by reviewers had not the Web-based subject mater of the studies been perceived as "new" and "innovative."

But new communication tools are not an excuse for ignoring established communication research techniques. In conclusion, the microscope of content analysis can be applied to the moving target of the Web. But researchers must use rigor and creativity to make sure that they don't lose focus before they take aim.

Chapter 10

Content Analysis of Online News

The landscape of news consumption is in the midst of a dramatic transition. As online news attracts more news consumers than ever before, Yahoo!News and Google News have, for now, established a stronghold in the news aggregation market. Aggregators produce little original news content, instead providing a platform for established news producers and access for users to multiple news sources. Arguably the most popular online news portal, Yahoo!News3 allows users to identify favourite topics-politics, business, science, entertainment-from various sources including Associated Press (AP), Agence France-Presse (AFP), Reuters, CNN, and others.

A recent Pew study determined that 23% of online news consumers chose Yahoo!News, and while Yahoo!News usage has continued to increase, competitor aggregators, such as Google News, and online news providers, such as MSNBC.com and CNN.com, have lost users. In the fickle world of online credibility ratings, YahooiNews is considered by consumers to be as trustworthy as national television and newspaper producers' Web sites and more credible than the online versions of local news media. And Yahool's customers are satisfied, with satisfaction scores increasing from 2006 to 2007.

This increased reliance on online news consumption brings with it many opportunities and challenges for mass communication research. Rich sources of text and images fundamental to mass communication research have never been more accessible, and while data can be gathered relatively easily, the sheer volume of available data can be overwhelming. The choice of appropriate sampling procedures is always a critical methodological decision, but unlike traditional print and broadcast media, the question of how much is enough to adequately represent online news content is yet to be rigorously addressed.

This chapter evaluates constructed week samples in terms of efficiency for representing online news content. Five sample sizes, ranging from one week (n=7 days) to five constructed weeks (n=35 days), are compared for their ability to accurately represent six months of content. Eight different content measures are used: four different news categories, plus average length of story, average number of photos, average number of videos, and the average number of "most popular" stories. In addition, the results are compared with the results from two other sampling techniques: simple random sampling and consecutive day sampling.

In her review of nineteen studies that applied content analysis techniques to the World Wide Web, McMillan found that few provided any discussion of sampling decisions and some applied statistics that "assume a random sample to analyse data sets that were not randomly generated." She concluded that the findings and conclusions of such studies must be viewed with caution and that the requirement for rigor in drawing a sample "may be one of the most difficult aspects of content analysis on the Web."

Sample selection is a critical content analysis design decision and must assure that each unit has the same chance of being represented in the collection of sampling units.10 In the early 1990s, Riffe and Lacy began a programme of research on sampling standards in the content analysis of traditional news media coverage. The recurring question for content analysts is, they argued, "how many sampled edition dates are needed to adequately represent the population during a particular period in time?"

More than half a century of news media research, beginning with Stempel's 1952 study of sampling daily newspapers, has shown that "the cyclic nature of media content can render simple random sampling inefficient compared to other types of sampling." Stratified sampling that yields constructed weeks has been the most convincing response to the problem of systematic content variation in media content. Constructed week samples "involve identifying all Mondays, and randomly selecting one Monday, then identifying all Tuesdays, and randomly selecting one Tuesday, etc., to 'construct' a week that ensures that each source of cyclic variation-each day of the week-is represented equally."

For example, after comparing different sampling methods, one study found that one constructed week was adequate for representing a six-month "population" of editions for a daily newspaper, but that two constructed weeks were better. While stratified sampling has some efficiency compared to random sampling for weekly newspapers and magazines, the influence of cycles in weekly or monthly content is not as strong, and so the relative efficiency of stratified (constructed) sampling compared to random sampling is not as high.

When studying sampling efficiency for nightly network newscasts, researchers found the selection of two days stratified by month to be most efficient. In contrast, simple random sampling demanded selecting thirty-five days to match the efficiency of the twenty-four-day-per-year sample required using stratified sampling.

The requirement for stratification has also been explored in the context of longitudinal studies of news content. In a study of sample size for newspaper content over multiple years, researchers deemed the selection of nine constructed weeks from five years to be more efficient than selecting two constructed weeks from each year or ten weeks in total, but only when the variables being measured had small variations. An important caveat for this finding was that, when variations in the variables under consideration are large, the sample size of ten constructed weeks should be used.

A review of online news research applying the content analysis method shows limited evidence of the application of random sampling techniques that might lend efficiency and support claims of representativeness and generalizability. Most researchers opt for sampling approaches that are purposive, convenience, consecutive days, or some combination therein. Stratification of sampling in published studies of online news is rarely discussed and even more rarely applied.

Sampling stratification decisions in the content analysis of online news coverage continue to be guided by the conventions developed by Riffe, Lacy, and others for traditional print and broadcast contentnewspapers, magazines, and network newscasts.

For example, Hoffman compared the content of online and print newspapers for differences in the frequency of mobilizing information, selecting a sample of one constructed week for each version to represent a seven-week period. This sampling approach assumed no difference between print and online news, and cited guidelines for sampling for newspapers from Riffe, Lacy, and Fico. In Lim's cross-lagged analysis of agenda setting among online news media, a sample of two constructed weeks was selected to represent a twelve-month period.

Bucy content analysed the home pages of four network affiliates, sampling purposively during approximately the same time (mid-October) in two years-1998 and 2000. The reasons for choosing this sampling approach are given limited explicit attention.

To compare online news sites with their printed counterparts, Boczkowski and de Santos collected online news content from three Argentine sites on two days per week, Monday through Friday only, for ten weeks. Schwalbe recognized that generalizations beyond the days and sites studied could not be made in her content analysis of the home pages of twenty-six mainstream news sites on every Wednesday for the first four weeks of the 2003 Iraq war.

Despite extensive research into sampling issues for newspapers of various types, as well as TV news broadcasts and news magazines, little is known about sampling for studying online news content. In the few instances where researchers have attempted to randomly sample online news content, they have relied on the research from traditional news media to guide sampling decisions. Do the same guidelines apply? Is online news content affected by daily variation similar to that in daily newspapers? How much content needs to be sampled to estimate the content in a longer time period? To address these issues, this study attempts to answer two research questions:

RQ1: What is the minimum number of randomly constructed weeks necessary to accurately generalize to a population of six months of online news?

RQ2: Is a constructed week sample more efficient than simple random or consecutive day samples of comparable size?

METHOD

Testing sampling efficiency for generalizing to a six-month population of online news content requires knowledge of population parameters to compare with obtained sample statistics. This study used data from a content analysis of news content on the Yahoo! News portal collected daily between 11 a.m. and 2 p.m. (EST) from December 15, 2005, to June 15, 2006. Data collected included the top five stories listed for each of the three wire services (Agence France Presse-AFP; Associated Press-AP; and Reuters), two newspapers (Christian Science Monitor-CSM and USA Today) and one cable TV news channel (CNN). Also captured were users' top five most-viewed, most-recommended, and most-e-mailed stories.

After approximately twelve hours of training, five coders examined each of the 7,438 separate articles collected during the 183-day period. Coding categories included news source, article length (in paragraphs), whether the story was a news source's top story, and whether the story was one of the top five most viewed stories, most e-mailed (one of the top five stories most often e-mailed by a reader to someone else), or most recommended story (one of the top five stories based on user ratings). Also coded were whether the story had a link on the home page and whether it was accompanied by still images, video footage, or audio clips. Additionally, adapting the YahooiNews categories, coders organized the articles into one of nine topics: world, business, entertainment, sports, health, technology, U.S. government/politics, science/education, and odd news. The coders used data from days not coded in this study to pretest the coding schedule and work out coding disagreements.

Intercoder reliability was calculated with Holsti's coefficient of reliability using data from the first seven days of December and the first fourteen days of February (11.5% of the data). Agreement was 100% for the "Most Popular" variable and 98% for "Story Length," "Photos," and "Video." For the nine news topic categories, the intercoder reliability outcomes are as follows: "World," 93%; "Business," 92%; "Entertainment," 97%; "Sports," 100%; "Health," 99%; "Technology," 90%; "U.S. Government/Politics," 90%; "Science & Education" 99%; and "Odd News," 90%.

For this study, the 183 days were treated as the population, and data were used to create, for this study's purposes, eight variables describing the content for each day. The eight variables showed a degree of variation in their means and standard deviations that would provide a more conservative test than using just a single variable. The variables were:

News Category 1: Percentage of "Odd News" stories each day

News Category 2: Percentage of "Sports" and "Entertainment" stories each day

News Category 3: Percentage of "Health," "Tech," "Science," and "Business" stories each day

News Category 4: Percentage of "U.S. Government/ Politics," and "World" stories each day

Story Length: Average number of paragraphs in each story coded each day

Photos: Percentage of stories containing photos/slides each day

Video: Percentage of stories containing video each day

Most Popular Stories: Percentage of stories each day that are simultaneously featured as a Top 5 story among online users (most e-mailed, most viewed, or most recommended) in addition to being a Top 5 story for at least one of the news sources.

Once population parameters were known, the first step involved drawing constructed week samples in sets of fifty. Originally, fifty samples of one constructed week (n=7) were drawn, as were fifty samples of two constructed weeks (n=14), fifty samples of three constructed weeks (n=21), and fifty samples of four constructed weeks (n=28). However, after analyzing these samples, an additional set of fifty samples of five constructed weeks (n=35) was also drawn.

The second step involved drawing comparable sets of fifty samples for comparison using both simple random sampling and consecutive day sampling. Fifty 7-day samples were randomly selected, as were fifty 14-day samples, fifty 21-day samples, fifty 28-day samples, and fifty 35-day samples.

For consecutive day samples, fifty random starting points were generated and, for each, seven consecutive days were selected to form a sample week. The same process was used, again with random starting points, to create fifty two-week (fourteen consecutive days) samples, fifty three-week (twenty-one consecutive days) samples, fifty four-week (twenty-eight consecutive days) samples, and fifty five-week (thirty-five consecutive days) samples.

The third step was to compare the efficiencies of the various sampling methods and sample sizes. These comparisons are based on the distribution of sample means predicted by the Central Limits Theorem. Because this distribution is based on a normal curve, in 68% of the samples, the population mean should fall within plus or minus one standard error of the sample mean, and in 95% of the samples, the population mean should fall within plus or minus two standard errors of the sample mean.

The percentage of times the population mean fell within

the ranges predicted by the theorem was then computed for each sample size and sampling method.

The CV is the standard deviation divided by the mean and represents the variability of the units in the population. A higher CV indicates more variation among the cases. In this population of news stories, three variables show relative low variation: News Category 4 (CV=.11), average Story Length (CV=.10), and Photos (CV=.17). On the other hand, two variables, News Category 1 (CV=.86) and Most Popular Stories (CV=.81), have very high coefficients of variation. Past research has shown that high variability requires larger sample sizes in order to be representative of the population.

RQ1 asked: What is the minimum number of randomly constructed weeks necessary to accurately generalize to a population of six months of online news? As noted earlier, constructed week sampling assumes that there is systematic, or cyclic, variation of content by day of week. For example, Sunday has the highest average number of sports and entertainment stories (News Category 2), but the lowest average number of health, tech, science, and business stories (News Category 3) as well as the lowest average number of videos.

Data present the results for fifty samples of 7-, 14-, 21-, 28- and 35-day constructed week samples for each variable. Each underlined percentage indicates that the sampling percentage exceeded the values determined by the Central Limits Theorem (68% for plus or minus one standard error; 95% for plus or minus two standard errors).

Based on the decision criteria used in previous research,36 sample size was efficient if both its percentages equaled or exceeded the expected percentages, provided that the next larger sample size did not drop below either of the expected percentages.

Using these criteria, a sample of two constructed weeks (n=14) was efficient for four of the variables. These four variables, News Category 3 (CV =.31), News Category 4 (CV=.ll), Photos (CV=.17), and Video (CV=.49), had coefficients of variation that were less than.50.

The remaining four variables still did not meet the efficiency criteria when an additional week was added to form a sample of three constructed weeks (n=21). Instead, a sample of four constructed weeks (n=28) was required for two variables, News Category 2 (CV=.48) and Average Story Length (CV=.10), despite the fact that Average Story Length had the lowest CV of any variable tested.

The Most Popular Stories (CV=.81) variable did not meet the efficiency criteria until five constructed weeks (n=35) were used. None of the sample sizes tested were efficient for the variable with the highest CV, News Category 1 (CV=.86). This variable reached the expected percentages with one constructed week (n=7), but then dropped below the criteria levels for the remaining sample sizes.

RQ2 asked: Is a constructed week sample more efficient than simple random or consecutive day samples of comparable size? For simple random samples, only the 21-day sample for one variable (Video) and the 28-day sample for one variable (Most Popular Stories) meet both sets of decision criteria (equaling or exceeding the expected percentages, provided that the next larger sample size did not drop below either of the expected percentages). For the consecutive day samples, the 28day sample for one variable (News Category 3) is the only sample meeting both sets of decision criteria. Compared to constructed week samples, simple random and consecutive day samples are much less efficient.

Based on the results of this study, sampling requirements for online news content are somewhat different from those of traditional media. Constructed week sampling is still the most efficient type of sample, but sample size needs to be much larger. While previous research concluded that a single constructed week would allow reliable estimates of content in a population of six months of newspaper editions, this study shows that, at a minimum, two constructed weeks are needed. Moreover, as many as five constructed weeks may be needed for some online news content depending on the type of variables being analysed. In addition, both simple random and consecutive day samples performed particularly poorly and should probably be avoided.

As a general rule, variables with high variability need larger samples. Among the variables in this study, the one with the highest level of variability, News Category 1 ("Odd News," CV=.86), never reached the established efficiency criteria for the sample sizes tested, while the variable with the second most variability, Most Popular Stories (CV=.81), needed at least five constructed weeks to represent six months of content. On the other hand, some low variability samples such as News Category 4, Photos (CV=.17), and News Category 3 met the efficiency criteria with just two constructed weeks.

Previous research suggests using a coefficient of variation of.5 as the criterion for increasing sample size. The results of this study imply that this approach may not be sufficient. Two variables in this study, Video (CV=.49) and News Category 2 ("Sports" and "Entertainment;" CV=.48), had almost identical coefficients of variation but required very different sample sizes, two and four constructed weeks, respectively. One possible explanation is the difference in population percentages. The population mean for the Video variable (15.24) was higher than the population mean for the News Category 2 variable (9.50). A similar pattern is seen in comparing the four news category variables.

The two news category variables with highest population means (News Category 3 and News Category 4) also require the smallest sample sizes, two constructed weeks. In addition, the variable with the lowest CV (.10) and a relatively low population mean, Average Story Length, required a sample of four constructed weeks to meet the threshold while other variables with low CVs but higher population means required only two constructed weeks. Future research should investigate the relationships between population means and CVs, along with other indicators of variability, as criteria for determining sample size.

Of course, this study cannot be generalized to all online news content because only one news aggregator, YahooiNews, was examined. Additional research is needed to examine other sources and types of online news content. In addition, news content was gathered only once each day. Research is needed to determine if variation in news content throughout the day affects sampling requirements.

Like most of the previous research on sample size for content analysis of the media, the variables in question are the types that are simply counted. Future research using different types of variables common to media content analyses (tone, frames, etc.) would also be a very useful contribution to the content analysis sampling literature.

Research shows a decline in voter turnout since the 1950s, while other forms of political participation also have declined over the past four decades. Reduced newspaper readership has been named as one precursor to this falloff in participation, with newspaper readership decreasing from 47% in 2000 to 42% in 2004.

Some scholars hail the Internet as a possible route for reinvigorating the democratic process and encouraging citizens to become more involved. Others have argued the Internet could negatively affect the electorate, much like other media such as the telephone and television, which at first were thought to enhance participation. However, a study by Kraut et al. suggests that such negative effects of the Internet have dissipated. "Changes in the Internet environment itself," they noted, "might be more important to understanding the observed effects than maturation or differences between samples."

Those seeking news online increased from 23% in 2000 to 29% in 2004. Reading political news is also popular: 40% of Internet users reported this activity in 2002. This suggests that news and politics online could have substantial effects and that systematic analysis of this content could be fruitful.

Communication scholars have long advocated examination of content10 in addition to time spent with a medium. Content, more than just the diverse materials presented on various media, changes from day to day. Analysis of content is important in understanding what information people are exposed to, above and beyond measures of time spent with media.

Content analyses of the Internet, though, have generally focused on how messages are presented rather than what is communicated. Thus, in the absence of a true theoretical framework, many Internet studies fail to come to replicable conclusions.

Bucy asserted, "Web content is often measured and described in a theory-free context, adding little to our conceptual understanding of the online medium." Although effects cannot be ascertained from a content analysis, the absence of content research in the Internet-effects debate ignores the importance of studying content before effects. As Riffe, Lacy, and Fico argued, "in the long run, one cannot study mass communication without studying content." One type of content that has been studied in analyses of news and that is the focus of this study is mobilizing information (MI), defined simply as information found in news that aids people to act on attitudes they already hold.

THEORETICAL FRAMEWORK

The introduction of a new communication technology, such as the Internet, allows scholars to "rethink, rather than abandon, definitions and categories," including conceptualizations like MI. This shady seeks to answer the question: Does the presence of MI differ in online versus print newspaper contexts? Eveland suggested applying uniform analyses to media, assessing "mixed attributes" to differentiate media. This study assesses print and online content in as uniform a way as possible to evaluate whether new technology has changed the content of newspapers.

Importantly, new technology alters the sociology of news production, which suggests that content differences may be found. For instance, Pavlik predicts that new media will encourage journalists to move beyond norms of objectivity. Some cases of what Pavlik calls "contextualized journalism" have already occurred. For example, reader feedback via e-mails to journalists has changed the way future stories are written, readers can create unique content, and journalists have relinquished some control to consumers who can customise their news experience. Newspapers, in particular, are being forced to make their Web sites "commercially viable" to compete with other sources.

Boczkowski found that online newsrooms differ from print newsrooms in the amount of autonomy they have, policies, and definitions of Web site users. He suggested that online, news "moves from being mostly journalist-centered...to also being increasingly audience-centered." The Internet could also have advantages over other media because reduced material cost can provide more incentive for consumers to search for political information as well as decrease production costs for news producers.

THE INTERNET AS A PARTICIPATORY MEDIUM

Much debate surrounding the Internet as a political and participatory medium relates to its ability to create new relationships; function as a virtual forum; or enhance social networks. Findings generally show that this social aspect of the Internet is ineffective in producing social trust or engagement. Some research has found, however, that online users who search for information and exchange e-mail, rather than those who chat or play games, are more active in civic life.

Thus far, no empirical research directly links the Internet to political participation. Indirect effects have been monitored, and "political learning and motivation for participation are enhanced through various types of communication, which in turn increases the level of political participation." In this way, the information that so many users seek online could encourage participation.

MOBILIZING INFORMATION

MI can be found online via hyperlinks, contact information, and linked content on other Web sites. Although it does not inherently motivate citizens, MI enables them to act on existing motivations by providing information on how to follow through with an action. Research on MI has declined since the 1980s, yet the concept continues to be cited in the context of media's role in mobilizing political participation and civic engagement, as well as in health communication.33 MI is relevant to the discussion of media effects and political participation because MI has the potential for directly encouraging citizens to become involved in politics.

Lemert and his colleagues, credited with the term, acknowledged that MI originated in publications on environmental and media studies. Two articles, published mere months apart, are cited as the concept's inspiration. Murch's content analysis of newspapers revealed that local media focused more on national rather than local pollution issues, excluding information that could provide information on which to act.

Rubin and Sachs's report correlated increased public interest in environmental issues and increased media discourse on the environr .nt during the 1970s.

While "mobilizing information" was not referenced explicitly, Rubin and Sachs referred to "specific information, and the day-to-day alerting which is necessary for any citizen to participate effectively in the legislative process," which "the public at large still expects the news media to provide." They asserted that the public does not have access to such information outside the media and "one cannot become involved without at least knowing when and where hearings are being held, and who it is that should be contacted in order to voice an opinion."

THREE TYPES OF MOBILIZING INFORMATION

Locational MI provides information about the time and place of an activity; identificational MI provides names and contact information for people or groups; and tactical MI is the explicit and implicit instructions for certain behaviors, such as tactics used in a strike. Because some MI could be controversial or even harmful, Lemert argued that mainstream media are reluctant to provide coverage of such events, let alone publish information that might encourage participation.

Lemert also differentiated between "political MI," (locational, identificational, and tactical) and nonpolitical MI (such as advertisements, cooking recipes, or garden tips). He admitted, however, that MI "needs to be described in more detail" and that it is "a relatively new concept, and our thinking about it is still changing."

How does one move forward, then, in a meticulous study of MI in news content? Lemert provided calls for research, most of which centered on reasons MI is excluded from media content. He claimed, however, that there is so little MI in news that it becomes difficult to test for it. Previous work on MI has focused on environmental or specialized contexts. The present study seeks to analyse the concept in a more general news context.

Where Is Mobilizing Information? MI is essential in advertising; the advertiser wants potential customers to know where and how to purchase a product or service (e.g., "in your grocer's freezer"). In news, however, MI varies depending on the type of news presented. Positive and noncontroversial items are most likely to include MI because they are "harmless" or "good for the community." Local items are more likely than nonlocal and wire items to include MI. Editorial pages, including letters to the editor, are extremely unlikely to contain MI because of a journalistic emphasis on an opinion forum rather than a "bulletin board" of community or political causes.

A contemporary content analysis of MI must acknowledge that there could be differences between Lemert's conceptualizations and the reality of today's news content. Online mobilizing information can take the form of e-mail links, discussion boards, or links to government agencies, interest groups, political candidates, and other sites.

MOBILIZING INFORMATION ONLINE

There are multiple reasons for revisiting MI, particularly in light of new media technology. Hyperlinks lead Web users to new information, either within a site or outside it. Some online newspaper sites provide audio/video links or interactive links to discussions, polls, and chat rooms, which may also provide further mobilizing information. While much online newspaper content is loaded by "shovelware" straight from print content, the possibilities for additional MI arguably abound in this new technology.

Because online newspapers are nonlinear, they may provide the user with more control and make information more readily available. Hyperlinks are common in online news. Tewksbury and Althaus claim that hyperlinks in online newspapers provide access to information that is often buried in print newspapers. Hyperlinks represent a shift away from the traditional gatekeeping role for mainstream media, by providing the user with more control and interactivity, enhancing comprehension. Moreover, online newspapers can cross-link to related sites and potentially provide more in-depth articles in the nearly limitless space available.

In addition, online newspapers might present different content because, "to attract and serve a younger demographic, [they] must live by different rules." For example, SFGate.com (the portal for the San Francisco Chronicle) published a photo of barebacked runners; the print Chronicle took a more conventional approach, printing photos of clothed runners. Lawrence.com (Kansas) published an entertainment column online with numerous profanities that, in the paper version, were printed with asterisks.

Although these are by no means examples of MI, they provide anecdotal evidence that online newspapers do not always publish exactly the same content or follow the same rules as print papers. If online newspapers need to make themselves "commercially viable," they may differentiate themselves from their print counterparts through inclusion of MI, which could be considered unsuitable for print.

Scholars have already assessed some differences between online and "offline" content. For example, traditional print and broadcast campaign information has been found to differ from campaign Web sites, which actually conformed to look like each other by including similar portals of content. This suggests that if content tends to become homogenized, as

Bagdikian claimed, online newspapers may resemble other Web sites more than their print counterparts.

Therefore:

H1: Online newspapers will have more MI than print newspapers.

Additionally, a question that has not been clarified in previous research is whether one type of MI is more prevalent in news content. A first step toward understanding the types of MI is assessing which appears most often.

RQ1: Does one type of MI (locational, identificational, or tactical) exist more than another in print news content?

RQ2: Does one type of MI (locational, identificational, or tactical) exist more than another in online news content?

METHOD

SAMPLE

This study sampled a broad selection of American newspapers, both print and online, selected to include a variety of communities, ownership statuses, circulation rankings, content, and regions. News media are subject to publication cycles, so this analysis used the "constructed week" method, which randomly selects an issue for each day of the week to account for systematic variation due to the day of the week.

Riffe, Lacy, and Fico recommended two constructed weeks from a year for daily newspapers (randomly selecting two Mondays, two Tuesdays, etc.). For convenience purposes, and to obtain the most current sample, this study analysed one constructed week (seven days) during the seven-week period from 19 October to 3 December 2003. The days within each week were selected using a random numbers table without replacement. Online content can vary from hour to hour, so online news was downloaded and archived at the same time for each day sampled.

MEASUREMENT

The unit of analysis was the individual news story. Print

newspapers were analysed for presence and type of MI in text. However, online newspapers require a different set of indicators to identify MI. Web-specific elements such as discussion boards and hyperlinks cannot be ignored. Therefore, nonlinear elements-audio/video links, interactive links, and hyperlinks-were coded. Definitions were created to differentiate between types of pages and types of links.

CONCEPTUAL AND OPERATIONAL DEFINITIONS

Because explicit coding rules and criteria for analyzing MI have not been published previously, both conceptual and operational definitions of locational, identificational, and tactical MI were constructed for this analysis. Although MI can be found within different contexts, this study examines only political news, as derived from Perloff's definition of politics: "a process whereby a group of people, whose opinions or interests are initially divergent, reach collective decisions which are generally regarded as binding on the group, and enforced as common policy."

Therefore, political MI contained only those news stories about decisions that are regarded as binding on the group and enforced as common policy. Specifically included were stories in National, International, Political, and Local/Metro sections.

Only MI that fit this definition of "politics" was coded. Operationally, this means that to be included, each instance of MI had to represent a decision to be made regarding public policy or government. Because this is still quite broad, an example may help demonstrate criteria for inclusion. An announcement for a neighborhood social where community members are welcome to share food and play games would not be included, while an announcement for a neighborhood meeting to discuss new regulations enforced by city council would.

The question to be answered in deciding what content should be included was, "Does this represent the fact that multiple opinions exist and a common policy should or will ultimately be enforced by political actors?"

The three types of MI are not mutually exclusive and more than one type may exist in a unit of analysis, particularly with tactical MI (i.e., a unit may describe specifically how to accomplish an activity, but also provide the time and place for that activity).

Locational MI provides information about a time and place for an activity. Excluded from examples of locational MI were programme listings for television and radio, as well as obituaries. The fundamental attribute of locational MI is that it provides a time and place for a political activity or event. An example of locational MI from this study's sample provided information about a Philadelphia City Council committee: "The committee meeting will be at 3 p.m. tomorrow in Room 696 at City Hall."

Online, there are multiple opportunities for locational MI that may not exist in print. A meeting announcement might be hyperlinked from a story about a new residential development, or a hyperlink could link to details on a weekend rally. For both print and online, the question to ask when assessing locational MI was, "Does this give me enough information to attend an event in which I might be interested?"

Identificational MI provides names and contact information for a political candidate or representative, interest group, political party, corporation, or government agency. Examples include names and addresses or phone numbers; names and positions in relatively stable, easily locatable organizations (i.e., Vice President Dick Cheney); and company or group names.

Again, the emphasis is on strictly political or publicpolicy contexts and the key element is contact information. Online, a hyperlink is inherently identificational if it links to an e-mail address or a Web site of a person or organization. Reporters often provide a link to their e-mail address in their byline. Because this study examined political news, these links were included, as they allow readers to act on information they read. Not all newspapers provided this information. However, the Philadelphia Inquirer, for example, provided both a phone number and e-mail address for each article. Tactical MI makes available explicit and implicit behavioral models for action.

In this study, only explicit tactical information was coded. Explicit tactical MI tells a person exactly how to accomplish a political activity without necessarily providing a time, place, or contact information. The chief component of tactical MI is that it tells a reader how to do something, such as how to participate in a rally or how to affect the legislative process.

An example comes from the San Francisco Chronicle, which encouraged citizens to contact officials when things went wrong in their neighborhoods. The Chronicle provided specific information on how to make a complaint to be published in the newspaper and, once complaints were published, contact information for officials in charge was given.

This represents tactical MI because explicit directions are provided for how to accomplish the activity. The question asked in ascertaining tactical MI was, "Does this give me enough information to become involved in some way, based on the attitudes I may already hold?"

PROCEDURE

Print articles were collected through subscriptions to each newspaper during the sampled period. Online articles were collected using WebZIP software (version 5.0.5.896) from Spidersoft and were downloaded only at the first level-the news article page and subsequent pages for that same article. The content beyond the news article page(s) was not downloaded for analysis.

Online and print articles were selected based on whether they fit the coding criteria, then assigned numbers. Links were assessed for mobilizing information based on the information they provided on the news article page(s) (i.e., if information provided on the page indicated that MI was accessible by clicking on that link).

An a priori power analysis was conducted using GPOWER software (version 2.0) in order to minimize the sample size while maintaining sufficient power. The total sample before this analysis was 1,418 articles. It was concluded that 65 articles per version of each newspaper (online and print) were adequate to maintain power, and the sample was reduced to 780 articles. Because some issues did not include enough articles to reach this total, the final sample was 763.

RELIABILITY

Two coders assessed reliability after being trained with coding rules and definitions. Reliability was analysed for locational, identificational, and tactical MI. Eighty-seven articles were sampled from the same seven-week period from days on which sampling did not take place. This meets Wimmer and Dominick's recommendation of coding 10% to 20% of the total sample for reliability. Krippendorf's alpha was used because it takes into account chance agreement.

All reliability coeffiecients met standards set by Krippendorf and Riffe, Lacy, and Fico (above.80), except tactical MI in online text (0.76), tactical MI in print text (0.72), and locational MI in online text (0.66). Latent content is admittedly more difficult to assess; therefore, those coefficients above.65 were deemed acceptable. Disagreements were addressed by the coders until understanding was reached before actual coding began. In order to prevent biases due to coder fatigue or repetitive stress, care was taken not to code articles in any systematic order and coding was completed in one- to two-hour increments.

RESULTS

MI IN NEWSPAPERS BY TYPE

Of all MI found in the sampled articles, identificational was the most plentiful. Lemert's definition, which stated simply that this type of MI "usually requires" both identification (such as a name) with locational information, did not provide specific coding rules or operationalizations. Therefore, coding rules were created. This may explain the differences in MI found here when compared to Lemert's and colleagues' findings.

Hungerford and Lemert found that 20% of environmental stories had some form of MI, while Lemert, et al. reported that 22.8% of main news stories had some form of MI. Similar results were gleaned from Stanfield and Lemert who found that, in two mainstream dailies, between 13% and 17% of all stories had some form of MI. Perhaps because of a more inclusive operationalization of identificational MI, 99.5% of articles in the present study contained some form of identificational MI, while 9% of all articles contained locational MI, and 5.1% contained tactical MI.

MI by Medium: Online versus Print. Hl predicted more MI overall in online newspapers than in print because of added space, technological advances, and relative freedom. But even with the inclusion of hyperlinks, video/audio links (of which there were zero occurrences with MI), interactive links, and online artwork, this hypothesis was not supported. There were indeed more occurrences of MI online than in print, but this relationship were not significant. When all the online-specific links were excluded, and only MI in text was included (i.e., the body of the story without any links), print newspapers had slightly more MI in text than online newspapers. Again, results were below the standards for marginal significance.

RQ1 asked whether one type of MI was more prevalent in print and online newspapers. There was significantly more identificational MI than locational MI online. Identificational MI also occurred more frequently in print than locational. Online, identificational MI had significantly more occurrences than tactical MI. In print, identificational MI occurred significantly more frequently than tactical MI.

The comparison between locational and tactical MI yields the only nonsignificant difference, and this is specific to print. There were no more occurrences of locational MI than tactical MI in print. The difference online, however, was significant, with more locational than tactical. Thus, identificational MI occurred with more frequency in both print and online contexts than either locational or tactical MI, and locational MI occurred more frequently online than in print. However, this last difference is most likely due to the enormity of the San Francisco Chronicle's archival links in its "ChronicleWatch."

Online newspapers do not differ significantly from print newspapers in terms of presence of mobilizing information, and look much like the "shovelware" versions Singer suggested.

The relative similarity between print and online versions of the newspaper-even accounting for value-added items such as links to archived content, audio/video links, and discussion boards-is startling.

This was not a print-to-print or text-only comparison; on the contrary, this analysis took into account those elements that make online newspapers different from print newspapers. This would suggest that the same fears Lemert cited as reasons journalists exclude MI in print newspapers might also apply to those publishing online.

That said, however, online newspapers are certainly not the only political and news content available online. There are countless government and interest-group Web sites, discussion boards, and "blogs," as well as nontraditional news sources unavailable in other media formats.

Moreover, non-newspaper sites may create "runoff" to newspaper sites. Therefore, although this study was limited to print and online newspapers, it provides a first step in examining MI online.

In addition to journalistic fears of endorsement, partisanship, or libel, there might be other factors acting to keep online newspapers similar to print versions. It has been argued that powerful media corporations establish norms and routines that keep journalists deferential to the media structure and that normalize content. Journalists who adhere to these routines are considered professional and rewarded, while those who oppose them might be reprimanded.

The most widely discussed of these norms is objectivity or neutrality-the desire to be fair and present "both sides" of an issue-a norm particularly widespread in American journalism.83 The adherence to norms could deter journalists from publishing MI online that threatens the status quo. However, online newspapers might simply be seeking consistency with their print counterparts in order to maintain a common voice. Interviews with online journalists could provide useful insights into these dynamics.

This study operationally distinguished among the three types of MI-locational, identificational, and tactical. Past research has focused on the reasons MI is excluded from news, and recent work on political participation that alludes to, or sometimes assumes, the presence of MI in news often fails to differentiate among the three types.

The near exclusion of tactical and locational MI in this study indicates that explicit MI is rare in both print and online newspapers. This raises questions about the validity of differentiating among these types that occur so infrequently. However, the volume of identificational MI begs important new questions: Is identification of a political individual enough to mobilize action on the part of the reader? Moreover, in this era-when to find more information, all a person has to do is "Google" someone-are mobilizing possibilities greater than they were before these technologies were available? Surveys and experiments with online users could provide us with answers.

Future studies could expand on this analysis by conducting similar research in health, environmental, and other contexts. Health communication researchers have already adopted the MI concept, although the conceptual and operational definitions used here have diverged substantially from those in the political and environmental contexts. A useful study would apply the same operationalizations to each context. Additionally, Lemert and Ashman, as well as Dunwoody and Griffin, examined mobilizing content in controversial or negative contexts, suggesting that tone also influences inclusion of MI.

A second, and laudable, addition to this content analysis would be an expanded examination of all content in online newspapers, including that found on discussion boards, chat rooms, hyperlinked sites, and audio/video clips. This information is inherently different from what is in print newspapers.

An expanded sample of newspapers including more regional variation might also find more differences. Examining news content on blogs, portal sites, and search engines could also yield new and interesting findings. Additionally, as Tremayne found, Web sites affiliated with broadcast networks are more "linked" than those affiliated with newspapers. An interesting direction for research would be to compare these two in terms of their mobilizing information.

Beyond examining MI in content, researchers could assess the cognitive processes involved in reading and understanding MI. Eveland and Scheufele argued that those in a community with higher SES are more likely to see MI and, perhaps more important, "they possess the information processing strategies and cognitive skills necessary to identify mobilizing information, even if it is less prominently placed or mentioned only implicitly." Individual and socioeconomic differences could play a key role in the usefulness of MI.

Finally, a reliability assessment for inclusion of political news in the sample would make the interpretation of these results more powerful. Print newspaper readership has consistently been correlated with higher rates of political participation, voter turnout, and civic engagement. If Internet news use is on the rise while print news use declines, what does this mean for the link between political participation and media use?

This study suggests that online newspapers provide content that simply reinforces print content. But even if mobilizing information in print and online newspapers is not significantly different, the effects may differ across readers. Because this study examines only content, effects cannot be ascertained, but this is clearly an area for further research. Indeed, the Internet could draw new readers who would not have otherwise been exposed to mobilizing content. In this case, more people may be exposed to more mobilizing information, despite declines in print newspaper readership.

Some researchers have noted that higher levels of Internet use are associated with higher levels of political participation. Johnson and Kaye asserted that Internet users represent "model citizens" and are more likely to be politically interested, efficacious, and seek information from the media. Moreover, evidence suggests that both gender and race gaps in Internet use are closing or closed, and children increasingly use the Internet at school and home. Improved understanding of how individuals use the Internet, as well as what content they view, will clearly add meaning to the present study's findings. The changing nature of the Internet environment demands that researchers take into account how both its audience and its content must continually be monitored.

Chapter 11

Peril of Anecdotes in News Coverage

Journalists for print and broadcast media often use anecdotes about individuals to illustrate larger points. Research on the use of examples about individuals, such as anecdotes, in news coverage has shown that exemplars shape people's perceptions of social issues. But even journalists understand the difficulties posed by anecdotes. Gina Kolata, a science reporter for the New York Times, said:

I think anecdotes are actually almost too powerful. I always call it the "tyranny of the anecdote." You have to be really careful with anecdotes because people will remember the anecdote and it will mean more to them than anything else you say. So you have to be very, very careful, I think, about how you use them, but I think that they're so powerful that they sort of cry out to be used if they can.

Rather than testing effects of anecdotes on audience understanding, as exemplification researchers have done, this chapter assesses the use of anecdotes on ethical grounds. It evaluates the ethical strengths and weaknesses of anecdotes as a journalistic device.

The analytical groundwork for ethical evaluation comes from a framework used earlier for assessing news coverage of ethical issues; Christians, Ferre, and Fackler's communitarian media ethics; and Gilligan's relationship-oriented feminist ethic. These perspectives hold that news coverage should address topics at the individual level and within broader contexts as well.

The three perspectives will be used to analyse some news coverage of human embryo research, physician-assisted suicide, and the practices of health maintenance organizations. The anecdotes used as cases for analysis are from major print and broadcast news organizations, organizations that presumably reflect the state of the art in use of anecdotes in reporting, however flawed that art may be.

This chapter will also discuss how journalists can choose anecdotes more critically, building on Boeyink's discussion of casuistry in journalistic decision making. Finally, it suggests an adaptation of the anecdotal form that is ethically supportable.

Studies of framing effects have found that episodic and human interest frames-in which anecdotes are often an element-affect audiences' thinking in important ways. In particular, Iyengar found that episodic framing, focusing news coverage on individuals and events, tends to prompt television news audiences to attribute responsibility for issues to individuals rather than social factors. Valkenburg, Semetko, and de Vreese found that crime stories framed in human interest terms prompted readers to emphasize emotions and implications for individuals more often, and to recall less information about an issue.

The literature on exemplification, because it focuses explicitly on the use and impact of examples, carries particular significance for an ethical analysis of anecdotes. Zillmann and Brosius address the problematic nature of anecdotes in noting that the concept of exemplification calls for the representation of groups of events "by single events that are typical and characteristic of the group.

Exemplification by atypical and uncharacteristic events is deemed inappropriate because it fails to provide reliable information about the group." Given the inherent difficulties of accurate representation through anecdotes, the prevalence of anecdotes in journalism stands out as an ethical issue.

Psychological research shows that exemplification can overwhelm the influence of base-rate information-broader figures or statements about the frequency or typicality of an event. In one study, subjects shown an article about a welfare recipient and an interview with a prison guard changed their minds about the population as a whole, regardless of what kind of information they received about how typical the case was.

Mass communication researchers have found that different distributions of exemplars have differing effects on audience perception of issues. Zillmann, Perkins, and Sundar varied the ratio of exemplars to counterexemplars in a story about keeping weight off after dieting.

The exemplars either all followed the focus of the story (selective exemplification), or were proportional to the situation in the broader population (representative), or disproportionately favored one side (blended). Audiences' perception of the overall incidence of weight regaining proved most accurate for the representative condition and least accurate for the selective.

Likewise, Brosius and Bathelt found that the perception of majority and minority opinions on public issues followed the distribution of exemplars. Zillmann et al. found that changes in the kinds of exemplars used in a news report on the plight of family farmers altered readers' perceptions of the prevalence of family farm failures.

Other research has examined the impact of using examples from extraordinary or highly emotional cases. Gibson and Zillmann found that estimates of the frequency of deaths in carjackings increased as exemplars were tilted more and more toward the unusual case of a fatal carjacking. A study of television news found that exemplification using emotional victims fostered perceptions that food poisoning problems and random violence were more severe than when unemotional or no victim exemplification was used.

Even the use of quotations in exemplars, a conventional journalistic practice, has been found to influence audiences. Gibson and Zillmann found that direct, one-sided personal testimony in print reports changed perceptions of amusement park safety. They also found that personal testimony about the plight of family farmers swayed readers' views. In addition, studies have found effects from the use of both threatening images and innocuous images, for example, changes in perception of risk of skin cancer. Findings about use of images are relevant to the evaluation of anecdotes in broadcast news because of its dependence on images. Viewed as a body, empirical studies on the power of exemplars indicate a need for careful consideration of the ethical implications of anecdote choice.

ANALYTICAL PERSPECTIVES

Three analytical perspectives are useful tools for assessing these ethical implications because they point both to the potential ethical good and the ethical dangers of anecdote use. A framework developed previously for studying coverage of news with an ethical dimension involves evaluating stories based on how thoroughly they portray the ethical issues relevant to a topic, the parties connected with those issues, the levels at which the ethical issues play out (individual, organizational/institutional, professional, and social), and the legal backdrop for those issues.

Although each story about ethics-laden topics cannot be expected to address all four of these elements comprehensively, coverage that addresses these areas well is considered to be ethical. The normative assumptions about journalism in this framework are in keeping with social responsibility and communitarian press theory, both of which emphasize the importance of not merely reporting events but also serving society.

The attention to levels of analysis reflects the importance of portraying individuals in news coverage. News coverage should include the ways that individuals and families are affected by decisions or events-such as a health maintenance organization's decision about whether to approve or deny coverage for a kind of cancer treatment. Anecdotes shine light on the difficulties that individuals face, and as such they are tools of ethical journalism.

The importance of the individual notwithstanding, journalists should go beyond that level to examine issues at the organizational/institutional, professional, and social levels. Attention to only one level of analysis, in an in-depth piece or a body of coverage, falls short of the moral obligation of journalists.

In this light, anecdotes are morally a double-edged sword. While they can bring attention to the plight of individuals in riveting fashion, and even place that plight in institutional, professional, and social contexts, the attention remains on a representative, or perhaps unrepresentative, individual or family, as exemplification studies have shown.

Furthermore, previous work suggests that news coverage should include an array of sources, including neither exclusively professionals (such as doctors or businesspeople) nor nonprofessionals (patients or customers). Good anecdotes, although they focus on an individual, may point out how that individual interacts with other people, as well as with organizations and institutions.

Attention to a range of relevant parties at a variety of levels, both in the anecdote and elsewhere in the story, can mitigate the potential ethical harm from anecdotes' narrow focus. But the exemplification literature suggests that the anecdote still would have power to shape readers' or viewers' perception of the broader issue.

Christians, Ferre, and Fackler's communitarian media ethic also provides ethical justification for using anecdotes to highlight the situations of individuals while it draws attention to the limitations of anecdotes. The idea of mutuality is central to this perspective, which has a variety of intellectual underpinnings including communitarian political theory and theology. Mutuality views humans as having their identity in relation to others and living both for others and themselves.

The relationship of persons and communities takes priority over either alone. This ethic is profoundly concerned with both society and the individual. The priority of justice creates a profound interest in the needs of the hurting or marginalized. "A press nurtured by communitarian ethics requires more of itself than fair treatment of events deemed worthy of coverage. Under the notion that justice itself-and not merely haphazard public enlightenment-is a telos of the press, the news-media system stands under obligation to tell the stories that justice requires." Part of telling "the stories that justice requires" involves telling the stories of individuals. This is because justice addresses fair treatment of individuals. One of the most powerful ways, in fact, to draw attention to such individuals is through the telling of their stories, in words and images, in print and broadcast media.

Even as it provides an ethical underpinning for use of anecdotes, communitarian media ethics, with its deeply grounded concern for the good of society, calls into question the structure and choice of anecdotes. Again, this ethic does support the use of compelling individual cases to highlight broader social injustices. However, sloppy use of anecdotes can undermine an effort to portray the broader issue, not simply because of the natural tendency of anecdotes to highlight individuals, but also because the particular choice of individuals can skew understanding toward one side of a controversial issue, resulting potentially in neglect of social justice.

The issue is not formulaic balance in news coverage; communitarian ethics calls for more than "fair treatment of events." Consonant with Durham's notion of "strong objectivity," Christians, Ferre, and Fackler call for highlighting the perspectives of the marginalized and, where needed, giving those perspectives attention that is out of balance with the play given to the stories of the powerful. However, since communitarian ethics also implies a concern for faithful portrayal of the whole community, it implies a need to portray the breadth of the community's concern.

Gilligan's feminist ethic of care supports the use of anecdotes because it, too, is concerned with persons in relationships. This perspective, developed out of psychological studies of women's distinctive conceptions of morality, underlines the importance of relationships and responsibilities. Discussing one of her interviewees, Gilligan writes: "Her world is a world of relationships and psychological truths where an awareness of the connection between people gives rise to a recognition of responsibility for one another, a perception of the need for response." Commenting on how another interviewee viewed activities of care, she writes: "The ideal of care is thus an activity of relationship, of seeing and responding to need, taking care of the world by sustaining the web of connection so that no one is left alone." This ethic of care in relationships, however, is not relevant only to women, Gilligan argues. "To admit the truth of the women's perspective to the conception of moral development is to recognize for both sexes the importance throughout life of the connection between self and other, the universality of the need for compassion and care."

Anecdotes are ethically significant in the context of this perspective because they can help to portray the web of personal relationships and responsibilities involved in ethical situations. Anecdotes can dramatically represent the difficulties that individuals, including women facing illnesses such as breast cancer, face in relation to their families and others outside their families, such as physicians. In fact, use of anecdotes are in keeping with the attention to particulars that Gilligan found women bringing to their moral analysis. She discusses what happens when women go beyond hypothetical dilemmas:

> However, the reconstruction of the dilemma in its contextual particularity allows the understanding of cause and consequence which engages the compassion and tolerance repeatedly noted to distinguish the moral judgments of women. Only when substance is given to the skeletal lives of hypothetical people is it possible to consider the social injustice that their moral problems may reflect and to imagine the individual suffering their occurrence may signify or their resolution engender.

This passage implies that anecdotes may awaken attention both to the suffering of individuals and the social context of their difficulties. It suggests that, despite the danger of distortion of the broader picture that the exemplification literature suggests, deep concern for the people behind issues that journalists report may arise only through telling the stories of individuals. Even as it underpins the ethical value of anecdotes, the ethic of care also implies a need for careful attention to what anecdotes are chosen and what they portray. It implies a need for accurate understanding of responsibilities of individuals in the broader context of society, so that the web of relationships and people's responsibilities within them is rightly understood.

All three perspectives suggest that anecdotes are best when they situate individuals they mention in the broader context of the issues being discussed. These three perspectives all draw attention to the value of the individual and therefore imply that it is ethically justifiable to use anecdotes to draw attention to the needs and concerns of individuals.

The communitarian ethic and the ethic of care complement the ethics coverage framework by emphasizing the individual in relationships. Communitarianism puts priority on the hurting and marginalized. The ethic of care draws attention to the importance of the circumstances of the lives of individuals in prompting a depth of concern for them. Even as they draw attention to the individual, however, all three perspectives emphasize the need to think beyond the individual to the broader contexts of a problem, thereby implying that anecdotes should be carefully chosen for how they may limit or draw attention to these contexts.

METHOD FOR CASE ANALYSIS

These three analytical perspectives will be applied to three anecdotes taken from larger bodies of stories about human embryo research, physician-assisted suicide, and HMOs, all topics that have received attention from the media and professionals during the past decade. These topics lend themselves to powerful use of anecdotes because of their life-and-death import.

Even though both the exemplification literature and the analytical perspectives used here suggest this power may be a mixed blessing, it is appropriate to study these kinds of topics because of the priority that journalists place on powerful, compelling anecdotes.

Stories used here were published or aired during a key period of public discourse on each topic. For human embryo research, this was 1994-1995, amid federal debate on the subject. For physician-assisted suicide, it was 1997-1999, which encompassed a Supreme Court ruling that there is no general constitutional right to assisted suicide, passage of law in Oregon legalizing the practice, and the trial of Dr. Jack Kevorkian for euthanasia. For health maintenance organizations, 1997-1998 was a time of increasing legal and political attention to HMO practices. For each topic, both print and broadcast stories that dealt significantly with the ethical dimension of the issue were examined.36

The anecdotes analysed as cases were chosen for their vivid language and emotional power. In these respects, they represent the kinds of anecdotes that journalists strive to include in stories on many topics. Thus, while it is inescapable that they cannot fully represent the range of anecdote use, even in the topics studied, they represent an aspect of standard journalistic usage. They are, therefore, appropriate for ethical analysis of the strong and weak points in this usage.37 Although space limits consideration to one anecdote from each topic, both print and broadcast cases are included to make the ethical analysis more relevant to both.

ANALYSIS OF CASES

George Strait used an anecdote to help illustrate an ABC TV news story about human embryo research, aired just after a federal advisory panel recommended that federal funding be used to pay for research on human embryos. The story outlined arguments for and against human embryo research. This anecdote, shown in the middle of the piece, was the second of two that illustrated potential benefits of human embryo research. The story showed a girl born after genetic testing of her mother's embryos, and Strait talked with the girl's father. Strait described the treatment that enabled this girl to be born, against the backdrop of video that included shots of her:

This research on human embryos has vast potential, from

improving fertility and contraceptives to better screening for genetic diseases.

Take Brittany Abshire [baby is shown wearing a bow on her head and a fançy dress]. Her parents, Rene and David Abshire, were afraid they might never have a healthy baby. Their first child, Meaghan [face is shown close-up in a still portrait], died of a rare genetic disease called Tay-Sachs. They got help here at the Jones Institute, where doctors recently developed a way to test an embryo for defective genes. Her deformed embryos were discarded; only healthy ones were implanted through in vitro fertilization. The result is Brittany [the dressed-up baby is shown again].

By showing compelling video of real people affected by embryo research-especially children-Strait brought home the reality that this ethical topic touches individuals deeply. He thus drew attention to the individual level while remaining consistent with the ethic of care, by showing the web of family relationships in which the individuals are affected profoundly by decisions made about in vitro fertilization. In addition, he used professionals elsewhere in the story to show others involved in these kinds of cases, including a doctor at the institute the Abshires used. He thus represented a range of parties.

In this case, the communitarian ethic does not apply as strongly in the sense that the people involved were not poor or marginalized. But the decisions paralleled those faced by thousands of other families-all of whom, in communitarian terms, should be concerned about people who face similar situations. The story served to highlight the difficulties faced by couples seeking in vitro fertilization, and it pointed appropriately to ethical questions raised about embryo research as well as the benefits.

However, especially given television's ability to use emotional visuals, the use of anecdotes may overshadow broader issues. Strait's anecdote about the Abshire family used a still portrait of their now-deceased child, Meaghan, and shots of dressed-up baby Brittany, born after tests of other embryos for genetic defects and the use of in vitro fertilization.

The story also used as sources two doctors, a Catholic leader critical of embryo research, and a member of a National Institutes of Health panel on human embryo research. This sourcing shows that Strait was seeking to place the issue in broader organizational, professional, and social context. But shots of a child who died and of a cute, living baby may overshadow the discussion of the broader context, especially since this and the only other anecdote in the story were used to illustrate potential benefits to individuals.

The second anecdote examined came from an NBC Nightly News story reported by Mike Boettcher. After anchor Brian Williams' introduction, Boettcher opened his reporting this way:

Mike Boettcher reporting: No matter what Barbara Oskamp does, no matter how simple the act, the terminally ill woman writes it down [video shows list of simple things she must write down to remember], otherwise she'll forget when she takes a bath, when she washes clothes. A brain tumor slowly is taking her memory as it takes her life, and she wants the option to end her suffering before the pain becomes unbearable [close-up of her]. She supports Oregon's Death With Dignity Act, the only assisted suicide law in the nation.

Ms. Barbara Oskamp: I don't know I'd be brave enough to actually do it. But the feeling that I had a choice, if the pain, maybe, was too awful, just as I said before, gave me a feeling of relief.

The use of this anecdote is commendable from the standpoint of the ethics coverage framework in that it drew attention to the difficulties of the terminally ill at the individual level. From the standpoint of communitarian ethics, with its priority of mutuality and its attention to the marginalized, it amounted to a call for better support-emotional and medical-for this woman and others like her.

Similarly, through the lens of the ethic of care, this examination of the particulars of Oskamp's daily life might evoke empathy for her suffering and consideration of the justice of the system of care for her (as well as concern about what seems in this anecdote to be an absence of relationships).

However, again these perspectives point to ethical lapses. Oskamp's plight was heart-rending, and it likely would evoke empathy from the audience because she was suffering. However, the very power of this portrayal of suffering may obscure consideration of issues such as, at the professional level, the role of better pain management or counseling, and, at the social level, the implications of legal assisted suicide for people with disabilities and terminally ill individuals who cannot pay for insurance.

Social-level issues would be particularly important in the communitarian ethic-which, while supporting the attention to Oskamp and the concerns her situation raised, would also call for more direct attention to these other areas. A doctor was quoted as raising concern about impact on the poor-also important context under the ethic of care -but this professional voice was not as compelling as Oskamp's.

The third anecdote case concerns HMOs, which have become controversial in recent years because of the impact of HMO cost controls on patients. One repeated feature in the HMO stories, particularly the television pieces, was the use of anecdotes that were sympathetic to patients dealing with the fallout of HMO cost controls and related issues. A lengthy story in the Los Angeles Times, part of a series on "The HMO Backlash" in Ventura County, opened with that kind of account:

Norma Barry had been treated by Simi Valley family doctor Elvin Gaines all her life. She trusted him so much he delivered both of her babies. She believed in his judgment to such a degree that she never argued when Gaines prescribed common painkillers after she complained of headaches and dizziness. Then, in late 1996, she died at age 26 of a massive brain hemorrhage, and evidence suggests she may have suffered from a series of small brain bleeds.

"I blame myself so much for not making her go to another doctor," said her husband, Simi Valley truck mechanic Jerome Barry.

Just a few years ago, the Barry case would have represented nothing more than a routine, though tragic, claim of malpractice-a lawsuit not yet resolved in court: Gaines insists he did nothing wrong, and his attorney says medical records do not show a history of chronic headaches.

But in this y ear of HMO reform, it stands as a purported example of how HMO financial incentives to cut costs can interfere with a doctor's treatment of his patients-and as a reason that lawmakers, doctors, and patients are trying to change managed-care medicine. Jerome Barry claims not only negligence, but that his wife was mistreated by Gaines because an HMO contract required the doctor to pay out of his own pocket for the costly special test the young mother needed, but never got.

This anecdote, too, riveted attention on the plight of an individual, consistent with the three analytical perspectives and especially the ethic of care's concern with the particulars of such a plight. It also placed Norma Barry in the context of her relationship with her husband, who was obviously agonizing over her death, and a relationship of trust with her doctor-in keeping with both the communitarian ethic and the ethic of care.

The account also drew readers toward the organizational/institutional and professional levels because the example was placed in the context of the HMO reform debate that touched on business, medicine, and politics. This paragraph of context also implied concern with the justice of HMO interference in the treatment of patients.

Again, though, there are ethical problems, particularly in the fact that the anecdote, although couched in broader terms, may limit attention at the broader levels. Medical costs must be controlled. Because of the serious nature of medical problems, how costs are to be controlled becomes a profound issue of social ethics. Even though the story pointed to the broader issue of cost-cutting, exemplification research suggests that readers may better remember the individual, tragic case and thus miss the broader attention to economic reality.

Daniel Callahan, a medical ethicist, sees the use of anecdotes as hindering consideration of broader resource questions. His comment regarding use of anecdotes in the assisted-suicide debate is also cautionary regarding HMO coverage and portrayal of other topics that involve social ethics: "I'm endlessly on programs with people who tell these sad stories, and it's very hard to talk about the larger social dangers of physician-assisted suicide when somebody's got a sad story."

The analysis of anecdotes about assisted suicide and HMOs bolsters the argument that anecdotes are ethically problematic if they ignore broader consideration of social-level concerns, such as just treatment of the terminally ill and just allocation of health care resources.

Applying the three analytical vantage points to the three examples suggests the importance of careful consideration of how and when anecdotes are to be used in news stories, especially against the backdrop of the exemplification literature's findings on the influence of exemplars. This section will suggest an approach that adapts the advantages of anecdotes but avoids some of their liabilities.

The suggestions for more critical thinking about choice of anecdotes arise out of an application of David Boeyink's discussion of use of casuistry in journalists' ethical decision making. Casuistry is an appropriate method here because it is case-based, as is anecdote choice. Casuists consider comparison of cases to be highly important in determining whether an action is morally justifiable.

The anchor for the comparison and judgment is a paradigm case (or cases), in which the decision made is morally unambiguous. In classical Jesuit casuistry, such a case might involve a clear breach of the biblical command against killing.

In terms of journalism ethics, it might mean taking an expensive gift from a news source - or, at the ethical end of the spectrum, accepting a free cup of coffee. In either realm of decision making, ambiguous cases are compared to clear-cut cases before choices are made. The choice of paradigm case thus becomes critical to the decision maker's understanding of the ethical issues at hand.

In situations in which reporters are striving to portray the ethical dimension of a news story, the notion of a paradigm case could be applied in two senses: anecdotes (cases) could be chosen to represent the possible extremes (the clearly ethical and the clearly unethical), or-in a twist on the notion of paradigm case-an anecdote could be chosen to represent the most morally ambiguous situation (as perceived in relationship to clear-cut cases).

Without referring to casuistry, many reporters undoubtedly already seek to choose anecdotes that represent the ethical topics they are covering, and they focus on cases that highlight the difficult choices people face. However, the analysis in this chapter suggests that anecdotes could be used more appropriately if more conscious attention were given to how they represent the ethical issues in the situation being covered.

Two examples using stories about the topics discussed above will suggest more concretely how this adaptation of the use of casuistry could refine journalists' choices of anecdotes:

1. Use of two anecdotes from "ethical extremes": a story on assisted suicide could use one anecdote that reflects a situation in which both opponents and proponents would come closest to seeing it as ethically unsupportable and one in which they would come closest to agreeing that it was supportable. The writer or TV reporter using this approach need not ignore the ethical concerns of opponents who would object even in this case, but by using this kind of template for choosing anecdotes, the reporter would reflect the breadth of viewpoints more fully.

A review of the body of stories on assisted suicide from which the case anecdote was taken did not show any single story with both kinds of anecdotes. However, examples of anecdotes that come close to reflecting both ethical extremes appeared in separate television stories. One depicted Emerson Hoogstraat, whose body was "in excruciating pain from bone cancer" and whose wife said, "He would go to bed at night and say to me, 'I hope I don't wake up in the morning.'" If this pain were too excruciating to be relieved, both sides would be closer to agreement on the appropriateness of assisted suicide than in other cases. Another story had an anecdote that portrayed Karen Mortensen, for whom better pain treatment had made her able to sleep at night and able to think about things other than dying. In this case, both sides might agree that assisted suicide would be inappropriate. Using both these anecdotes in one story would present the viewpoint spectrum.

This suggestion is not meant to imply that balance of ethical viewpoints should be the norm for all ethics coverage. In fact, writing which makes explicit a journalist's ethical views may do more for readers' understanding than ethical neutrality. But this suggestion retains the notion that audience understanding is enhanced by exposure to more than one viewpoint.

2. Use of one anecdote with maximum moral ambiguity: a story about the practices of health maintenance organizations could use one anecdote that reflected the difficulty of moral choices involved by showing both ethical and unethical sides of HMOs. An ABC story about how to get the care one wants from an HMO focused on Cathy Patti, an Olympic skiing champion who had lost her right leg to cancer at age 9. She was initially denied the kind of prosthetic leg she needed, but eventually the company responded to her research and to her efforts to answer its questions by compromising on price with the prosthetic maker so she could get the leg, at no cost to her. The two sides in this case each individually represent clear-cut cases, but combined in one situation they reflect the ethical tension that arises in connection with HMOs.

Although this application of casuistry applies most directly to stories with a clear ethical dimension-such as stories on bioethical topics, or controversial practices in business or government-it also has implications for stories where ethics may not be as prominent. Use of anecdotes reflecting extremes of the positive or negative impact from a public issue, such as a city council decision on subdivision zoning, would help to paint a broad picture for readers or viewers. Similarly, an anecdote that reflected the most mixed impact would, in a different way, represent more than one side of the issue.

Yet another way that journalists can personalize topics while keeping attention to their broadest dimensions is to accompany a broad issue piece with two or three sidebars, each centered on how the issue is playing out in the life of an individual or family. This idea of expanding anecdotes-personal stories-to full sidebars is not unfamiliar to journalists, but the use of more than one person-centered sidebar would broaden reader or viewer understanding of the impact of the issue beyond what might be gained from a single sidebar. In addition, applying the discussion of casuistry above to the choice of these "superanecdotes"-by using the notions of ethical extremes and maximum moral ambiguity-could help make journalistic portrayals more ethically balanced.

These sidebars could be written in third person like conventional news stories, with the sources cited, or they could be first-person pieces by the individuals themselves. In either case, they are consistent in particular with Gilligan's emphasis on the importance of relationships and voice. This approach can address the relationship dimension better than conventional anecdotes by shedding more detailed light on individuals and how they are wrestling through an issue such as genetic testing for a disease that runs in the family.

A sidebar with an issue piece from the first day of the Los Angeles Times series on HMOs noted earlier provides an excellent example of use of "super-anecdotes." The sidebar, headlined "Faces and Voices," looked at the perspectives on HMOs of ten people including doctors, a nurse, and a hospital administrator. Each person was introduced in the reporter's voice; then each was quoted directly for several paragraphs, which empirical studies suggest will be more engaging to readers than paraphrasing. In addition, the series that day included a sidebar focusing on one surgeon. The ten-person sidebar provides one example of "maximum moral ambiguity": a cardiologist cites improvement in the quality of health care and greater accountability for time and resources, but also a deterioration in relationships among doctors and between them and patients as medicine becomes more competitive.

Training readers and viewers to expect anecdotes is problematic if stories without anecdotes are ignored or devalued. But, it is unrealistic to expect journalists to avoid using anecdotes, given their potential power to get the attention of readers and viewers. Thus, both journalists and researchers should think critically about the choice and use of anecdotes.

This analysis suggests that a good anecdote:

- Provides the fullest possible insight not merely about an individual but also about individuals in relationship with one another.
- Provides the fullest possible insight about the broader organizational, professional, and social contexts of a topic.
- Illustrates the tug of different viewpoints within the same situation or works with one or more other anecdotes to reflect multiple viewpoints.
- Is not so highly emotional that it overshadows the broader point of a story.

These criteria suggest lines for further research. Additional studies growing out of this analysis could provide ethical evaluation of the use of anecdotes in larger sets of stories on a variety of topics, with an eye to how well the stories reflect these criteria. This kind of research would further the kind of critical analysis that can help bring readers and viewers stories that have both a powerful personal dimension and the context of social meaning.

Chapter 12

Methodological Comparison with Human Coding in Content Analysis

Computers have played an important role in the advancement of content analysis as a tool in the study of media messages and can cut hours of human coding and analysis into seconds or minutes. Content analysis has been one of the most popular methods in top communication journals during the past quarter-century and the time-saving characteristics of computers have become so popular that "it's rare to find a text content analysis today that does not use computer analysis."

Because most studies using computer-assisted analysis do not employ human coding as a check, researchers rarely know if decisions made along the way to customise the computer programme for analysis have altered the results. This project compares both the process and results of human versus computer-assisted coding in a content study of newspaper coverage during a political campaign. Both the human coders and those using a computer programme started with the same sample, research question, and codebook, and progressed independently. This design was chosen to answer questions of whether or not results would be different between the two approaches and if the processes themselves could influence the outcome.

In the 1960s, Lasswell envisioned computers providing a "fresh start" for content analysis, which he believed had been languishing because of the work involved in coding and processing content. Danielson and Mullen in this era described human coding as "time consuming, tedious, and demoralizing."

They hinted that researchers were limiting the time element or content scope of their projects because of the work involved. Researchers at Harvard developed a computer system, the General Inquirer, in 1961 to analyse content quickly.

The programme was used on several content analysis projects including a study of Soviet and Chinese perceptions of U.S. policy, and a look at twenty presidential nomination acceptance speeches.

Danielson and Mullen used a computer to create a new level of analysis, the Basic Space Unit, to provide a uniform method of comparing content across print media. The 1980s started an explosion in the use of computer-assisted programs because of faster, more nimble, and accessible computers, as well as optical scanners.

Hart created Diction, a programme utilizing 10,000 search words in thirty-three different lists/' using it to examine presidential campaign communication from Truman to Clinton. Danielson used his GENCA programme to analyse one hundred years of front-page content of both the New York Times and Los Angeles Times." Lind and SaIo used a word proximity programme to study framing of feminists and feminism in U.S. electronic media.

Another popular set of computer programs, VBPro and VBMap, compute word frequencies and co-occurrences. VBPro and VBMap were used to compare candidate framing in press releases versus news coverage in the 1996 Republican Presidential Primary. Andsager and Powers employed VBPro and VBMap programs to study what kinds of frames were used in magazine stories about breast cancer and silicone breast implants.

COMPARISONS

Few attempts have been made to compare human coding

and computer-assisted projects. In one case, researchers employed a computer programme to replicate a human-coded project on policies and coverage of six national crises. The computer group could only compare two, the invasion of Grenada and Three Mile Island, because of electronic database limitations.

The computer programme and the human coding exhibited strong agreement (.90) concerning Grenada, but only after a "neutral" category was eliminated. The authors called the comparison using the Three Mile Island coverage "clearly a failure" based on between-method correlations.

In another comparison, Linderman used a previous project's Swedish news editorial data. The original study sampled thirty years of news editorials, but once again the computer comparison severely limited the scope, in this case, from thirty to three years.

The two studies came up with similar results (a correlation of.908) in the number of cultural indicators in the editorials. Further analysis showed that in some areas of the study, only 56% of the editorials were found in samples of both studies.

Therefore, the correlation was strong, but the two studies were not analyzing the same sample. Linderman concluded that comparing human and computer-assisted coding depends on the complexity of categories, with computers working best when categories are "easy to operationalize," but human coders working better with complex categories.

Two main research questions guided this project and the specific methods used to compare human-coded and computer-assisted content analysis.

The first question probed the correlation between the results produced by the two methods of data collection. The second question involved the divergent methods used for the two forms of content analysis.

RQ1: To what degree do the two methods of content analysis, human and computer-assisted coding, starting with the same sample, research question, and codebook, produce the same results?

RQ2: Keeping the sample, research question, and codebook

constant, are there methodological differences between human and computer-assisted coding which could lead to different results?

METHOD

This methodological comparison was part of a larger study of newspaper agenda setting in a state-wide political race (the 2002 Texas gubernatorial primary). The Democratic primary signaled the first time in Texas history that two minority candidates ran against each other for a statewide office: Tony Sanchez, a multi-millionaire banker, and Dan Morales, a former state attorney general and legislator. Republican Governor Rick Perry did not have any competition. In the Democratic primary, Sanchez easily defeated Morales, and Perry easily defeated Sanchez in the general election.

INITIAL PROJECT

The research question for the initial content analysis involved how the candidates were portrayed in the media: namely, what were the substantive and affective attributes and issues used in the newspaper coverage to describe the candidates and which of those attributes and issues were used most frequently?

The newspaper and issues (print copies) picked for study were the Austin American-Statesman for the period from 1 January 2002 through the day of the primary, 12 March 2002. Any articles referring to any of the three major candidates became the sampling unit for the project.

Graduate students under the supervision of a senior faculty member read the 107 articles in the sample to create and test the initial codebook and undergo coder training. The coding unit was every paragraph mentioning a candidate. Because a single paragraph could have more than one reference to a candidate's image, the unit of analysis became the assertion. An assertion was any word, phrase, or sentence that conveyed an issue or attribute pertaining to the campaign or a candidate.

The final codebook included 96 specific issues and

attributes mentioned in media coverage as well as categories from previous research in this subject area. Twenty-five per cent of the content was used for a test of inter-coder reliability among four coders.

Among the issues and attributes that emerged as the most important for comparison purposes, the highest reliability was found in campaign (.91) and experience (.88), with the lowest numbers for education (.78) and Hispanic/minority (.79). Others included politics and wealth (.86) and debate (.83).

COMPUTER-ASSISTED CONTENT ANALYSIS

After the codebook was finalized, the computer-assisted and human-coding groups worked separately. This procedure promoted objectivity and ecological validity in the application of both data collection methods. The purpose of this comparison was not to mimic human coding methods to ensure similar results. Instead, it allowed both methods to run their course independently to avoid a potential weakness of previous comparison studies. In both the Nacos et al. and Linderman comparison studies, the human coded-project had already been completed and published when the computer-assisted method was utilized for comparison. Therefore the computer-assisted groups knew the human-coded results before they started their study, giving them at least an opportunity to shape or alter the method to aim for the desired results.

The computer-assisted group (two people) employed the VBPro and VBMap computer programs used in previous content analysis studies published in top peer-reviewed communication journals and edited volumes. The process of turning the final codebook for the human coders into a computer-assisted study will be discussed in the results section since it is at the heart of the second research question.

RESULTS

RQ1 asked to what degree do the two methods of content analysis, human and computer-assisted coding, starting with the same sample, research question, and codebook, produce the same results? The human coders and those using the computer programme came up with dramatically different results on how the newspaper portrayed the candidates and issues during the campaign. However, in order to compare the two coding efforts, the results first had to be narrowed down to the top seven attributes or issues that surfaced in both processes: campaign, debate, education, experience, Hispanic/minority, politics, and wealth.

The total occurrences of the seven issue/attributes for each candidate are listed and rank ordered in both the computer and human coding efforts. To compare the issue / attribute agendas of the two methods, a rank-order correlation is shown for each candidate. One of the most obvious differences in the methods is the number of issues or attributes found in the coverage. On average, the human coders found only one quarter of the occurrences as compared to the computer-assisted method. The numbers for Perry are lower than the other two candidates because he ran unopposed in the primary.

For both Sanchez and Morales, politics was the most important issue in coverage for the human coders, but the least important in the computer-assisted results. In the computer-assisted coding process, the campaign was the top issue for all three candidates. One reason politics ranked so high for human coders and low in the computer process was the computer-assisted researchers chose to only use variations of the word "politics" or "politician" to define this category, while the "campaign" word index contained 16 different words. That being said, the "debate" word index contained only six words, yet the computer process came up with many more occurrences than did human coders.

The Democratic candidate debate coverage emerged as one of the defining issues for computer-assisted coding, but ranked near the bottom for the human coders. Morales had challenged Sanchez to a series of debates during the campaign. They settled on one two-hour debate, one hour in English, the second hour in Spanish. The importance of experience for all three candidates was noted by both processes, with that attribute coming in at the same ranking for Sanchez, and differing by only one rank for the other two candidates.

Comparing the rank orders for the candidates on the seven issues/attributes reveals the disconnect between methods. The rank-order correlation between the human and computer-assisted coding for Sanchez coverage is barely positive at.071, far from significant. Morales' coverage results diverged even more, with a negative correlation of -.214. Computer-assisted and human coding were more closely aligned, at.607, for Governor Perry. Overall, the two methods yielded different results about the important issues and attributes in the newspaper campaign coverage.

AFFECT RESULTS COMPARISON

The differences are even more pronounced when judging affect. The results were so different that only three of the categories-campaign, debate, and experience-could be analysed across all three candidates using the human and computer-assisted coding methods. In addition, the computer method did not include "neutral," so those results could not be compared. In order to compare the coding of affect, data for the three candidates were combined. This combination allowed a more direct comparison between human and computer-assisted coding.

The positive, negative, and net difference scores for campaign, debate, and experience issues were compared across methods using a t-test. The net scores were calculated by subtracting the number of negative instances of issue coverage from positive stories. This approach provided a sense of the overall valence with which issues were covered.

The difference between the two processes on the campaign issue coverage is significant in both positive and net results. The computer process revealed a campaign defined in positive terms for the combined candidates. The results from the human coders show a much more negative portrayal of the campaigns. On the experience issue, the combined coverage of the three candidates was significantly different across methods in positive affect and approached significance in both negative and net affect. This time, both methods indicated more positive than negative coverage for the candidates, but the human coders found a wider margin of positive to negative coverage. The closest the human and computer-assisted coding efforts came on affect was for debate coverage, with both showing a negative tone in stories concerning the Democratic debate.

METHODOLOGICAL COMPARISON

How could two processes of content analysis come up with such different results when analyzing one medium's coverage of a single primary campaign using the same sample? One answer lies in the differences between human coding and the computer-assisted method. For this methodological study, a look at the divergent processes is just as important as the results themselves, and permits examination of RQ2: Keeping the sample, research question, and codebook constant, is there methodological differences between human and computer-assisted coding which could lead to different results?

The reason for at least some of the differences in results starts to become clear when the two methods of content analysis are compared.

After the codebook was finalized and an acceptable level of inter-coder reliability was achieved in the human-coded project, the researchers coded the sample and computed frequencies of attributes and issues. For the computer-assisted programme researchers, the final codebook for the human coders became a starting point for a series of decisions that affected the direction of the research.

Sample Differences. The computer team used the Lexis-Nexis database of newspaper content to find relevant articles from the American-Statesman. This computerized search failed to find 6 of 107 articles that ran in the print edition of the newspaper, 2% of the total paragraphs in the sample. These articles were added to the electronic database for a more direct sample comparison.

WORD INDEXING

For the purpose of this study, the process of building the word files to represent attributes or issues is referred to as "word indexing," an important, but little-discussed process in computer-assisted content analysis. Word indexing is critical in computer-assisted content analysis but the process affects everything from the unit of analysis to the scope of attributes to be studied, which makes subsequent comparisons to human coding more difficult.

The human coders used the assertion as the unit of analysis. Computers are best at counting words but cannot find an assertion. Therefore, each assertion had to be turned into a list of words, or word index. Therefore, for the computer-assisted process, the unit of analysis became the word index defining each issue or attribute.

In the human coding project, a single assertion could be anything from a word or phrase to a sentence. But in word indexing, every time a word from the index is found in the content, it is counted as an occurrence of that issue or attribute. This difference in unit of analysis is the main reason why the computer-assisted coding came up with a higher number of issues and attributes than the human coders.

Another major difference is the selection of attributes or issues to analyse. A codebook for human coders often casts a wide net for potential answers. But in computer-assisted content analysis, steps are taken early in the process to narrow the potential areas to be analysed.

In this study, the final codebook for the human coders included 96 potential attributes or issues and 3 different candidates, adding up to 288 possible answers for each assertion. Developing 288 separate word indexes would eliminate the speed benefit of computer-assisted projects. Instead, researchers often first check the frequency of all words in the sample. Using the frequencies, word indexes were created for the issues and attributes most prominent in the sample.

Another part of the computer analysis, using VBMap, plotted words on a graph depending on co-occurrence with other words. Through this method of successive filtrations, the first set of word indexes included 25 of the 96 attributes and issues from the final human codebook. At this point, the two members of the computer programme team split up, with each taking steps and developing separate methods to improve the word indexes. Through alterations to word indexes and more filtrations, the number of issues and attributes was reduced to the top seven categories: campaign, debate, education, experience, Hispanic/minority, politics, and wealth.

Matching an Attribute or Issue to a Candidate. While the VBPro programme can quickly find how often attribute words appear in text, those words must also be linked to a particular candidate. To isolate each of the candidates, then, three separate searchable files were created. Each contained every paragraph that mentioned the specific candidate by name.

Obvious distinctions between the candidates started to emerge when the separate files were analysed using the seven word files. Sanchez's wealth was an important attribute in newspaper coverage; it was associated with him 65 more times than with Morales. At the same time, Morales was more often identified by his experience; he had been involved in state-wide politics for several years while Sanchez was running for his first political office. As expected, both Morales and Sanchez were associated with ethnicity.

This method of linking a candidate to an attribute does have a serious flaw. Condensing the data set into a file for each candidate does not guarantee all terms in the file pertain to that specific candidate. Therefore, each of the three candidate data sets was searched for mentions of the other candidates.

Both Morales and Sanchez's names appear in roughly half of each other's paragraphs: Sanchez appears in 50% of Morales paragraphs while Morales is mentioned in 46% of Sanchez paragraphs. Thus, when an attribute word appears in the Morales or Sanchez file, there is a good chance that the attribute could be linked to the other candidate. Only Perry appears to have separation from the other candidates.

The effect of co-occurrence of the two Democratic candidates' names in each other's file is apparent. The human coders found "wealth" the third most important attribute for Sanchez, a multi-millionaire who financed much of the campaign with his own money. But for Perry and Morales, "wealth" came in last in their order of attributes. In the computer-assisted list, "wealth" came in second for Sanchez, but it also finished third for Perry and fourth for Morales, likely because of the overlap of candidate files.

An attempt was made to cut down on the co-occurrence of candidates in each others' attribute and issue files by revising the coding unit from a paragraph to each individual sentence with a candidate's name. But this only cut the co-occurrences to around 30% and lost valuable context needed in assessing attributes and issues. Therefore, the paragraph was retained as coding unit for analyzing the attributes and issues.

Affect Word Indexing. Even more difficult than linking attributes to candidates is discerning the affective directions of the attributes. Because the affective dimension (positive or negative) must be linked to the substantive dimension (attribute or issue), and then to a specific candidate, the complexity in finding a way for a computer programme to dig out this information is even greater. Twenty-one new files had to be created, linking one of three candidates to one of the seven attribute/ issues.

Two new word indexes were created, one for positive and one for negative affect. These indexes were comprised of positive and negative words found at least five times in the sample. Then the affect word indexes were analysed against the 21 candidate-attribute data sets. In most of the attributes the tone of the coverage was the same for the two Democrats. The coverage of Morales and Sanchez was more positive for campaign and experience, and was more negative for the debate and Hispanic/minority. Concerning wealth, Sanchez's coverage was more negative and Morales' was positive. The news stories tended to focus on how Sanchez's personal fortune was bankrolling his campaign. Republican incumbent

Perry's only large numbers were for positive affect for both campaign and experience. Because Perry had no competition in the primary, he was spared negative coverage.

Overall, the human-coded process revealed a more negative tone to campaign coverage than the computer-assisted process in the directly comparable areas. The difference in tone cannot be explained by the size of the word indexes. The negative affect word index contained 53 different words while the positive word index had only 30 words. Still, the computer-assisted results showed more positive coverage than the human-coded data.

RESULTS COMPARISON CONSTRAINTS

Thus, the steps that had to be taken to turn the final human codebook into word indexes for the computer programme altered the study's direction and results. Because of the two different methodological paths, direct comparisons of results were problematic. As shown, the two methods did detect some of the same general areas of coverage, such as campaign, debate, experience, Hispanic/minority, and wealth.

But the human coding also revealed more nuanced results, which could not be matched by the computer. Human coding hinted that the coverage of Sanchez brought into question his credibility and morality as well as other negative personal traits.

For Morales, human coding also suggested negative personal coverage, especially his role in a major tobacco company settlement. Human coding showed that incumbent Perry was not subjected to as much coverage on his personal qualifications, and was identified mostly by major issues confronting the state, such as economy, health care, insurance, and transportation.

Another decision made to ensure comparable results could also have altered the overall analysis of the coverage: to compare affective dimensions, the "neutral" category had to be eliminated from the human-coded results. The computer could find only positive and negative affect, but not neutral. While the elimination of "neutral" is hardly an optimal solution, it is an approach taken in a previous methodological study to permit comparisons.

Questions of Word Index Reliability. This comparison raises questions about reliability in computer-assisted content analysis. One of the strengths of the approach is the precision of the computer programs, to the point that inter-coder reliability is rarely, if ever, discussed. But the computer-assisted method here led researchers to create detailed word indexes so the computer could search for the attributes or issues. After the two people in the computer-assisted group separated, each separately created and refined word indexes, with no systematic method to check decisions. While these choices were no doubt informed by specific knowledge of candidates and campaign, the computer content analysis requires no specific reliability measure justifying the word indexes.

This methodological comparison illuminates different paths taken by researchers attempting to answer the same question with the same research method and sample. Unlike previous comparisons that applied computer-analysis programs to completed human-coded projects, this study's two analyses were carried out concurrently, with neither group knowing the other's results. The divergent results are a reminder that the two processes, even within the same general rubric of "content analysis," need to be assessed for their merits and shortcomings.

In general, the computer-assisted approach highlighted broad categories of coverage, while human coders gleaned more nuanced attributes and issues. The computer-assisted results focused on the heavy attention to the campaign itself; the human coders highlighted coverage focused on issues for the uncontested incumbent, and on negative personal characteristics for the Democrats. These results are consistent with previous comparisons that found computer-assisted coding best at simple word counts and less effective at more nuanced analysis. Nacos et al. concluded that the computer "does not recognize ambiguities or problems as an attentive human coder would" while Linderman found human coders more effective at finding "the complex, wide-ranging and inclusive categories."

The differences in the two approaches began with the sample. While the computer team attempted to use the same sampling unit as the human coders, that was not possible through Lexis-Nexis. Six articles were not available online. Concerns over what could be missing in electronic text services are as old as the services themselves, of course, but what is most troubling is the fact that without a direct comparison, analysts using computer-assisted projects may never know what print content has been excluded.

This case study may have pushed the limits of VBPro because of its complexity. To answer the overall research question, the method had to identify and quantify the attributes, and link them to a specific candidate. VBPro and VBMap and other computer programs seem more suited for recognizing and counting words or syllables. In Andsager and Power's study on breast cancer framing, the sample included only stories about breast cancer. A study on presidential primary candidate frames in news coverage did not attempt to link attributes to different candidates within one newspaper article; to simplify the connection between the frame and the candidate, the authors analysed only articles that focused primarily on one candidate.

This step avoids the problem of linking frames or attributes to a candidate, but could potentially ignore important campaign content. In this case study, the majority of the articles included both Sanchez and Morales as they fought for the Democratic nomination. If those articles had been eliminated from the study, the process of preparing the computer programme for analysis would have been simplified, but the resulting sample would not be a representative picture of how the newspaper covered the primary.

This case also may have strained the capacity of reliable computer coding by exploring affective dimensions. According to Poindexter and McCombs, content analysis computer programs are "less useful" when trying to determine positive or negative context. In this case study, the two processes yielded significantly different conclusions on extent of positive or negative coverage.

Another important question about computer-assisted content analysis involves reliability. Typically, a major issue in human-coded content analysis has been inter-coder reliability and one presumed benefit of using a computer has been elimination of multiple coders. This, in turn, allows researchers to avoid questions of inter-coder reliability. But while between-human differences disappear, the researcher must develop precise word indexes to provide a roadmap for the computer to analyse the content. Currently, there is no systematic method for ensuring that the researcher's word indexes are effective at finding the unit of analysis.

Computer programs do help the word indexing by providing lists of words in the sample and how often they occur. Programs like VBMap can show words that occur together. But consider the fact that one researcher made decisions here on using words such as "Harvard" and "attorney general" to count as "experience" for Morales, and "bank" and "regent" for Sanchez. These decisions were made because of knowledge of and research into the backgrounds of the candidates, but with no assurances that other researchers would create the same word indexes or agree with the choices.

Early users of computers for content analysis were concerned with this issue, which Smith called "internal consistency." He suggested a form of inter-coder reliability among researchers to determine if the proper words were being chosen for the word indexes.

Different people would create word indexes for a category, with reliability estimates computed for their choices. "The principal purpose of assessing the internal consistency of a category is to aid the researcher in category construction and interpretation of his results." Despite this early concern, internal consistency in word indexes has received little attention. In the future, researchers should consider instituting some test of inter-coder reliability for the creation and refinement of word indexes. The same rigor considered critical to human coding should be applied to the process of building word indexes.

These results open the door to more comparison studies of human and computer-assisted coding. While both approaches fall under the "content analysis" umbrella, they do entail different processes to analyse the data. Computers allow large data sets to be analysed quickly, but there may be trade-offs in the level of complexity involved in the results. Future studies could map areas of content analysis that might not be best suited for computer programs. In this case study, the programme employed had difficulty detecting valence, recognizing subtle nuances in the coverage, and linking an attribute to a specific candidate. In general, computer-assisted content analysis is most effective when studying text that is readily available in electronic form. Computers are less effective in projects involving photographs, graphics, or video.

Moreover, as analysis advances beyond word counts and indexes, researchers must be particularly careful in interpreting the results. Riffe, Lacy, and Fico caution researchers to consider computer-assisted content analysis only if it will produce valid measures, cut the study's cost, and improve reliability. As computers and programs become more sophisticated, so will the scope and depth of computer-assisted content analysis. With future research, computers may be used more reliably and with more confidence, perhaps in combination with human coding. In the end, the choice of human or computer-assisted coding should be made for the same reasons as all methodological decisions in communication research: because that method is the best way to answer the research question at hand.

Chapter 13

Audience Story Selection: A Web-tracking Analysis

"When a dog bites a man, that is not news. But if a man bites a dog, that is news." Deviance is one of many news values widely used in practice and research in journalism. The deviance level of an event predicts whether journalists will select it and how prominently they will present it. For decades, Shoemaker and her colleagues have developed the concept of deviance as a useful predictor of media coverage. According to their newsworthiness model, deviance is a construct encompassing other news values, such as novelty, oddity, unusualness, conflict, controversy, and sensationalism. And, deviance is one of two main factorsthe other is social significance-that influence how prominently a news event is covered.

However, there is little research on the effect of deviance on news audiences. Journalists believe that news values they use for news production also work effectively for audiences. They assume that deviant stories they selectively present are also readily selected by their audience. But is deviance a useful predictor of audience selection of news stories? According to Shoemaker's conceptualization of deviance, human beings instinctively attend to deviant events or information because they need to detect threatening factors in their environment. This tendency to pay special attention to deviant stories, she argues, is true of both journalists and audience members. However, little evidence has been provided to support this idea.

This study examined the impact of deviance on audience members' news selection. Two types of deviance-story deviance and contextual deviance-were proposed as influencing audience news selection. In addition, an audience-driven factor, personal involvement, was predicted to moderate the effect of deviance on news selection. The findings will contribute to understanding the role of deviance in news processing and help journalists use deviance effectively as a news value criterion.

DEVIANCE

Deviance has been developed by Shoemaker and her colleagues as a news value. According to their newsworthiness model, deviance and social significance of an event predict how importantly the event is presented by news media. Recently, Shoemaker and Cohen's ten-country study confirmed the universal role of deviance as a significant predictor of new coverage. This deviance consists of three dimensions. Statistical deviance refers to events that are unlikely to occur and perceived as odd, unusual, or novel. Social change deviance refers to events that have a potential to make a difference in the existing social structure or order. Normative deviance refers to events that may violate or break a norm or a law in a society.

Shoemaker explicates the concept of deviance using a perspective of evolutionary psychology. She suggests that human brains are hardwired by biological instincts to pay attention to deviant occurrences in their environments. Based on Charles Darwin's theory of biological evolution, she argues that organisms competing for survival face unpredicted changes in the environment and those who adapt their ways of life to the environment pass their superior genes to their descendents.

For adaptation and survival, human beings also need to monitor their environments and pay special attention to deviant occurrences that may threaten their lives. Watching the environment enables human beings to run away from or fight against threatening events. Those who monitor their surroundings carefully can adapt themselves to the environment better than those who do not monitor their surroundings. According to Shoemaker, this biological instinct to monitor the surroundings accounts for human beings' interest in news. For people who monitor what is going on, a deviant event or story is something to be attended to and informed of because the event may become a threatening factor in their lives. In modern society, it is impossible for individual human beings to monitor every event, and, thus, they rely on news media to detect deviant events. Thus, deviance plays a significant role as a strong news value that influences audience members' selection of and attention to news stories, as well as journalists' selection and presentation of events.

Though they may not use the term "deviance," other researchers focused on human beings' instinctive reaction to events or information that signal a potential risk.8 Studies in cognitive psychology also point out that human brains are evolutionary set to react to threatening features automatically. In sum, deviant news stories elicit human beings' interest and reactions because they should be detected as soon as possible for human beings to survive in their environment.

DEVIANCE AND STORY SELECTION

In addition to Shoemaker's evolutionary explanation,10 other communication and psychological theories predict that deviant stories are specially attended to and likely selected: e.g., the limited capacity model of mediated message processing, schema theory, and cognitive mediation theory.

According to the limited capacity model of mediated message processing," information processing consists of three sub-processes such as encoding, storage, and retrieval. The initial step, encoding, is broken down into two steps. Only a certain amount or some aspects of information are selected from the entire information set and the selected information is transformed into activated mental representations in shortterm memory. The selection is either a controlled or an automatic process. Controlled selection is initiated by an audience member's goal whereas automatic selection is activated by the nature of given messages. Specifically, information describing change or an unexpected occurrence in the environment is automatically selected. This information elicits an orienting response, which calls for automatic attention, and much cognitive resource is allocated to encode the information. Deviant news stories describe unusual events that threaten the statusquo or break norms, which are unexpected occurrences possibly indicating potential risks for audience members' survival. Thus, deviant stories are likely to be selected, allocated cognitive resources, and readily encoded.

From the perspective of schema theory, deviant news stories can be considered information that is not congruent with schema. Schema refer to knowledge structures that form our expectations of events and help us evaluate new information. In general, deviant news events violate our expectation and therefore evoke schema incongruence. According to Berlyne, this incongruity leads people to show special interest in the information. Along the same line, scholars using the associative network model in cognitive psychology argue that an item incongruent with existing schema is salient among the surrounding items and this salience leads the item to be specially attended to and recalled. Information processing of a new item involves a search for information that helps to interpret the item in memory stores. It is difficult to find information congruent with a deviant item, and therefore a wide search is carried out until useful information is found. Thus, deviant information tends to be encoded more thoroughly than non-deviant information.

The cognitive mediation model proposed by Eveland explains information processing of political news in relation to the uses and gratifications approach. This model is theoretically based on McLeod, Kosicki, and McLeod's O-S-O-R perspective, which indicates that a person's characteristics (first O) influence the person's reception of a stimulus message (S) and then information processing-related variables (second O) influence the person's response to the message (R). Borrowing the concept of a surveillance motive from the uses and gratifications research, proponents of the cognitive mediation model argue that surveillance motivation (first O) of an audience member influences his or her attention to and elaboration (second O) of news stories and finally the motivation indirectly influences the audience member's knowledge about the stories.

In sum, researchers using the cognitive mediation model found that the surveillance motive influenced the level of attention and elaboration and the attention and elaboration led to knowledge gain. For human beings who have a certain level of surveillance motive, deviant news stories containing potential danger will be the information they need to detect and be aware of. If a person encounters a deviant story, he or she will be motivated to survey details of the story. According to the cognitive mediation model, this motivated person will pay special attention to the deviant story and elaborate it thoroughly.

These theories predict that deviant news stories are more likely to be selected with special attention than less deviant stories. Thus, the first hypothesis was proposed:

H1: The more deviant a news story is, the more likely the story is to be selected.

Story selection has two dimensions: selection probability (probability of a story's being selected) and selection order (the order of a story's being selected among all presented stories). The two dimensions are correlated with each other. The same prediction was made for selection order:

H2: The more deviant a news story is, the earlier the story is selected.

STORY DEVIANCE AND CONTEXTUAL DEVIANCE

Day by day, the number of deviant stories presented by news media differs. One day a news Web site may have only a couple of deviant stories while the next day it may be filled with many deviant stories. Thus, this study proposes another concept, contextual deviance, in addition to story deviance. Story deviance refers to the degree of deviance of a given story, whereas contextual deviance refers to the degree of deviance from neighboring stories. For example, a mass murder story is deviant itself, which indicates story deviance. However, the perceived degree of deviance of the mass murder story can differ depending on the degree of deviance of neighboring stories. The mass murder story is perceived as more deviant when it is presented along with non-deviant neighboring stories. However, if it is presented with stories about other types of murders, which are deviant as well, it may not be perceived as quite as deviant. The two types of deviance are theoretically based on Schmidt's categorization of distinctiveness."

According to Schmidt, primary distinctiveness occurs when an item stands out from the immediately surrounding context, whereas secondary distinctiveness is gained when an item is not congruent with people's existing cognitive structure or past experiences. Story deviance is related to secondary distinctiveness because the content-unusual, threatening to the status quo, or breaking norms-is not congruent with people's existing cognitive structures or past experiences.

Contextual deviance is based on primary distinctiveness because the deviance of a story makes the story stand out as a deviant one in a set of less deviant neighboring stories. In the context of high deviance, the same stories may be perceived as less deviant than in the context of low deviance because deviant neighboring stories "interfere" with the target stories' deviance. This underestimated deviance in the context of high deviance may lead stories to be less attended to and less likely selected than in the context of low deviance. Based on this logic, the following hypotheses were proposed:

H3: News stories are less likely to be selected in the context of high deviance than in the context of low deviance.

H4: News stories are selected later in the context of high deviance than in the context of low deviance.

PERSONAL INVOLVEMENT

Literature on personal involvement abounds in many academic areas, such as communication, advertising, marketing, and social and cognitive psychology. Krugman defines personal involvement as "the number of connections, conscious bridging experiences or personal references per minute that the subject makes between the content of the persuasive stimulus and the content of his own life." Zaichkowsky's view is a person's perceived relevance of an event based on inherent needs, values, and interests. Some studies found that personal involvement has two dimensions, cognitive and affective. Based on McQuire's conceptualization of motivation, Park and Young state that cognitive involvement refers to the degree of personal relevance of message contents or issues based on the brand's functional performance, whereas affective involvement refers to the degree of personal relevance of a message based on emotional or aesthetic appeal.

How is personal involvement related to deviance effects? According to Krugman, a high level of personal involvement refers to numerous connections between given stimulus information and an audience member's experience. In contrast, as schema theory implies, highly deviant information has few connections between given information and an audience member's experience. When audience members are exposed to a highly deviant story, they may think that the information is not connected to them. However, some of them who are personally involved in the story may find that they are somewhat connected to the story though the story is very deviant.

For example, a mass murder story is quite deviant for most people, which indicates that the story does not have many connections with people's overall experience. However, some people with personal involvement with crime stories-for example, those who are interested in crime stories or recognize the need for crime stories-may find more connections with crime news than those without personal involvement with crime stories. Those who value the crime stories may perceive a given story as less deviant than those who do not because they find more connections with the stories. In other words, those with personal involvement with the content of given stories may underestimate the level of deviance of the stories more than those without personal involvement. The underestimated deviance, therefore, reduces the probability of the stories' being selected. Therefore, personal involvement was predicted to negatively moderate the influence of deviance on story selection.

H5: Personal involvement with the content of news stories will attenuate the effect of story deviance on the probability of story selection.

H6: Personal involvement with the content of news stories will attenuate the effect of story deviance on the order of story selection.

METHOD

Design. An experiment was conducted to test the hypotheses. This study employs a 4 (story deviance) x 2 (contextual deviance) x 4 (presentation position: control variable) mixed-factor design. Additionally, measured personal involvement and its interaction terms were included in the analysis.

Story deviance is a within-subject factor, and contextual deviance and story order are between-subject factors. Story deviance has four levels: no deviance, low deviance, medium deviance, and high deviance. Contextual deviance consists of two conditions: less deviant context and more deviant context. Story order is a control variable that has four groups according to a Latin square rotation. Each group of stories with different four-level story deviance is positioned in each of four rows alternatively.

Participants: The participants were 111 undergraduate students enrolled in mass communication classes at two universities-a private university in the northeastern United States and a public university in the mid-eastern United States. All the students in the classes were notified about this experiment, and those who participated received extra credit.

Procedure: The experiment procedure consisted of two parts: Webtracking and questionnaires. Before the Webtracking part, all participants were randomly assigned to one of eight different conditions made up of two between-subject factors (2 contextual deviance x 4 presentation position). Then, each participant received an e-mail message leading to the experimental Web site. On the first page of the site, they saw a greeting message, a consent form, and an introduction to the experiment.

In the first part, participants saw a Web page with twenty-one crime news stories in the form of a 3x7 table, and were asked to select any stories they wanted to read for as long as they wanted to read them. They were asked to browse the Web page freely in such a way that they would click a story, read it, return to the previous page, select another story, and so on. While the participants were browsing the Web page, a Web-tracking programme recorded their behaviors: which story each participant selected and how long the participant read the selected story. After the participants finished reading stories, they were led to another Web page and answered questions about their personal involvement in crime news.

WEB-TRACKING PROGRAMME

A Web-tracking approach is useful in analyzing people's selective exposure to and navigation behaviors regarding information on the Internet. This method provides unobtrusive and objective data about a participant's behaviour on a Web page. This study uses HIOX Visitor Tracking (HVT) 2.0. This programme records the IP addresses of all the visitors, and the time and date when the visitors click on each Web page.

STIMULI AND MANIPULATION

Twenty-one crime stories were presented as stimuli on a Web page. The stories were selected from two sources: Associated Press (AP) in the Lexis/Nexis database and the Yahoo! news database. The length of all the stories was adjusted to about 150 words and references to specific locations in the stories were eliminated. The Web page had a two-layer structure, consisting of a main page and story pages. The main page presented each story headline and initial parts of the stories in the form of a 3x7 table. If a story headline was clicked on, the corresponding story page was displayed. Of 21 stories, 12 target stories were manipulated into 4 different levels of deviance, and 9 contextual stories were manipulated into more deviant and less deviant conditions. Four groups of target stories were positioned in the first, third, fifth, and seventh rows, and contextual stories filled up the rest of the rows between the target stories.

STORY DEVIANCE

Shoemaker and Cohen suggested complexity of deviance, which refers to how many dimensions of deviance-statistical, social change, and normative deviance-are involved in a news event.

Based on this conceptualization, this study selected four groups of stories: no deviance (no dimensions), low deviance (1 dimension), medium deviance (2 dimensions), and high deviance (3 dimensions). Of 100 potential stories, two trained coders rated the number of deviance dimensions involved in each story.

Two coders showed an agreement for 85 stories out of 100 (Scott's pi =.79). Among the agreed-upon stories, three stories were randomly selected for each of four story deviance levels.

CONTEXTUAL DEVIANCE

Two different Web pages were created: one with high deviant context and the other with low deviant context. Neighboring stories for high deviant context were randomly selected from the groups of stories with medium and high deviance, whereas the neighboring stories for low deviant context were drawn from the groups of no and low deviance.

PRESENTATION POSITION

To control the effect of presentation position of stories, the stimulus Web page presented four groups of stories with different levels of deviance at each of four rows alternatively. A Latin Square rotation was used.

MEASURES

Selection probability was operationally defined as the probability of a story's being selected for each story group of deviance. Since each group has three stories, this study divided the number of selected stories by three, which led to a maximum score of 1 and a minimum of 0. For example, if only one story is selected from three in the low deviant group, this group's selection probability was.33. Selection order was operationally defined as the order of a story's being selected among all the stimuli stories.

After examining in what order all the stories were selected, this study gave the highest score (1) to the first selected story and the lowest score (0) to non-selected stories. For example, if a participant read 10 stories out of 21, the selected stories were first coded from 10 (first selected story) to 1 (last selected story), and non-selected stories were given a score of 0. To control for the different number of stories read by participants, the scores were divided by the total number of stories selected. Thus, the first selected story was coded 1 for every participant, and all scores range from 1 to 0. The average score of the 3 stories was used in each group of deviance. Personal involvement in crime news was measured by employing Zaichkowsky's PII (Personal Involvement Inventory) questionnaires, which is a context-free 10-item scale.

Factor analysis was used to classify the items and two types of personal involvement emerged as previous studies indicated: cognitive involvement and affective involvement.

Among the 111 participants, 73.9% were female and their average age was 22. Most of them were Caucasians (77.5%) and citizens of the United States (92.8%).

MANIPULATION CHECK

This experiment has two manipulated variables: story deviance and contextual deviance. For story deviance, three Likert-scale questions based on the three dimensions of deviance were prepared for each story: (a) this story event is unusual, (b) this story event may lead to some kind of change in society, and (c) this story event may be unconventional or may break norms. A mean of the three scores was calculated for every story and the average scores of three stories in a group of deviance were compared.

A repeated-measure ANOVA with 4 groups of story deviance showed a significant difference among four groups. The mean deviance score was 2.42 for no deviance, 2.65 for low deviance, 2.96 for medium deviance, and 3.65 for high deviance. This showed a significant linear trend. For contextual deviance, the average scores of three deviance dimensions across nine contextual stories were compared between high deviant and low deviant contexts. High deviant context was scored significantly higher than low deviant context.

HYPOTHESIS TESTING

H1 predicted a positive effect of deviance on story selection probability. The main effect of story deviance was significant.

The means for each group were.61 for no deviance,.64 for low deviance,.78 for medium deviance, and.81 for high deviance. They also showed a significant linear trend. H1 was supported. H2 was about the effect of deviance on story selection order. The means for each group were.31 for no deviance,.28 for low deviance,.44 for medium deviance, and.53 for high deviance. High scores close to 1 indicate that the story was selected early. A significant linear trend was confirmed. H2 was also supported.

The third and fourth hypotheses predicted that contextual deviance had positive influences on story selection probability (H3) and story selection order (H4).

H5 predicted a negative moderating effect of personal involvement on the influence of deviance on story selection probability. Affective personal involvement showed a significant interaction with story deviance. To visualize this interaction, this study recoded affective personal involvement into high (above the mean) and low (below the mean) groups and analysed the data again with all other variables in the previous analysis included. As predicted, the increasing rate of story selection probability over the level of deviance was decreased for the high personal involvement group, compared to the low personal involvement group. H5 was supported.

The last hypothesis (H6) was about the same moderating effect of personal involvement on the influence of deviance on story selection order. The direction of moderating effect was negative as predicted.

Thus, H6 was supported. This study investigated how deviance influenced audience selection of news stories and how personal involvement moderates the influence of deviance on story selection.

For both probability and order of story selection, story deviance turned out to be a significant predictor. This finding is consistent with the predictions of previous theories: Shoemaker's evolutionary account, the limited capacity model's automatic selection, schema theory's incongruity, and the cognitive mediation theory's surveillance motivation and resulting elaboration. Online news reading is a type of an audience member's information processing. This study suggests that that there are three phases of this process: before story exposure, during exposure, and after exposure.

Before the exposure to news stories, audience members, as human beings, are biologically hard-wired to attend to deviant events or information and this human tendency leads them to be equipped with a basic and common surveillance motivation. As soon as they are exposed to stories with different levels of deviance, deviant stories describing unexpected events draw uncontrolled attention by eliciting an orienting response. In addition, much cognitive resource is prepared to process the deviant stories (limited capacity model and orienting responses).

After exposure, the audience members realise that the deviant stories should be learned for a good surveillance of their environment. The motivated members concentrate and elaborate on the stories with a special attention (cognitive mediation model). As a result, audience members are likely to select deviant stories rather than less deviant stories and, if multiple deviant stories are presented, they are likely to select the most deviant story first.

Contextual deviance, however, did not make any difference in the audience's story selection. This study predicted that if a story is presented with highly deviant neighboring stories, the chance of the story's being selected would decrease.

However, participants selected almost the same number of target stories between high and low deviant contexts. This may be due to their being given unlimited reading time. The experiment allowed participants to spend as much time as they wanted to read stories. The participants in the highly deviant context felt free to read many target stories and neighboring stories. Target stories did not necessarily compete with neighboring stories to be selected. Thus, an interference of deviant neighboring stories with target story selection did not take place.

An interesting finding is a significant moderating effect of personal involvement. Affective personal involvement interfered with the effect of deviance on story selection. Those who reported being highly involved in crime news reacted less sensitively to different levels of deviance than those with low personal involvement.

Theoretically, deviance and personal involvement are measured by counting the number of connections or shared items between a given stimulus story and old information stored in an audience member's mind (schema theory and Krugman's definition of personal involvement). A news story with high deviance has few connections between the story and old information held in audience members' minds. However, people who are highly involved with this story have more connections than those who are less involved with the story.

The increased connection due to personal involvement then makes audience members undervalue the deviance of the given stories and this decrease in perceived deviance leads to less likely selection of the story.

For example, the experiment participants with high

affective involvement rated crime news as more exciting, appealing, interesting, and fascinating than those with low involvement. Their somewhat positive ratings on crime news had been formed based on frequent exposure to and familiarity with crime news. They might have had more connections between the presented crime news and the information held in their minds and thought of the news stories as less deviant than those who showed little involvement with crime news.

Overall, this study provided empirical evidence supporting journalists' assumption that deviance is a working news value for audience members' news selection as well as journalists' news presentation. However, as the findings indicate, the magnitude of any deviance effect could be different depending on an individual's level of involvement with the stories. This conclusion could help journalists use the deviance criterion more effectively considering audience members' involvement as well as the nature of a given news event.

This study has some limitations. It examined only crime news stories. Other topics of news stories should be examined to generalize the findings to other news. The form of stimulus stories, a Web site presenting twenty-one headlines, was designed to control other interfering variables such as photos, related links, and different space of each story. However, this might have been too artificial. Another limitation is the uneven distribution of gender. Female participants were almost evenly assigned to each condition of contextual deviance. However, story deviance, a within-subject measure, may be affected by gender.

Lastly, the story deviance was operationally defined as the number of deviance dimensions a story has. Alternatively, it could be defined by measuring degree of deviance on each dimension. According to Shoemaker and Cohen, the former indicates the complexity of deviance whereas the latter indicates the intensity of deviance. Intensity measures of deviance could show how each dimension of deviance is associated with story selection.

Future studies may expand the scope of this study by including more variables. Grabe, Lang, and Zhao suggest that forms of news stories such as tabloid packaging as well as news content also influence audience members' information processing. According to the uses and gratifications approach, audience members' various motives, such as guidance, entertainment, personal relationships, and diversion as well as surveillance, may initiate audience members' story selection. Audience members' personality, such as sensation seeking, may be another factor that needs to be considered. In terms of dependent variables, other information processing measures rather than selection, such as comprehension, recognition, and recall, could be examined in relation to deviance of news stories. Specifically, the distinctiveness theory in psychology could be a useful theoretical framework to study the recall of deviant information.

Chapter 14

News Paradigm: A Multi-national Comparative Analysis

For the press in the age ofglobalization, there is a need to sort out and make sense of the world. The concept ofglobalism has provided a new mandate for a different order of coverage of international affairs, especially economic connections. The mass media often act as agents of globalization. Sports events like the Olympics or World Cup and political events like the collapse of the Berlin Wall or the Gulf War have been covered by the news media across countries. More recently, the reporting of antiglobalization demonstrations in Seattle and Washington, D.C., in 2000 has kindled debate about the economic globalization process by multinational organizations, such as the World Trade Organization (WTO) and the International Monetary Fund (IMF).

This is a multi-national comparative study of major newspaper reporting of the 1997 Asian economic crisis and subsequent economic interventions by the IMF, a topic directly addressing the phenomenon of globalization and its associated problems. The media construction of meaning (or framing) of international economic crises and the responses of multinational monetary organizations was examined in the context of the newly emerged "globalization" paradigm.

"Globalization" has been discussed widely in the tradition of international communication. Thus far, however, news media reporting has not gained much attention in the globalization debate. Instead, there has been much research on the power of media, especially the technological or economic aspects, to act as globalizing forces. The question remains open about the reporting of globalization news.

After World War II, the mass media of most countries, particularly the United States and the Western alliance, adopted a Cold War perspective defining the world in a particular fashion, such as East against West, or socialism versus the democratic Western countries. It has been natural for the media to follow this perspective in reporting international affairs. Indeed, the media relied heavily on the Cold War as a frame in understanding and interpreting world events during the last several decades. In 1989, however, the collapse of the USSR ended the Cold War, leading the Freedom Forum Media Studies Centre to observe:

The end of the Cold War has opened new horizons for the world media, but it has also confronted them with new challenges. One of the overarching issues for the media today is finding ways to make sense of a world in which change is the only constant. The old criteria for covering international affairs and many of the old standards of newsworthiness no longer apply in the post-Cold War world.

In the last decade, the world has witnessed the emergence of "a new world order" where, in the words of former Prime Minister Margaret Thatcher, "there is no alternative" to free market economics and neoliberalism. This new world order has come to be known as "globalization."

Obviously, considering the important role mass media play in disseminating globalization news, empirical research about that news coverage permits examination of how the media "construct" the meaning of globalization. With recent changes in technological, political, and economic structures, how have the media interpreted globalization, especially economic globalization? What frames have emerged as the world has become more economically interdependent and globalized? Is globalization news framed differently given the relative economic positions of countries?

The term "economic globalization" has been widely discussed. The primary assumption of economic globalization in which the IMF plays an important role is that unfettered free market competition leads to an efficient allocation of resources for the economy as a whole, as both producers and consumers act in their own self-interest. This is the essence of neo-liberalism.

Under the guidance of a new guard of liberal thinkers, the IMF or the World Bank developed "Structural Adjustment Programs" (SAPs) that sought to alter the nature of the economies requiring assistance.

For example, since the mid-1970s and the 1980s, the IMF imposed SAPs on more than seventy countries in economic crisis. Through integration of the isolated domestic economy into the global market by exploiting their comparative advantages, struggling nations would, it was believed, emerge from crisis and find prosperity. The IMF lends money to member nations in economic or financial trouble, as it did to Mexico in 1995. Taking advantage of the huge indebtedness of these countries, the IMF has demanded extensive economic reforms, including reforms toward radical liberalization or free-market systems.

How did the IMF respond to the 1997 Asian economic crisis? Along with forceful SAPs demanding reform of banking and industrial systems in Thailand, Indonesia, and South Korea, the IMF approved about $117.7 billion of financial support for reform programs in these countries ($57 billion for Korea, $43 billion for Indonesia, and $17 billion for Thailand). However, the crisis and IMF bailout have touched off a debate over the appropriateness of such IMF responses and free-market economic policies, and even about the creed of globalization.

Before the crisis in 1997, the IMF and World Bank proudly pointed to the success of Asia as a model for other less developed countries. The "Asian tigers" were bright and shining examples of free-market globalization. For instance, in 1993 the World Bank attributed these Asian countries' success to "sound macroeconomic management... improving the business-enabling framework, and liberalizing markets and prices. "

However, the economy could not grow forever. Vast savings saturated the financial market so that all productive investment opportunities were funded. When surplus funds could not be invested productively, they were funneled into property and stock market speculation as well as into corrupt borrowing practices by Asian industry. Along with these signs of an unraveling East Asian economy, investors also became reluctant to invest more, and the Asian countries faced paying about a hundred billion dollars in outstanding loans. Unable to meet this heavy debt obligation, three Asian countries turned to the IMF.

The 1997 economic crisis calls into question "the miracle of East Asian Tigers." What happened to the miracle? How is it that these Asian countries went from a "showcase" economy to the acceptance of the IMF bailout package? Some identify two major causes, neither recognized by the IMF: global "overcapacity" and "deflation." Both are the natural result of the free-market system. For example, many Asian countries, especially the three IMF-supported nations, found success in a "growth-at-all-costs" strategy for development.

In a report by staff economists, the IMF acknowledged that it made some mistakes in its rescues of the Asian countries in crisis-Thailand, Indonesia, and Korea, in 1997 and 1998 -notably in understanding the severity of those countries' recessions. The IMF largely dismissed criticism that it made the crisis worse by its insistence that the Thai, Indonesian, and Korean governments adopt painful economic policies such as high interest rates.

Similarly, World Bank chief economist Joseph E. Stiglitz has suggested that the fund committed a key error by imposing high interest rates on countries that were already headed for recession. Also, in the report on global economic prospects, the bank even criticized the U.S. Treasury and the IMF for imposing overly harsh economic measures on nations in crisis in 1997.

Criticizing the "one-size-fits-all" policy of the IMF, especially regarding to its responses to the Asian crisis, Jeffrey Sachs said that "a careful examination of the actual record shows that the IMF, loyal to financial orthodoxy and mindful of creditors to the neglect of debtor countries, often pours oil on the flames." According to a report recently released by the Heritage Foundation, of the ninety developing countries that have accepted IMF programs in the last thirty years, forty-eight are no better off while thirty-two are actually poorer.

Proponents of neo-liberalism still argue that such sacrifices must be made in the short-term for long-term economic stability. Milton Friedman, the American economist responsible for reviving laissez faire thinking, argues that such countries need to "take the bitter medicine" of structural adjustment if they ever hope to climb out of their financial morass.

As mentioned earlier, the Asian crisis and the IMF bailout have cast doubt on the appropriateness of IMF responses and free-market economic policies. If so, how did the media report this newly revived globalization controversy?

RESEARCH QUESTIONS AND HYPOTHESES

To date there have been several critiques of media coverage of "globalization." According to McChesney, news media content largely serves to perpetuate the conservative status quo. He warns that globalization, especially economic globalization, has a distinctly undemocratic edge as it effectively forces national governments to comply with the needs of the world capitalist system in which the inequality between countries exists. The media's event-based news coverage on globalization issues has been criticized by McChesney, who argues that "by defining the news as being based on specific events or the activities of official sources, the news media neglect coverage of long-term social issues that dominate society."

Well-known critics of globalization like Mander and Sachs argued that the media have largely misunderstood the major problems of globalization because they have failed to recognize the root causes of globalization itself. According to them, the media rarely report the connection between specific crises and the larger process of globalization, especially in terms of globalization and its accompanying problems.25 Journalist Timothy Lamer also observed problems in globalization news coverage:

In most of the reporting recently on the economic troubles worldwide, something has been missing, namely any hint that there are economists who believe the International Monetary Fund (IMF) has made matters in Asia and Russia worse. Most stories simply ignore the role the IMF has played in the problems overseas, but even when stories acknowledge criticism, it isn't the criticism coming from conservatives.

In sum, while the topic of globalization has gained a very prominent position in the media, the portrait of it has not necessarily attained a "globalized" view. Instead, its coverage has been heavily influenced by a "particularized" view with which the media have been more likely to embrace the Utopian vision of globalization. This study seeks to answer the question of how the media interpret (or frame) "globalization" by generating empirical data to make sense of the complex globalization phenomenon.

Many argue that a multidimensional approach is needed to detect the complexities of news frames. For example, media frames have been conceptualized in many different ways: as thematic or episodic; as abstract or concrete news coverage; as having cognitive or affective dimensions; as problem definition, attributed causes, moral judgments, and proposed remedies; and as causes and solutions of an issue.

This study assumes that the news frames of globalization in the case of the Asian economic crisis can be detected by examining the following four dimensions: major themes of each news story, story context, and informative (primary causes and solutions to the crisis) and affective dimensions (tone of news coverage). It attempts to answer the following research questions:

RQ1: What types of news themes are emphasized in the stories? Are there any similarities or differences among countries?

RQ2: What kinds of story contexts, such as global or domestic perspectives, were used in the story? Are there any differences between the United States and Asian countries?

In addition to these general research questions, four hypotheses were proposed based on the findings of previous studies about news coverage of international events. These were based on the assumption that the press of the United States and the three IMF-supported Asian countries-Thailand, Indonesia, and South Korea-would be more likely to report positive news regarding the IMF bailout for the crisis.

In the absence of a counter-superpower, the United States has assumed leadership of the global economy. Economically, the United States has perpetuated the spread of globalization by influencing the policy of inter-governmental organizations like the IMF.

In addition, this study included Malaysia to look for possible differences in news coverage of countries directly involved with the IMF programs compared to a country not so involved. This study expects that newspapers of Malaysia would differ in news coverage of the other countries directly involved with the.IMF programme.

H1: Considering the level of involvement with the IMF programs, the press of the United States and the three IMF-supported countries will be more likely to report news stories supporting (positive) the IMF, especially as compared with Malaysia.

H2: Considering that the criticism of the IMF has increased over time and the U.S. government's position on the IMF policy has changed, especially after the Russian government's moratorium announcement in August 1998, the press of all five countries will be more likely to report negative news stories about the IMF during the second year (August 1998-July 1999) than the first year of the time period (August 1997-July 1998).

H3: In the reporting of causes of the Asian economic crisis, news reports of the United States and the three IMFsupported countries will be more likely to focus on internal problems of Asian countries as the IMF prescribed, especially as compared with Malaysia.

H4: In the reporting of solutions to the crisis, news reports of the United States and the three IMF-supported countries will be more likely to focus on structural reforms of Asian countries as the IMF demanded, especially as compared with Malaysia.

METHODS

SAMPLE DATA COLLECTION

This is a comparative study based on data collected from major newspapers published in the United States, Korea, Indonesia, Thailand, and Malaysia. Four elite U.S. newspapers were selected-New York Times, Washington Post, Los Angeles Times, and Wall Street Journal.

Five national Korean-language newspapers-DongA llbo, Chosun Ilbo, Joongang Ilbo, Hankeoreh (formerly, Hankeoreh Sinmun), and Hankook libo were chosen. Three national Indonesian-language newspapers-Kompas, Suara Pembaruan, Republika-and the Jakarta Post, the most influential English newspaper in the country, were analysed.

Two Thai-language newspapers, the Krungthep Turakij and Chiang Mai News, and two national English newspapers-Bangkok Post and the Nation-were selected. Finally, two Malaysian-language newspapers, the Utusati Malaysia and Nanijang Siang Pau, and the Star, a national influential English paper, were chosen.

The publications are widely recognized by national audiences, opinion leaders, and decision makers as influential publications in each of the five countries. Asian newspapers were selected based on the preliminary review of the country's press system and interviews with journalists who are well aware of each country's newspapers. Also the coders who participated in the content analysis for this study helped in the newspaper selection process. As a result, most of the non-U.S. publications were selected based on their circulation and prestigious status in each respective country.

The U.S. data were collected from the electronic indexes of the four newspapers located in the Lexis-Nexis database. The Korea Press Institute Database (KINDS) was used for the Korean data.

Each newspaper's own electronic data indexes or microfilms were used for the Indonesian, Thai, and Malaysian data sets. Given that the first IMF bailout of the Asian economic crisis was officially announced in August of 1997 for Thailand, the study examined articles published during the two years between 1 August 1997 and 31 July 1999.

Two complementary methods were employed to obtain more representative samples and to ensure an equivalent number of news stories for the United States and the Asian countries.

For the former, the initial number of pertinent stories was determined by checking with each newspaper's electronic data base services. The population for U.S. papers was all news stories, commentaries, and editorials mentioning the Asian economic crisis and the subsequent IMF bailouts. Excluded were letters to the editor, reader opinion items, and obituaries. Based on the primary focus of news coverage, the collected news articles were sorted by countries-South Korea, Indonesia, Thailand, and Malaysia. Thus, a total of 649 news stories were coded from the U.S. newspapers.

The selection of newspapers and news articles for the Asian countries involved several steps. First, we investigated whether the full text and electronic files or microfilms of those newspapers were available. Then the news stories to be content analysed were selected by conducting a keyword search or by examining specialized data files for the subject so as to obtain all pertinent stories in the Asian countries' publications.

Due to a huge number of news articles (news stories, commentaries, and editorials) about the economic crisis, systematic sampling methods were combined with randomly constructed weeks so as to make the sample data more manageable.

First, a total of eight weeks was randomly constructed to limit the number of articles. Then all pertinent articles from each newspaper were sorted by date, Monday through Sunday. Next, stories for each weekday were systematically selected from all Asian newspapers published on the same days. After conducting these procedures, this study contained 201 articles for Korea, 180 for Indonesia, 210 for Thailand, and 186 for Malaysia. In the end, a total of 1,426 news articles were content-analysed.

CODING PROCEDURE

Coding team members (students and the author) were composed of two American coders, two from Indonesia, two from Thailand, two from Malaysia, and two from Korea. All were fluent in English. Before coding the sampled stories, one formal test and several pilot tests were conducted. Also, each coder assisted in the development of the coding procedure and participated in the coding process. Materials used in the training and pre-test sessions were not included in the study's data.

As mentioned earlier, it is assumed that news frames of globalization can be detected by investigating the following major dimensions of news coverage: major themes of the news story, story context, primary causes and solutions of the crisis, and direction of news coverage of the IMF bailout programs. The categories were generated inductively as the analysis proceeded. For the test of hypotheses, simple percentages were used.

Considering that this research is based on analysis of different language news content, special attention was given to test the reliability and validity of the categories used in the measurements. All stories sampled for this study were used for intercoder reliability tests.

More specifically, for the English newspapers, the codes of the two main coders were compared to determine a percentage of agreement on each variable. After calculating intercoder agreement, the items on which the two coders disagreed were given to a third person who served as an additional coder to decide which choice to use. For non-English news articles, at least two independent coders content-analysed all sampled stories. After calculating the intercoder agreement between the coders, the items on which they disagreed were translated into English for final determination by the author.

Then final agreement levels were calculated by using alpha as the average percentage of agreement among all involved coders. The final coefficients across the five countries were.78 for major themes;.82 for story direction;.91 for story context;.86 for primary causes; and.85 for primary solutions. The overall coefficient of news analysis for total sampled stories was.84.

FINDINGS

Overall, the examination of major themes, story tone regarding IMF programs, primary causes and solutions to the crisis, and story context helped not only to assess attributes of news reports about the Asian economic crisis and subsequent IMF bailouts, but also to detect a free-market supportive "globalization" news frame.

Major Themes. RQ1 asked what types of news themes were emphasized in the stories. In order to assess the nature of news coverage, this study identified the major themes of each story. The theme was defined as the "article's prevailing message or primary emphasis or concern." Because multiple coding was allowed (primary and if possible secondary theme), a total of 2,490 story themes in 1,426 news reports was categorized.

Overall, the newspapers of the United States and the three IMFsupported countries-South Korea, Indonesia, and Thailand- were fairly similar to one another in their distribution of story themes.

The category of "demanding reforms of the Asian countries," especially "reconstruction of industrial or financial systems," was the most common theme, accounting for 20.6% in Thailand and 26.5% in the United States. It also included "Asian governments' corruptions and demanding political reforms," "demanding a change of cultural mentality of Asian countries," and "opening regional markets to foreign investors," which are largely consistent with the IMF's goals.

On the other hand, the themes covered the most frequently by the Malaysian newspapers included "suggesting capital control policy" (13.9%), which is counter to the IMF's deregulation approach for a capital system, "IMF programs' inappropriateness and/or demanding the IMF policy reform" (13.6%), "reporting updated news of the IMF and the Asian countries" (9.0%), and "reporting international economic conferences or forums" (8.1%). Compared to news reports in the United States and three other Asian countries, less coverage (5.4%) emphasized "demanding reforms of the Asian countries."

FAVORABILITY LEVELS OF THE IMF PROGRAMS

Hl predicted that the press of the United States and the three IMF-supported countries would be more likely to report news stories supporting the IMF, especially compared with Malaysia.

Overall, the findings confirm the first hypothesis about favorability levels. The combined favorability score of the United States and the three IMF-supported countries was 3.04, whereas the level of Malaysia was 2.72, measured on a 5-point scale (3.0 indicates a neutral or balanced level).

A f-test between two mean scores also indicated that the favorability levels of news stories in the United States and the three IMF-supported countries were significantly more positive than Malaysian news coverage, although the absolute difference in average scores was small and both scores were close to the midpoint, suggesting mostly neutral or balanced coverage.

More specifically, the favorability scores of the United States (3.05), Korea (3.12), and Thailand (3.06) were notably higher than that of Malaysia (2.72), especially during the first year of the study, and also slightly higher than that of Indonesia (2.97). Also, of interest is favorability level of news reports about IMF programs in Asia before and after Russia's Moratorium Announcement in August 1998. H2 predicted that the press of all five countries would be more likely to report negative news stories about the IMF during the second year than the first year of the time period.

The results of the t-test show a significant difference in favorability levels across the examined time periods, except in the Malaysian press, generally confirming H2. The newspapers of four of the five countries were more likely to include negative reports about the IMF during the second year of the two-year time period, after Russia's moratorium announcement. More specifically, the average level of favorability of all news reports combined dropped significantly in each country, except Malaysia which was already somewhat negative about the IMF in the first year, from the first to the second year, indicating a more negative slant on the IMF programs.

PRIMARY CAUSES OF THE CRISIS

H3 predicted that news reports of the United States and the three IMF-supported countries would focus more on internal problems of Asian countries as the IMF prescribed, compared with Malaysia. About 70% of the total stories examined (1,006 in a total of 1,450 stories) reported some discussion of causes.

Internal factors in the Asian countries, such as economic structural problems, insufficient regulations, heavy reliance on foreign loans, and political corruption, accounted for 46% (United States) to 51.5% (Indonesia) of all causes discussed in the newspapers of the United States and the three IMF-supported countries.42 Only 28% of all causes discussed in the Malaysia newspapers were devoted to these internal factors. Financial factors, such as currency problems in general (22.5% on average) and speculative foreign investors (6.4% on average), were also discussed as important causes. Next, the IMF's inappropriate response to the crisis was a distant third cause in the United States and the three IMF-supportive Asian countries (17% on average), while it was reported as the primary cause in Malaysian newspapers (40%).

As hypothesized, while Malaysian newspapers put their emphasis on the IMF's inappropriate approaches to the crisis, the other four countries primarily named internal factors or currency problems in general as the more important causes rather than the IMF's inappropriate responses.

PRIMARY SOLUTIONS TO THE CRISIS

About 75% of all stories (1,065 of 1,426 total stories) included some discussion of solutions. H4 predicted that news reports of the United States and the three IMF-supported countries would be more likely to focus on structural reforms of Asian countries as the IMF demanded, especially as compared with Malaysia.

More specifically, various reform programs in Asian countries, such as industrial and/or financial reforms and political reform and cultural reforms, were discussed as primary solutions by the newspapers of the United States and three IMF-supportive countries (which ranged from 50% of the United States and Korea to 58.2% of Indonesia). Financial stabilization, such as currency stabilization in general (18.9% on average, and 25.7% in Korea) and restoring investors' confidence (9.7% on average), were also discussed as important solutions. However, the discussion of the IMF's policy reforms was mentioned relatively less (16.4% on average), especially in the United States, Korea, and Thailand.

The "others" category included such solutions as capital control, creation of the Asian Monetary Fund, and so on. Specifically, 30% of the solutions portrayed in the Malaysian newspapers mentioned capital control policy, which is in direct contrast to the IMF's deregulation approach for a capital system. Story Context. RQ2 asked what kinds of story contexts were used in the story. To answer the question, this study also coded the context or perspective of each news story as "global," "regional (Asian)," "domestic," or "mixed."

Slightly over half of the U.S. stories (58.4%) looked beyond the national realm into the broader realm of international affairs, employing either a global perspective (34.1%) or an Asian perspective (24.3%). By contrast, only about 10% (ranging from 4.4% in Indonesia to 14.4% in Korea) of the Asian countries' news stories were reported within a global context, such as the influences of their domestic economic crises on the world economy. By contrast, a majority of news stories of the Asian countries, except for Malaysian newspapers (24.2%), were strictly within each respective country's context (domestic issues).

Overall, news reports in the U.S. press were more likely to treat the Asian economic crisis in a broader context. For example, many stories in the U.S. newspapers dealt with the impact of the Asian economic crisis on the U.S. or global economy. These differences can be easily understood: the United States is an economic leader in the world economy and favors a global free-market economic system, while Asian countries are newly industrializing countries confronted by an unprecedented economic crisis.

The Asian countries' media, especially the three IMF-supported countries, focused on internal economic problems and reform programs that must take place under the IMF guidelines. The U.S. press, however, looked at the crisis from an outside perspective-seeing the crisis in the context of other crises or developments in the world market system, such as economic problems in Russia and Brazil.

Overall, the findings support the conclusion that the press of the United States and the three IMF-supported Asian countries largely used free-market supportive news frames that were mostly uncritical of the process of globalization, whereas Malaysian newspapers diverged from the news coverage patterns of the other directly involved countries. The most common theme found in the United States and the three IMF-supported countries' newspapers, the category of "reconstruction of industrial and financial systems," serves as compelling evidence for the existence of such a frame. Also, news coverage in these countries employed the same standards as the IMF for measuring primary causes and solutions to the crisis and the success of IMF programs in the Asian countries. By focusing on a certain theme or solution to the crisis above all else, the media accept the neo-liberal reasoning that austerity in the short-term would lead to prosperity in the long-term as the nation became a participant in the world market system.

Interestingly, the second most common theme in U.S. newspapers was that IMF policies in general and/or the IMF programs in Asia were inappropriate. However, the subject matter of these critical stories had largely nothing to do neither with the economic theories underlying the programme nor with the human suffering accompanying austerity. Instead, these stories addressed political issues surrounding

IMF programs. In the spring of 1998, for example, austerity was linked to the political unrest and riots culminating in the toppling of President Suharto in Indonesia.

A second common topic of stories coded as "IMF policies' inappropriate" was the battle waged on the floor of the U.S. Congress over whether to provide $18 billion to build up the IMF's flagging reserves. Other critical stories reported the failure of the IMF programme in Russia during the summer of 1998 and later her moratorium announcement. The close examination of these news stories critical of the IMF suggests that politically oriented negative-toned stories did not question the soundness of neo-liberal thinking. Thus, these stories did not seem to temper the pro-neo-liberal frame.

We assume that the United States as a leader of the global economy has perpetuated the spread of globalization by influencing the neoliberal policy of the IMF. If so, the next question should ask how the free-market supportive news frame of globalization has become the one emphasized by media in the three IMF-supported Asian countries. We can possibly, but not necessarily, think of information concerning the crisis and bailout as being filtered down a chain of command-the IMF set the policy and the Asian governments, facing default, accepted it. In order for the country to emerge from the crisis, the government tended to embrace the IMF policy rationale and neo-liberal rhetoric. This line of thinking was then transmitted to the press, which passed it on by relying mainly on the IMF and World Bank, their respective governments, and economic analysts.

Moreover, there are several possible reasons why the Asian governments remained in the spotlight in newspaper coverage of the crisis. Perhaps the most important one is that during the last several decades Asian governments have been central figures in economic development of their countries and thus the most authoritative sources for economic information. Also, the presses of Asian countries have historically not been as free as the U.S. press to be critical of the government. A self-censorship mentality persists, so that the government line tends to be echoed in the press.

During the crisis, therefore, the Asian countries' presses focused largely on the government because it was responsible for negotiating the rescue package and, due to the nature of neo-liberal reform, the government had to agree to a process of radical economic transformation. As a result, the heavy reliance of the Asian countries' newspapers on government sources probably had a significant impact on the framing of the crisis in the Asian countries.

Some economists have regarded the IMF's response to the Asian financial crisis as inappropriate. Nevertheless, because of a heavy reliance of the press in the United States and the IMF-supported Asian countries on the IMF and their governments, a pluralistic interpretation of the crisis in the global context was seldom included in the coverage. Such limited diversity of news suggests that the media frames would fail to take into account other more critical perspectives.

The findings of this study also revealed that the human cost of the IMF programme may have been underreported in news coverage. In 1999, journalist Claudia Rosett wrote: "The real human-interest aspect of this saga is still playing out....Hundreds of millions of ordinary middle-class folks are still in shock. Whatever world has been saved, it's not theirs."

Along with reporting the bright side of globalization, journalists need to report critically the difference between the planned scheme and its actual implementation, and the difference between its impact on people as reported by the IMF and local governments, compared to its actual impact. Servaes wrote that people are still "voiceless" in news coverage not because they have nothing to say, but because nobody cares to listen to them. Despite the growing importance of the global economy and its influence on the lives of people, especially in developing countries, media coverage of global economics seldom includes the "voices" of these "voiceless" people.

Against the backdrop of rapid diffusion of a wide array of new media technologies such as personal computers (PCs) and the Internet, the phenomenon of non-adoption and characteristics of non-adopters have received increasing scholarly attention. Studies of nonadopters-also called "have-nots"-of the household telephone, PC, and cell phone show that age, income, and technological complexity are significant barriers to adoption. The concern of a "crisis of equality" or a "two-tier society" of new media haves and have-nots grew out of these studies.

Many of the previous non-adopter studies, however, were based on one-shot surveys and suffered methodological deficiencies. Longitudinal studies, on the other hand, better address extended social changes since they can track profound, long-term social changes associated with the uneven diffusion of new media technologies and can assess the consequences of non-adoption. By updating a previous survey study on cell phone have-nots, the present study aims to examine the enduring social-psychological characteristics of non-adopters. Such a longitudinal design facilitates a cross-time comparative analysis of the characteristics of the diminishing ranks of cell phone have-nots as well as the barriers that impede their adoption of the cell phone.

Why the cell telephone technology? As a mass medium and social instrument similar to the plain old telephone, the cell phone has plunged in cost and skyrocketed in popularity thanks to advances in wireless telecommunications technologies. More important, it is more than "a talking device on the move." The cell phone represents a converged new communication and information technology providing a variety of extensive interpersonal and mass communication services such as paging, voice-mail, news updates, e-mailing, and Internet surfing, to name a few. Cell phone users are no longer just well-educated, upscale business people, but also the general public, including housewives and students. The rapid diffusion of cell telephone technology worldwide is phenomenal and shows no sign of abating. For instance, even though the former British colony of Hong Kong has achieved almost 100 per cent penetration of the fixed household telephone (the telephone density was 58 lines per 100 people, among the highest in Asia), the number of cell phone users surged nine-fold to 1.21 million in 1996 from 133,912 in 1990. The total increased 4.5 times to 5.23 million in December 2000, penetrating 77 per cent of the 6.78 million population.

The adoption rate of cell phones between 1998 and 2000 in the Hong Kong Special Administrative Region (SAR) has been faster than any other time thanks to the region's advantages of a free market and an advanced telecommunication infrastructure. By 2000, almost eight of every ten residents owned a cell phone. Then, who remained a cell phone have-not in a cell phone-saturated society? As the secondwave survey of cell phone have-nots, the present study intends to trace the socio-psychological changes of the non-adopter population across time. The 1998 first-wave study identified cell phone have-nots as predominantly less educated, less affluent older women. Would these socioeconomic characteristics of non-adopters persist in 2000? Further, would non-adopters be doomed to be laggards (i.e., those who resist an innovation and are the last to adopt)? In other words, what are the key factors that prevent the persistent cell phone have-nots from becoming cell phone haves? Finally, what is the consequence of being left out of the current new media technology-driven social change?

New media technologies are increasingly crucial in the expansion of access to information and the skills to use it. Numerous adoption studies show that the members of higher socioeconomic groups have embraced new media technologies such as PCs and the Internet faster than any other social groups. Knowledge about non-adopters is an important but under-researched area compared to voluminous studies on adopters in the past fifty years. Given the growing concern about the "information gap" or the "digital divide," a longitudinal analysis of cell phone non-adopters is timely. Findings help shed light on what makes certain social groups continue to lag as the pace of the ongoing "information revolution" accelerates. They further address the fundamental issue of whether the cell phone as a massively popular new technology helps widen or narrow the digital divide in society. Theoretically, this empirical study offers insights into the dynamics of socioeconomic variables, attitudes, innnovativeness, and channels of communication on turning persistent non-adopters of cell phones into potential adopters at the late stage of adoption.

The conceptualization of the present study was informed by adoption theory and knowledge gap theory. Unlike past studies on adoption and use of new media technologies and on knowledgegap as a social phenomenon associated with uneven access to information and technological resources, this study integrates adoption and knowledge-gap theories into a unified analysis. A variety of socioeconomic and psychological factors are considered as determinants of a non-adopter's likelihood to convert. Further, the non-adoption status, conceptualized as a lack of access to information and resources originated from the cell phone technology, immediately affects the cell phone have-nots' gaining of general knowledge about information technologies (IT).

ADOPTION THEORY

The links between social-technological change and the adoption of new media technologies are complex. The wellestablished diffusion of innovation research paradigm holds that the adoption decision is subject to a wide range of factors. These factors group into four broad categories: (1) adopter-related personality variables such as traits and innovativeness (i.e., the degree to which an individual is relatively earlier to adopt than are others), namely the "people difference" factors; (2) socioeconomic status, including age, gender, education, and income; (3) the role of interpersonal communications channels and use of mass media; and (4) five attributes of an innovation, or the "technology difference" factors, such as relative advantage, compatibility, complexity, reliability, and observability.

Numerous adoption studies have been conducted to test the diffusion paradigm in the past. Age negatively correlated with adoption, while education and income tend to have a positive relationship with adoption.10 Large households were found more likely to be early adopters than were smaller households. Conflicting results were reported on the role of gender in adoption. These tested relationships intuitively make sense. Younger people tend to be more adventuresome in adopting new things. Higher level of education enables potential adopters to be more aware of a new technology's existence and benefits, while higher income lets them buy a new media technology.

In the 1998 first-wave study of the cell phone have-nots in Hong Kong, socioeconomic variables significantly influenced adoption likelihood. Age was a particularly strong variable in predicting the likelihood of a cell-phone have-not becoming a have. Older people were less likely to convert. Considering the 30 per cent increase in cell phone users in the former British colony since 1998, who still remained a have-not? Once they fell behind, would non-adopters be completely left out? This was the first research question that the present study addressed:

RQ1: Who still remained a cell phone have-not? Was there any significant change in the socioeconomic characteristics of cell phone have-nots between 1998 and 2000? That is, did the have-nots remain primarily less educated older women with less income?

A generalization of adoption theory proposes that early adopters of higher socioeconomic status tend to own a larger number of functionally similar new media technologies. In fact, adoption of new media technologies can be best predicted by the adoption of functionally similar ones. Empirical studies supported such a generalization. In the case of cell phone adoption, the 1998 first-wave study found that the have-nots owned or subscribed to fewer functionally similar telecommunication technologies or services as compared to their counterparts. Would this polarizing phenomenon in owning new telecommunications technologies persist across time? Specifically,

RQ2: Was there any change in owning new media technologies among cell phone have-nots across time? Would the non-adopters have fewer telecommunications technologies as compared to the non-adopters in 1998?

Adoption theory further holds that earlier adopters use mass media more than do later adopters, especially at the early stage of adoption. The patterns of media use of cell phone have-nots were found empirically different from cell phone haves in the 1998 survey.

Cell phone have-nots read fewer newspapers and magazines, which are paid channels of communication. Would there be any change in the pattern of mass media use among the non-adopters two years later? This is the concern of the third research question:

RQ3: Would the cell phone have-nots be consistently dependent on using free mass media such as TV as compared to the cell phone haves?

Further, past adoption research suggests that the adoption of new media technologies is related to potential adopters' needs as well as the perceived usefulness and ease of use of a given new media technology. Compatibility with users' existing values and meeting their needs play a significant role in the adoption process.

Past research shows that older people tend to hold more pessimistic views about information technologies. In the 1998 first-wave study, the have-nots perceived the attributes of the cell phone largely as disadvantages instead of advantages. Specifically, dependence on public phones led the have-nots to believe that cell phones were incompatible with their values.

They also perceived the cell phone as overly complex due to confusing services offered. They further considered that the cell phone offered no observable benefit for them because they had no need or opportunity to use it; and they considered the need to either turn off the phone or risk interruptions as a relative disadvantage.

The perceived disadvantages in turn shape subsequent adoption decisions. The more that cell phone have-nots perceived the attributes of cell phones as negative, the less likely they were to consider adopting it. Given that during the period, the cell phone became less expensive, massively popular, and more powerful in diverse functions, would its attributes still be perceived negatively among the non-adopters? The fourth research question asked the following:

RQ4: Was there any change between 1998 and 2000 in the have-nots' perceptions of the cell phone attributes?

Finally, adoption theory proposes that before a new technology reaches its critical adoption threshold, socioeconomic variables as a block play a significant role in differentiating adopters from non-adopters. On the other hand, socioeconomic influences arguably become less important once the new technology reaches a critical mass. Numerous empirical studies have found consistently that age has a negative correlation while education and income have positive correlations with adoption or adoption intention in the early stage of a new media technology. Several recent studies on household telephone use report that age, education, and income were significant adoption barriers for later adopters or discontinued adopters. The 1998 study of cell phone have-nots identified age and interpersonal influence as strong predictors of adoption likelihood at a stage when nearly half of the surveyed population had owned a cell phone: a diffusion stage close to "late majority." In fact, the combined influence of socioeconomic variables and change agent contacts topped that of the perceived technological attributes of the cell phone on the likelihood of converting non-adopters to adopters. Accordingly, it was hypothesized that:

H1: Socioeconomic variables would still be the strongest predictors of non-adopters' likelihood to convert as compared to other predictors such as perceived attributes of cell phones, contacts with change agents, and mass media use.

KNOWLEDGE GAP THEORY

What is the far-reaching consequence of non-adoption of a new media technology? One argument is that the distribution of information in society is related to differences in social economic status. Tichneor et al.'s seminal study of this issue led to knowledge gap theory, which states that the growth of knowledge is relatively greater among the higher social status segments. Similarly, information gap theory addresses the effects of uneven diffusion of new media technologies by differentiating adopters into "information rich" (those with superior levels of education, higher income, and access to information and technological resources) and "information poor" (those who have inferior levels of education, less income, and fewer resources). It states that the introduction of new information and communication technologies in the population will benefit both groups but will benefit the information rich more given their advantages in social-economic status and resources. As a consequence, the information rich get richer at a faster rate than the poor get rich, causing the information gap to widen.

The 1998 first-wave study did not test the differences between cell phone haves and have-nots regarding knowledge about information technology. The second-wave expands on the first by examining the consequence of non-adoption in terms of information gain; that is, it assesses the effects of uneven diffusion of the cell phone. Based on numerous empirical findings on knowledge-gap theory, it was hypothesized that:

H2: Cell phone have-nots would be less knowledgeable about information technologies than would the haves.

RESEARCH DESIGN AND METHODS

The present study employed a longitudinal design to address the four research questions and test the two hypotheses. Specifically, the design features a trend study that drew on a sample of different respondents from the same population at different time points.

Survey Sample. The sampling procedures followed the same used in the 1998 first-wave survey in Hong Kong. First, the three geographic areas of Hong Kong Island, Kowloon, and New Territories were used to construct a sampling frame using the latest telephone directories. Since the penetration of household telephone was almost 100% (Hong Kong's 2.115 million households were served by 2.209 million residential telephone lines, including second telephone line and faxlines in 2000), the sampling frame was adequate. Second, a household telephone number was selected randomly from the sampling frame. The Random Digit Dial (RDD) method was used. Selection of respondents in a household was governed by gender (to seek ratio balance) and by age (restricted to 18 years or older). The last birthday method was used to identify a qualified respondent. Up to four callback attempts were made for refusals, midinterview terminations, and busy numbers. A total of 2,492 residential numbers were successfully identified, out of which 1,190 interviews were completed in July and August 2000. The response rate of 47.8% was slightly lower than that of the 1998 survey of 52%, but comparable to similar surveys.

A comparative analysis of the demographic distribution of the two samples shows that gender is evenly distributed in both. With regard to age, the 2000 sample is older than the 1998 sample. Those under 30 years old account for 45.6% in the 2000 survey, while their counterparts are 36.5% in the 1998 survey. The percentages of those older than 41 years are 34.6% and 28.9%, respectively. The education categories are comparable across the samples with the majority finishing senior high school (44.1% in 2000 and 42.1% in 1998). For annual household income, the brackets are similar. The largest income bracket for both the 2000 and the 1998 samples are between US$15,425 and $30,840. More married respondents (60%) are found in the 2000 sample as compared to that in the 1998 sample (53.1%). The distributions of occupation of the two samples are also comparable, but with many fewer respondents in services and sales (12.3%) in 2000 (as compared to 30.8% in 1998).

Measurement

To ensure comparability, questions included in the 2000 survey were identical to those in the 1998 survey, including scales and wordings. However, as noted above, questions on knowledge of information technology were added to expand the firstwave survey.

Adoption Status. A single question was used to determine the adoption status of cell phones. Respondents were asked to indicate if they currently owned a cell phone. The scale was dichotomous. Respondents who answered "yes" were classified as "cell phone haves" while those who answered "no" as "cell phone have-nots."

ADOPTION LIKELIHOOD

As the dependent variable, this variable was measured by questioning respondents without a cell phone as to the likelihood that they would buy one in the next 12 months. The scale was 1 to 5, with "1" being "very unlikely" and "5" being "very likely."

ATTITUDES TOWARD THE CELL PHONE

The measures of respondents' attitudes toward the cell phone focused on their perceptions of its attributes. The 12 items used in the 1998 survey were repeated. They tap the respondents' perceptions of the cell phone in terms of its values, benefits, technical complexity and relative disadvantages.

Initial confirmatory factor analyses of the 12 repeat items reproduced a 4-factor model of the 1998 study. The four factors were: "incompatibility with existing values," "relative disadvantages," "complexity," and "absence of observable benefits." The model yielded a X^sup 2^ value of 73.11 with 48 degrees of freedom. Though a reasonable fit, cross-loading was allowed to modify the model to pursue a smaller x2/df ratio. One item ("cell phone usually has bad transmission"), which belonged to the "complexity" factor, was allowed to load on the "relative disadvantages" factor. The modification was justified because a close examination of the wording revealed that the quality of wireless signal transmission had more to do with perceived cell phone advantages or disadvantages than did complexity of use. The modified model was accepted in creating the fourattitudinal measures.

INNOVATIVENESS

This was measured by the ownership of a cluster of interrelated telecommunications technologies. A set of questions asked respondents to report if they had adopted a number of telecommunications technologies such as answering machines, voice mail, pagers, caller ID display, call waiting, a second household telephone, and a fax machine (yes="1;" "no"=0). A composite index was created by combining the 7 repeat items (ranging from 0 to 7). It was labeled "telecommunications technology cluster" (alpha=.64).

CONTACTS WITH CHANGE AGENTS

Two repeat questions measured face-to-face interpersonal communication with change agents: whether in the preceding six months they had talks with sales representatives about cell phones or talks with friends. The scale was "1" (yes) and "0" (no).

MASS MEDIA USE

Respondents were asked to indicate the number of minutes they spent watching TV and listening to radio per day as well as the number of days per week they read newspapers and magazines.

INFORMATION TECHNOLOGY (IT) KNOWLEDGE

As a new variable to test the hypothesis of IT knowledge gap, a 5-item index measured respondents' knowledge about basic IT terms (i.e., the "Information Superhighway," "World Wide Web" and "WAP"-wireless application protocol) and big IT names (i.e., Bill Gates of "Microsoft" and Jerry Yang of "Yahoo"). In a recall question format, respondents were requested to indicate whether they had heard of or knew the given term or name ("1"=heard of or answered correctly, "0"=no or answered incorrectly). The alpha of the five items was.62.

SOCIOECONOMIC VARIABLES

Repeat measures of socioeconomic variables, which were used as indicators of respondents' socioeconomic status, included age, gender, marital status, family size, number of children under 18 at home, as well as education, household income, and occupation.

RESULTS

Among the 1,190 respondents, 988 (accounting for 83% of the sample) had a cell phone and 202 (accounting for 17%) were have-nots. The corresponding percentages were 53.5 and 46.5, respectively, in 1998. The result marked a dramatic and significant increase of haves and a decrease of have-nots in a period of 25 months, during which almost one-third (29.5%) of have-nots had become haves thanks to the deregulation of cell phone services and lower prices of cell phones. However, a larger number of the have-nots in 2000 were less likely to convert than were their counterparts in 1998.

The first research question is concerned with changes in socioeconomic stratum of cell phone have-nots from 1998 to 2000. Results of a series of t-tests show that the cell phone have-nots were 16.1 years older than the haves in the 2000 sample. Age difference was 6.5 in the 1998 sample. A cross-sample analysis shows that the have-nots were 12.6 years older between 1998 and 2000.

Similar significant changes were found with regard to the difference in education levels and income brackets between cell phone haves and have-nots. The education attainment of the have-nots declined from senior high school to junior high school. So did their household income, from the mid-point of $30,849-$46,272 to the lower end.

In terms of owning other telecommunications technologies, the concern of the second research, changes from 1998 to 2000 were significant. The mean score of cell phone have-nots in owning other telecommunications technologies decreased to 1.15 in 2000 from 1.65 in 1998. This particular finding suggests a trend of "the media poor getting poorer," a phenomenon that is the opposite that of "the media rich getting richer" in adopting new media technologies.

Were cell-phone have-nots still more likely than haves to depend on using mass media, especially free radio and TV? Results were mixed. The former read newspapers and magazines less frequently, and watched more TV than the latter. But the difference in radio listening between the respondents who had a cell phone and who still did not have one was non-significant. As none of the cross-time t-tests was significant, the pattern was unchanged from 1998 to 2000; respondents without a cell phone depended more on free TV and less on paid newspapers and magazines.

The fourth research question concerned the attitudinal changes of cell phone have-nots toward the cell phone across time. Small but significant differences were found in two of the four attitudinal dimensions underlying respondents' perceptions of cell phone attributes. The mean score of "incompatibility" decreased from 3.46 in the 1998 sample to 3.27 in the 2000 sample; the mean score of "relative disadvantages" also showed a decrease from 2.85 to 2.70. These results suggest that the nonadopters became more positive in perceiving the cell phone as more compatible with their existing values and something advantageous to have at a time when cell phone use was sweeping through society.

Next, a discriminant analysis was performed to seek a comparative multi-dimensional profile of cell phone have-nots between the two surveys. Included in the discriminant equations were socioeconomic variables, telecommunications technology cluster, and mass media use. Almost 80% of cases were correctly classified in 2000 as compared to that of 67.5% in 1998. Four variables showed enduring discriminating effects: age, gender, income, and reading newspapers and magazines. Owning a fax machine shows significant discriminating power only in 2000, while occupation, having a pager, and not-having caller ID were significant only in 1998. A multi-dimensional profile of cell phone have-nots largely persisted in 2000. As nearly 80% of the population had had a cell phone in 2000, marking an increase of 30% from 1998, those who still remained behind were older, less affluent women who read newspapers and magazines less frequently.

Separate regressions treating adoption likelihood as the dependent variable were run for the 2000 and 1998 data to test the first hypothesis. Significant predictors shared by the two surveys included age, absence of observable benefits, and talks with friends about cell phones. Household income was significant in the 1998 survey, but it lost predictive ability in the 2000 survey. Consistently, none of the predictors in the blocks of innovativeness and mass media use was significant. These results suggest that after the dominant majority of the population had owned a cell phone since 1998, those who would likely convert in the near future were those respondents of younger age who had talked with friends about cell phones. Of particular theoretical interest is that the result suggests the socialization factor in adopting a mobile social instrument like the cell phone is indeed enduring. In addition, the more these potential adopters perceived the cell phone as offering observable benefits, the more likely they would convert.

A close comparative analysis of the regression coefficients of age and gender showed no major change from 1998 to 2000. Among the persistent non-adopters, older women were consistently less likely than younger men to change adoption status. However, cross-time changes were found in the influences of education, occupation, household income, family size, and the number of children at home.

Education did not affect non-adopters in 1998, but among the cell phone have-nots in 2000, the better educated would be more likely to become haves. Business and non-business people were equally likely to adopt the cell phone in 1998, but business people were less likely to adopt it in 2000. This is probably because cell phones had already saturated the business community. Thus, it was the non-business user who had become a factor in adoption. This result made sense for business people were the first to have the cell phone in the 1980s. By 2000, the cell phone had spread to all sectors, including blue-collar workers, homemakers, and students. Household income, a significant positive determinant in 1998, was less so two years later in predicting adoption. This particular result-that income became increasingly irrelevant-supports the notion of Dutton, Rogers, and Jun that some socioeconomic factors are transient at different stages of adoption.

Interesting changes were found from 1998 to 2000 in the influences of household size and number of children, two measures of family structure. Cell phone have-nots of small and large families were both likely to become haves in 1998; the have-nots of large families were more likely to do so two years later. In addition, in the 1998 survey, whether non-adopters had more and fewer children, they were equally likely to become adopters; however, the adoption likelihood for those with fewer children was less in the 2000 survey. At a diffusion rate of 80% in the general population, most small-size families with small children probably already had a cell phone.

More important; the 1998 pattern that socioeconomic variables made the largest contribution to the equation, followed by attitudes toward the cell phone and change agent contacts, remained unchanged in 2000. In fact, the contribution of the seriocomic block was four times that of the other two blocks in the second-wave survey. These results supported Hi. On the whole, the 2000 equation was more successful in accounting for the systematic variance in the likelihood of cell phone have-nots to convert. Measured by adjusted R2, the percentages of variance accounted for by the equation doubled to 30.5 in 2000 from 15.1 in 1998.

To examine if there were any interaction effect between socioeconomic variables and the year of survey, the 1998 and 2000 samples were pooled. Seven interaction variables were created and then entered in a separate multiple regression equation. None of the interaction variables was significant; there was no change in R-square, either. These results indicate that the impact of socioeconomic variables (i.e., their causal relationships with adoption likelihood) did not change across time. The possibility of changes in the variables across time simply due to repeated measures was thus ruled out.

Finally, significant differences in IT knowledge between the cell phone have-nots and their counterparts were found. Those respondents without cell phones were less knowledgeable about information technologies as compared to those who had cell phones. The result supported H2.

In Hong Kong's cell phone-saturated society, the divide between haves and have-nots shrank from 1998 to 2000.

Nevertheless, socioeconomic-based differences still significantly affect the likelihood that nonadopters will make the switch to cell phone haves. If the have-nots resemble the "late majority" in the s-shaped diffusion curve in the firstwave 1998 study, those have-nots increasingly fit the descriptions of "laggards" in the current 2000 second-wave study.

More important, the results of the longitudinal analysis of cell phone have-nots provide fresh empirical support for the concern about social inequality or a digital divide due to the uneven diffusion of new media technologies in society. People who did not have a cell phone were also bypassed by other new media technologies. These findings confirm a polarizing phenomenon in owning a cluster of new media technologies.

The results of the second-wave analysis also show that as the cell phone becomes cheaper, incredibly popular, and more powerful in functions, respondents' perceptions of its attributes are more positive. However, the attitudinal changes are of secondary importance in the adoption decision, while the combined socioeconomic and social influences once again far outweigh that of attitudes toward the cell phone in the late adoption process. This hierarchical pattern of influences is the same as that found in the 1998 study. For the 2000 study, the influence of socioeconomic variables is even stronger than in the previous study. The results validate the proposition that the case of non-adoption of the cell phone suggests "a process of social exclusion."

Finally, this study gathers fresh empirical evidence on the consequence of being excluded in owning and using cell phone technology and related wireless services, which are increasingly important in disseminating public information and news. The have-nots lagged significantly in their IT knowledge as compared to the haves, though the oneshot measure does not permit an argument for causality.

Theoretically, the present study also contributes to the adoption research paradigm. The cross-time analysis of the influences of socioeconomic variables suggests dynamic changes at the very late stage of adoption of the cell phone.

In a population with nearly an 80 per cent penetration rate, where the cell phone is hardly considered a luxury that only socioeconomic elites can afford, income indeed becomes a transient factor. On the other hand, contrary to the generalization that socioeconomic variables would be less important, age turned out to be an enduring determinant at the late stage of adoption. The influences of other socioeconomic factors such as education, occupation, and family structure also changed dynamically. Previous research rarely examined these patterns longitudinally.

This study has some limitations. It found no interaction effects between socioeconomic variables and year of survey, perhaps due to the relatively small size of the sample of non-adopters. Further, the effects on Hong Kongese bypassed by the cell phone wave may not occur in less saturated societies. Race and ethnicity, for example, are important factors that were not included in analysis because the samples were drawn from a homogenous population. A cross-country comparative analysis is one direction for future research. Methodologically, one more wave of study should be conducted in 2002, followed by more two-year largescale surveys, eventually leading to a time-series analysis. Such a design will be even stronger in examining long-term changes among the population of cell phone have-nots.

Chapter 15

Interactive Disaster Communication on the Internet: A Content Analysis

In recent years, rapid development of new communication technology has prompted a shift in communication strategies.' When one examines the interactivity of new communication strategies in the context of disaster relief on the World Wide Web, the extent of interactive communication on the Internet developed to deal with natural disaster crises can be identified. The current study employs content analysis to explore the interactive nature of some of the disaster relief information at Internet users' disposal.

It is intended that the identification and development of a typology for interactive dimensions on disaster relief web pages will provide a useful frame of reference for future research in interactivity on the World Wide Web. The emergence of the Internet as a prominent form of mass media and its potential for interactivity are discussed, and potential indicators of web site interactivity are identified and measured. This study concludes with a discussion about the extent to which disaster communication on Internet is interactive.

THE INTERNET AS A MASS MEDIUM

As of November 2000, the number of Internet users worldwide was estimated to total more than 407 million, up

242 million from January of that same year. CommerceNet projections estimate 490 million users by the end of 2002 and 765 million users by year-end 2005, which may be conservative estimates, considering it projected only 349 million users by the end of year 2000. Because of this rapid growth, the Internet provides an increasing opportunity to not only reach large numbers of people, but also the potential to mobilize immediate responses from those people regarding their needs and wants.

Such Internet availability has become a concern for government and corporate agencies alike, primarily because the rift between those with access to the Internet and those without has been growing as rapidly as the Internet itself. A number of corporations' have been leading efforts to help narrow this gap through special funding and grants used to provide computer and Internet access to low-income neighborhoods and minority populations. In addition, for fiscal year 2000 the Clinton administration sought $65 million in funding for community Internet centers. That figure is a $55 million increase from the previous year's budget request.

In light of these efforts, the Internet is evolving into a medium with the potential to engage a large segment of the general public in ways that were not possible in the past. Like mass media, the Internet has the capacity and the resources to send a tremendous amount of information to large numbers of receivers simultaneously; however, unlike traditional mass communication, it often gives the receiver the ability to respond immediately and directly to the information's source (or alleged source), as well as discuss the information with many other receivers, offering the opportunity to be both receiver and sender concurrently. In continuing efforts toward development and accessibility, the Internet has the potential to eventually become the first global interactive mass medium.

INTERACTIVITY AND THE INTERNET

The potential for interactivity has been among the more heavily discussed characteristics of the Internet. It is important to avoid making the assumption, however, that the Internet is synonymous with interactivity. Studies of on-line journalism and business web sites have indicated that despite the interactive capabilities of the Internet, designers do not often implement interactive designs into their web sites.

Rafaeli and Sudweeks acknowledge that interactivity is not necessarily a characteristic of the Internet since definitions of interactivity are contingent upon the context to which they are applied. For the purposes of interpersonal communication, they define interactivity as the extent to which a set of messages are related to one another in a specific sequence, particularly regarding the relationship that later messages have to earlier ones.

In the context of commerce, it can be seen as a varying combination of content and communication that creates a powerful consumer encounter, as well as a person-to-person or personto-technology exchange of information designed to influence the behaviour or knowledge of at least one person. In many cases these definitions are subject to individual interpretation, however, limiting their applicability to varying contexts.

Heeter suggests that a range of meanings has emerged in the study of interactivity as it has evolved into a multidimensional concept. She examined a range of areas that covered many of the different ways in which the term interactivity is employed. Her dimension effort users must exert is considered one of two general categories of interactivity identified in this study. This dimension is defined as "the amount of effort a user of a media system must exert to access information."

In his mathematical definition of interactivity, Paisley identified a spectrum along which interactivity varies between the user of the system and the system itself. At one end users simply observe or read the information that is supplied to them by a media system. At the other, the users deliberate and choose what they access by sending messages to the system. The increase in the requirement of such effort is indicative of increased interactivity. Three of the seven dimensions of interactivity that are measured in this study fall within this category: complexity of choice, ease of adding information, and facilitation of interpersonal communication.

COMPLEXITY OF CHOICE

Indicated by the incorporation of various topics such as current events, advertisements, or entertainment, complexity concerns the extent to which an audience is exposed to a variety of choices. As an audience is provided with more choices, the level of interaction that is required in order for a viewer to make a choice increases.

EASE OF ADDING INFORMATION

The extent to which users can actually influence information content through interaction with a medium accessed by a mass audience also indicates potential for user effort. As technology has evolved, so has an increasing number of opportunities for users to become a source of information that can be communicated to a mass audience. This also increases the potential for users to expend energy interacting.

FACILITATION OF INTERPERSONAL COMMUNICATION

Although not synonymous with human face-to-face interaction, new media technology does provide the opportunity for users to send and receive messages directly, such as teleconferences, on-line discussions, instant messaging, and Internet chat rooms. Such interactivity via technology varies in its synchronicity, however. In some situations, messages are sent, received, and responded to at different points in time, or in an asynchronous manner. Synchronous interaction, on the other hand, involves immediate, concurrent participation. Both, however, potentially increase the attention and effort users must give to a medium during periods of interaction.

Although the opportunity for interactivity on the Internet is certainly available, whether that opportunity is utilized is also determined by the designer of the web site, not solely its visitors. The second general category of interactivity, effort producers must exert, will identify four dimensions in which web producers strive to decrease the effort required of the user, yet must devote an increased amount of attention to design and interaction with the users of the site in order for interactivity to take place.

For example, efforts to increase the navigability of a site may result in a reduction in effort exerted by the user. Less effort in this case would not necessarily indicate a lower level of interactivity, but rather an increase in the web site producer's share of the effort expended. Dimensions in this category include: monitoring information use, responsiveness to users, facilitation of site navigation, and immediacy of information.

Monitoring Information Use" is the extent to which a media system can monitor its use. On the Internet, the use of cookies and on-line user surveys provide examples of attempts to trace audience usage patterns of the World Wide Web. The use of such design considerations requires increased effort on the part of the web producers if they wish to effectively analyse, interpret, and utilize the data that is gathered.

RESPONSIVENESS TO USERS

This dimension is based on Rafaeli's19 concept of how "actively responsive" a medium is to its users. Active response refers to the degree to which communication between a media system and its users can resemble the highly sophisticated processes of human interaction.

Rafaeli positions this level of sophistication at the far end of a continuum of communication involving varying degrees of speaking and listening. A declarative, one-way model lies at one end of the spectrum, while a reactive two-way model lies at the other end.

Interactivity also exists on different levels, including non-interactive, quasi-interactive, and fully interactive. For example, it takes little effort for a web designer to place an e-mail link on a site's home page to allow for one-way messaging; however, actually responding to users who contact the site's organization through that link can require much more time and effort. To respond in a timely manner requires more still, particularly for a site with many users.

Facilitation of Site Navigation

In the context of the World Wide Web, menu bars, search engines, and site maps all contribute to the clarity of a web site's structure and design. The use of such design approaches often means that making a site navigable for users takes increased effort and expertise on the part of the web designer.

Immediacy of Information

Massey and Levy2 added the dimension immediacy of information to Heeter's conceptualization of interactivity. This dimension indicates the amount of effort the web site producer has put forth in keeping the page current, in addition to saving the user effort spent trying to establish how current the information is.

This could be one of several ways to amend and organize the conceptualization of Internet interactivity provided by Heeter and interpreted by Massey and Levy. New media technologies, however, will continue to call for perpetual redefinition and interpretation of this concept. As models of interactivity continue to undergo evaluation through theoretical examination, so must the contexts to which they are applied.

THE INTERNET AND DISASTER COMMUNICATION

Voluntary disaster organizations perform any number of services to assist survivors with disaster response, providing food, water, shelter, counseling, advocacy, clean-up, education, training, repair, reconstruction, and consultation for community organizations. However, these organizations have now begun using the Internet in order to relay large volumes of information more effectively. For example, the National Organizations Active in Disasters includes a link that leads to more than 400 other natural disaster resources. As these fields of communication have progressed, attention has begun to shift from "what" the Internet can be used for to "how" it can be used as an interactive medium.

Having been described as a "lifesaver" in the flooding of Grand Forks, North Dakota, during the spring of 1996, Northscape News, the web version of the Grand Forks Herald, provided e-mail through which disaster victims could contact each other, bulletin boards for messages, and online video clips of damaged areas. Within a span of three weeks, site traffic skyrocketed from 4,000 to more than 75,000 page views a day.

This is but one indication of the powerful reach the Internet can have in disaster situations. To assist in flood mitigation efforts after a heavy rainfall in February of 2000, Palo Alto, California's city web site was used to provide frequent updates about rising creek levels.

In May of that same year, the Red Cross raised $340,000 in donations for disaster relief and other humanitarian services in its first national "virtual auction," believed to be the most successful Web charity auction to date. U.S. relatives of India's massive earthquake in January of 2001 used the Internet to follow updates and developments in their home country, as well as to search photographs posted on the Internet for familiar scenes.

RESEARCH QUESTIONS

Trends in disaster communication, coupled with the alleged potential for interactivity that is so prevalent on the World Wide Web, may lead one to expect that disaster communication on the Internet provides a predominantly interactive approach of communication among disaster victims, experts, volunteers, and agencies.

The objective of this research is to assess whether such methods are being utilized on disaster relief web sites, and whether disaster communication is indeed becoming more interactive. To test the application of interactivity to the design of disaster relief home pages, the following questions are posed:

RQ1: What proportion of disaster relief home pages have high, moderate, and low levels of interactivity?

RQ2: To what extent is on-line disaster relief information interactive in regard to the amount of effort web page users must exert?

RQ3: To what extent is on-line disaster relief information interactive in regard to the amount of effort web page producers must exert?

RQ4: What correlations exist among the seven dimensions of interactivity?

METHODS

UNIT OF ANALYSIS

Disaster relief organization home pages, as well as charity organizations' disaster relief front doors were chosen" as the unit of analysis for this study.

A home page serves as the front door to a web site, is usually the default page for the organization, and serves as the common link among all inner web pages. Most web site visitors base their decisions about browsing further into the site on the impressions they get of the home page, which often tends to offer an indication of the contents of internal pages.

There is also more consistency in looking at only the home page, as the size of web sites can vary a great deal, anywhere from one to thousands of pages. Front doors are similar to home pages, serving as the front page to a sub-dimension of an organization with multiple interests.

In order for site lists to be generated at a later time, a check list was developed of minimum criteria for a web site to be considered a source of disaster relief information, adapted from criteria used in a similar web analysis of family life education web sites:

- The site must have the obvious purpose of providing disaster relief information. Disaster relief information can be defined as that which pertains to the preparedness, recovery, relief, or mitigation of natural disasters. Although a site may contain other forms of disaster information (such as news coverage), it must supply basic information useful to volunteers and victims involved with some form of disaster relief.

- The site must be informative, providing facts, research, or recommendations about disaster relief, not solely links to other web sites.
- The site must emphasize one or more of the key elements of disaster relief: coverage, preparedness, recovery, relief, or mitigation, rather than coverage of the events surrounding one particular disaster.

For this study, a universe of regional, national, and international web sites accessible through search engines and other web sites was determined, and none of the sixty-four that turned up in such searches and met the above criteria was excluded.

It must be recognized, however, that less prominent sites with more localized interests could have been missed using this approach.

Therefore, this list excludes local disaster relief organizations that may have web sites that are not heavily trafficked, and therefore do not appear in web searches and are not linked to other web pages.

Units of Measure. Total interactivity score was strictly tabulated for descriptive purposes, and reflects the total of all seven dimensions of interactivity, including complexity of choice.

Although the complexity scores consist of half of the total interactivity score, it serves to describe sites' integration of all components of interactivity; therefore, a site that had a lot of content variety but none of the other six interactive design components, or vice versa, could not be considered as interactive as one that scored highly in all areas.

Effort users must exert is operationalized in three dimensions. Complexity of Choice Available is conceptualized as six content sub-dimensions: news, commercial, explanatory, agency, non-disaster, and commerce.

Ease of Adding Information is conceptualized as the presence or absence of opportunities to submit information, such as electronic bulletin boards and on-line polls. Facilitation of Personal Interaction is conceptualized as the presence or absence of moderated and unmoderated chat rooms.

Effort producers must exert is operationalized in four dimensions. Responsiveness to User is divided into potential for responsiveness, based on the number of e-mail links to the agency or institution employees, and actual responsiveness to a standardized e-mail requesting information.

Monitoring Information Use is conceptualized as the presence or absence of a site counter or user survey. Facilitation of site navigation is conceptualized as the presence or absence of a site map link or a search option on the home page. Immediacy of Information is conceptualized as the presence or absence of a web site publication date or "update ticker." Reliability coding of the interactivity dimensions, including all sub-dimensions of complexity of choice, was 83%.

RESULTS

RQ1: Proportion of disaster relief home pages with high, moderate, and low interactivity.

Total interactivity scores indicate that slightly more than half (53%) of the home pages exhibited moderate levels of interactivity, including both choice of content and interactive design strategies. Twenty sites contained low levels of interactivity, and only ten home pages exhibited high levels. No sites scored 0-1 or 11-12.

RQ2: Extent of interactivity regarding effort users must exert.

COMPLEXITY OF CONTENT CHOICE AVAILABLE

The 64 disaster relief home pages scored very highly on both the "news" (mean =.94, SD =.24) and "explanatory" (mean =.97, SD =.18) sub-dimensions of complexity. There was also a moderate amount of "non-disaster" information present (mean =.56, SD =.5), as well as "agency" content (mean =.47, SD =.5).

Both "commerce" (mean =.11, SD =.32) and "commercial" (mean =.06, SD =.24) information was sparse. Of the 60 disaster relief home pages that contained news content, 82% contained agency information or reports; 45% contained international, national, or local news stories; and 12% contained weather-related information.

EASE OF ADDING INFORMATION

Only about 23% of disaster relief home pages allowed visitors to add or create content through their home pages (SD =.43). A majority of those sites used bulletin boards.

FACILITATION OF PERSONAL INTERACTION

The use of on-line chat rooms among disaster relief home pages was minuscule. Only four home pages39 provided links to chat rooms in which site visitors could meet to converse with one another.

RQ3: Extent of interactivity regarding effort producers must exert.

MONITORING INFORMATION USE

Only about 23% of disaster relief home pages used site counters or user surveys to monitor the visitors' access to their web site (SD =.43).

RESPONSIVENESS TO USER

Most home pages offered potential responsiveness to users (mean =.84, SD =.37); however, only 21 (33%) agencies responded to a request for more information, suggesting that this dimension of interactivity continues to serve more often as a function of appearance instead of opportunity for response to user input. The average response time was 17 hours and 50 minutes.

FACILITATION OF SITE NAVIGATION

Slightly under half of the disaster relief home pages

contained site maps or search engines with which to assist visitors in navigating their sites (mean =.48, SD =.5).

IMMEDIACY OF INFORMATION

Slightly more than half of the 64 disaster relief home pages gave no indication of how recent the information on their web site was aside from a copyright date. Forty-eight per cent (SD =.5) of the home pages either provided an update ticker or a publication date.

RQ4: Correlations among dimensions of interactivity.

Each dimension used in the category effort users must exert, including facilitation of personal information, ease of adding information, and complexity of choice, were found to be correlated with one another.

Pearson Correlation Coefficients indicate that complexity of choice is highly correlated to ease of adding information, in addition to being correlated to facilitation of personal interaction.

Likewise, ease of adding information and facilitation of personal interaction were highly correlated. This indicates that sites with a greater variety of content were also more likely to employ the use of interactive tools such as chat rooms, bulletin boards, and polls.

Ease of adding information was also correlated to monitoring information use, indicating that pages using polls and bulletin boards could be more likely to use site counters and user surveys to monitor user activity.

In addition, complexity of choice was found to be correlated to facilitation of site navigation, indicating that site maps and search engines tend to accompany a larger variety of content.

Many dimensions of effort producers must exert, including monitoring information use, responsiveness to user, facilitation of site navigation, and immediacy of information, were also found to have correlations with one another. Monitoring information use was found to be correlated with immediacy of information, in addition to ease of adding information.

Therefore, not only may site counters and user surveys be related to the use of polls and bulletin boards, but such pages could be more likely to have the page dated as well.

Facilitation of site navigation was correlated with immediacy of information and responsiveness to user, in addition to complexity of choice.

This indicates that site maps and search engines are not only correlated with the use of e-mail addresses for contact information, but also with dated page material and variety of content.

DISCUSSION

Moderate would be the most appropriate way to describe the level of interactivity on these disaster relief home pages. The fact that roughly 84% of the home pages scored a 7 or below when design interactivity scores and content complexity scores are combined, and more than 30% scored a 4 or lower, indicates that there is still some room for increasing the level of interactivity in this area of web site development.

Although pages scored highly in news and explanatory content, all other sub-dimensions of complexity were moderate or low.

The sparse presence of such tools as polls, bulletin boards, and chat rooms indicate, however, that the level of effort users must exert is often contingent upon complexity.

Site producers fared little better in their category. None of the four dimensions in effort producers must exert scored above a 50%, and only a quarter gave indication that there was interest in monitoring user activity on their home page.

Although this may indicate a limited amount of interactivity for home page visitors, the elements used for measurement in this study only account for a tip of the iceberg when one considers the pace at which the Internet is continuing to evolve.

Software such as Flash(R) and Fireworks(R) continues to develop and contribute to the evolution of interactivity on the World Wide Web, in addition to features such as video conferencing and instant messaging that the Internet has to offer.

Further, many sites now require free plug-in software, such as QuickTime(R), RealMedia(TM), or Shockwave(TM), to use video or audio clips featured on that page. Newsgroups, listservs, and other e-mail messaging systems, along with online billing, shopping, and banking, have also contributed to the breadth and depth of opportunities for interaction between individuals, discussion groups, organizations, and corporations.

Money and time constraints may require that a novice undertake the design process, which could subsequently lead to the exclusion of many design elements of which he or she does not have an understanding or awareness. Despite the opportunity for anyone to post a web page, one should not underestimate the amount of training, knowledge, and experience necessary to truly manage all of the components involved in web design.

Since the quality of interactive components was not a focus in this study, suggestions for improvement are limited to three recommendations:

- Acknowledge the im ant tat professional design can have on the utility and productivity of a web site, and perhaps appoint an individual within the organization to seek training for such endeavors, if hiring a professional web page designer is not feasible;
- Strive to more fully utilize the interactive features already in place; for example, responding to visitor e-mails in a timely and professional manner; and
- Increase the opportunities for web page interactivity with care and deliberation, and make a concerted effort to be mindful of design principles and user-friendliness when deciding which and how many interactive elements to implement into a web page or site.

It may be more beneficial to provide a greater variety of

content and a more navigable site than to reformat current content in a flashy style.

LIMITATIONS

Several limitations to this study exist that must be considered. The fact that only home pages were used could provide veritable challenges to the application of this study to web sites in general.

For example, a home page with a complexity score of one or two could be the doorway to vast amounts of varied information.

Likewise, chat rooms and bulletin boards may be located on inner pages, which means that facilitation of personal interaction and ease of adding information scores would be higher for the site than measurements on the home page would indicate. In addition, conceptualizations used here may not be appropriate or applicable to all interactivity studies on the web.

For example, Heeter's complexity of choice was also conceptualized in a content analysis of health communication web sites. In McMillan's study, however, the number of links and presence of a search engine were used as indicators of complexity, which is vastly different from and even contrary to the conceptualization used in this study, since search engines were used here as an indication of navigability.

Furthermore, although the presence/absence coding enhances the feasibility of analyzing sixty-four web pages, it cannot adequately portray the depth or extent of each unit of measurement. For example, a site with one chat room was treated identically to one with seven. A study focused on the continued conceptualization of interactivity, coupled with a deeper look past home pages and into the interactive nature of entire web sites, is not only desirable but imperative to provide perspective for the results featured in this study.

FUTURE RESEARCH

One challenge for future research is a continued development of the conceptualization and typology of

Internet interactivity. For example, complexity of choice can continue to be developed into a more consistent and applicable measure that more aptly reflects the variation of content within a fairly focused source of information, and studies could avoid employing different measurements for the same concept.

The number of bulletin boards and chat rooms within a site, along with the extent of their use, could be measured to get a richer idea about ease of adding information and facilitation of personal interaction. Follow-up emails could be sent to further test the actual responsiveness to user of web pages.

In addition, facilitation of site navigation could also be isolated and broadened. There are many elements besides menu bars, search engines, and site maps that contribute to the navigability of a web site, including the design of the site itself. Download options to accompany special interactive elements, the use of passwords, recent web accessibility issues and the use of frames in web page design, and e-mail update notifications for regular site visitors are all examples of navigation elements this study did not consider.

Studies specific to the examination of monitoring information use could also be undertaken. For example, among the twenty-one agencies who responded to the e-mail requesting more information, nine reported using special tracking software or contractors that recorded things like search, visitor, and page traffic information.

Nine sites reportedly used only site counters, which indicate the alleged number of site visitors and provide no information about actual site visitor use. Five reported using information from e-mails, surveys, donations, and other submissions.

Two reported using no monitoring activities at all. Although this information was not acquired systematically and should not be treated as scientific data, it could lend itself to directing questions for future studies in this area.

In the application of an adapted conceptualization of Heeter's dimensions of interactivity and Massey and Levy's study of online journalism to disaster relief web sites, a more discriminate analysis of whether interactivity is becoming prevalent in online disaster communication can be provided. Although it perhaps presents as many questions as it attempts to answer, it also provides a useful framework that allows for examination of the development and utilization of the World Wide Web not only in disaster communication, but in areas such as business and health communication as well.

Analyses of how these web sites truly utilize the interactive potential of the medium, the funding and staffing constraints with which they are presented, and the economic utility of implementing interactive web page designs for nonprofit organizations are all areas in which more light needs to be shed upon the compelling, important topic of Internet interactivity.

Chapter 16

Internet Influence on the Coverage of Social Protest

Social movement organizations consider both social protest and news coverage of social protest to be major political resources. This chapter expores where the two intersect, by examining whether journalists follow a pattern in protest coverage.

This study inquires also into whether sourcing strategies and framing of social protest has begun to change as journalists gain access to contacts and debates/arguments/research over the Internet. A good location to study such information seeking by the press is within the info-activism created in cyberspace during the protests against the World Trade Organization's ministerial meeting in Seattle in November and December of 1999.

The WTO meetings between governments and trade organizations from across the world were shut down after human rights groups, students, environmental groups, religious leaders, labour rights activists, and other groups with diverse agendas thronged the streets of Seattle demanding fairer, less exploitative trade decision making. This mobilization of masses of people with non-violent as well as anarchist protest repertoires was one of the first examples of trans-border networking and activism facilitated by the Internet; activists used Web sites, e-mail, listserves, e-groups, and Indymedia to mobilize.

Even though the Internet provides movements such as this one a tool for political organization of those who are "accessible" (i.e., knowledgeable, interested, sympathetic Web surfers or those who devise their personalized political information networks over digital media), mainstream media are still the ones expected to provoke popular debate and public opinion. How the mass media respond to these debates themselves and how they access via the Internet the contexts and arguments behind the movement become questions fundamental to a democracy still dependent on mainstream media for generation of public opinion.

SOURCES AND SOCIAL PROTEST

Reflecting the hierarchy in government and society, scholars argue, journalists defer to a hierarchy in sourcing-official sources over unofficial ones, sources in government and industry over those outside. When covering social protests, even general reporters rarely interview ordinary protesters, and organizations that are resource-poor have problems gaining coverage. Cans noted that disorder news is affected by whose order is being upset and focuses on the restoration of order.

The strategies used by social protesters may involve different behaviors-even disruptive behaviour-to garner attention from the media, but protesters have little control over the aspects and actions that the media choose to highlight or underplay.

In a 1994 book on the media and the Vietnam anti-war movement, Small writes "Oppositional mass movements have a difficult time obtaining fair, much less favorable, coverage from establishment media, even in the freest of democracies. For a variety of economic, political and institutional reasons, journalists and their employers tend to denigrate those out of the mainstream...."

Small's content analysis of newspapers, magazines, and television coverage showed that journalists concentrated on violent and radicalalbeit colorful-behaviour on the fringes of the activity.

They undercounted the crowds and ignored political arguments the protesters' leadership presented. Moreover, the "fairness doctrine" had journalists going out of their way to carry the views of counter-demonstrators and the establishment whenever they covered the views of protesters. Research during the past few decades has shown that the media treat non-mainstream points of view as unduly deviant and thereby restrict the diversity of political discourse.

In the context of coverage of social movements and social protest, then, "framing" becomes as important to consider as sourcing.

THE FRAMES OF SOCIAL PROTEST

Iyengar and Kinder explored the direct impact of episodic and thematic news formats, or frames, on viewers' attributions of responsibility for political issues and the indirect effects of these frames on public opinion in general. The authors found that journalists routinely fail to provide the larger contexts (thematic frames) behind protests and cover them merely as disorder and violence news (episodic frames).

Scholars have also found that the media have the ability to define situations and label groups and individuals as deviant, to supply context, and to define issues, through selection, emphasis, exclusion, and elaboration. The effects of such coverage of social protest and political issues, then, leads to readers and viewers perceiving issues as "problems" and to offering status quo support to the establishment.

What does the theoretical framework point to in the context of media coverage of social movements and social protest? In other words, how do the media frame protest? According to scholars, novelty, polemic, confrontation, and controversy are the frames that win media attention for social movements. Studies have shown that news coverage of social protest marginalizes challenging groups and depicts selection bias or description bias.

SOCIAL MOVEMENTS, THE INTERNET, AND THE PRESS

Establishing a presence over the Internet, it is believed, will be one of the key factors that contribute to a social movement or contentious group rising to prominence. The Internet has been used with equal vigour by the right and left, and Internet skill is now considered integral to political communication among progressive intellectuals, students, and activists.

Mainstream media, meanwhile, are seen as becoming less approachable because of emerging ideologies and exigencies. As an alternative, the Internet is celebrated for contributing to political normalization, democratic pluralism, the development of a democratic media politics by the establishment of alternative media, and "the cyber-diffusion of contention."

Does the power of the Internet as a political and communication tool, then, circumvent the relevance of the mainstream mass media?

Research and practice suggest not, pointing out that mainstream media, in fact, gain particular importance in the "network information politics" of transnational advocacy networks. Network activists cultivate credibility with the press and package their information in a timely and dramatic way to draw press attention.

Even groups that circumvent a focus on garnering mainstream media attention do sometimes provide hypertext links and information as press releases on their Web sites.24 The Zapatista movement in Mexico used the Internet for everything from voting in plebiscites by participants from forty-seven countries, to drawing in the mainstream media to create awareness and outrage worldwide.

For a journalist seeking information on today's social protests, protest groups' Web sites present complex debates, research papers, rationales, and contact details, all of which may be expected to make the movement, its contexts, and its participants more accessible to journalists than ever before.

Studies on journalists' Internet use in the United States26 have chronicled the rapid increase in Internet use by journalists and the gradual shifts in attitude toward such use-journalists are using the Web for researching stories, finding new sources, receiving press releases and information, updating breaking news, interviewing sources, and engaging in dialogue with readers. Literature is now emerging on the nebulous relationship between bloggers and journalists and journalist-bloggers.

A next step in research into Internet use might involve how such use plays out in the final product of the journalist-the media story-and the decisions that surround it.

The two practices of sourcing/attribution and framing, in particular, are significant to this study for two reasons. First, as the literature review above shows, these two practices involve location of power in a given story.

Sourcing/attribution determines who gets a "voice," and whose interpretation of events gets reported in mainstream media. Framing, especially thematic framing, gives "context." In one recent study, television journalists covering breast cancer appeared to have increased their use of thematic frames and their discussion of research developments across time, but did not change other practices, such as the dominant citation of medical doctors as sources.

Most important, reporters today, as compared to reporters thirty years ago, can access material online and possibly provide a thematic, contextualized story on their own terms. So, did access to the Internet in 1999 enable reporters to expand their sourcing and/or provide greater thematic framing in their coverage as compared to reporters in 1967?

As evident from the literature, research into the relationship between movements and the media, and the role of the Internet in this relationship, stands at a juncture that is both exciting and undecided. An earlier study on the WTO protests points to the need to develop a new theory of media, political elites and social movement relations. Drawing on the literature and theory presented above, and using the case of social protest coverage as a lens to study this relationship, the following research questions were developed:

RQ1: Was there a significant difference in sourcing and attribution between press coverage of the Vietnam anti-war protests (March on the Pentagon) in Washington, D.C., in October 1967 and the anti-WTO protests in Seattle in November-December 1999?

RQ2: Was there a significant difference in "framing" between press coverage of the anti-Vietnam war protests (March on the Pentagon) in Washington, D.C., in October 1967 and the anti-WTO protests in Seattle in NovemberDecember 1999?

RQ3: Does the Internet appear to have made an impact on the sourcing and attribution in press coverage of the antiWTO protests?

RQ4: Does the Internet appear to have made an impact on the "framing" in the press coverage of the anti-WTO protests?

METHOD

Content Analysis. This content analysis compares the coverage of two separate movements. The longitudinal design compares not one publication's coverage with another's, but the totality of coverage given to one movement by a set of publications with that given to another by the same (or similar) set of publications. For this, coverage of the anti-WTO (World Trade Organization) protests in Seattle is compared with pre-Internet protest coverage given to the Vietnam anti-war protests.

The Vietnam anti-war protests, in particular "The March on the Pentagon" on October 21 and 22, 1967, in Washington, D.C., provide a good comparison for study with the anti-WTO protests labeled "The Battle for Seattle," held between November 30 and December 3,1999, in Seattle.

In both cases, these protests (a) came relatively early in the movement through coalition-building and mobilization; (b) used similar protest repertoires such as celebrity speakers, banners, slogans, and costumes; (c) involved some violence; (d) attracted police force; and (e) were relatively sudden, which gave the media little time to plan their sourcing/attribution, or frames for coverage. Even though the two protests are separated in time and in journalistic advancement, this very separation, in fact, provides the opportunity to study whether the manner of journalistic coverage stayed static.

The Sample: Newspapers and Magazines. The publications were chosen to represent national as well as local coverage and newspaper as well as magazine coverage. This was essential to tap into source use by local as well as national journalists, and episodic as well as "thematic" frames, the latter being more likely to appear in magazine coverage.

Three weeks' coverage was picked from each newspaper. The universe of coverage was examined, i.e., the entire newspaper was scanned for relevant coverage. The newspapers were from October 15 through November 4, 1967, for the Vietnam anti-war protests, and from November 23 through December 13, 1999, for the anti-WTO protests. This comprises coverage from the week before the protests, the week during the protests, and the week after the protest.

For The March on the Pentagon, the national newspaper studied was the New York Times, considered the newspaper of record even in the 1960s. The local newspaper was the Washington Post, which serves as the local newspaper for Washington, D.C.

For the Seattle Protests, the national newspaper was the New York Times, again, and the local newspaper was the Seattle Times. This, of course, raises the question of comparability between the Washington Post and the Seattle Times. However, during both protests, these publications were the local, big-city publications for the venues where the protests were situated. Moreover, the sourcing and framing practices of these two publications have been studied together and comparatively in the past, with researchers noting similarities between the two publications' coverage decisions.30

The sample for the newspapers was collected from the Lexis Nexis Academic database. The magazines sampled for both protests were three issues each of Time and Newsweek: the weeks before, during, and after the protests. The sample produced a total of 444 stories.

Of the 444 stories analysed, 232 were anti-Vietnam war protest coverage and 212 were anti-WTO protest coverage. A total of 330 of these were news stories and 114 were editorials. In the case of the anti-Vietnam war protest coverage, the local newspaper, the Washington Post, carried 106 stories, while the New York Times carried 109. Time provided three stories and Newsweek 14.

In the WTO coverage, the Seattle Times carried a total of 152 stories while the New York Times, the national newspaper, had 47.

Time magazine had 5 stories during the three weeks' issues examined, while Newsweek had 8 stories during this same period. In the total coverage of both protests, a total of 3,752 sources were used, with 39% as Official (Govt. and Trade) sources, 15% as Authoritative (Govt. and Trade) sources, 25% as Official (Protester) sources, 17% as Authoritative (Protester) sources, and 4% as Unknown Protester sources.

Analysis of Variance was used to see whether there were any significant differences between the anti-WTO coverage and Vietnam antiwar coverage on the "sourcing" and "framing" elements.

The five dependent variables (DVs) measuring sourcing patterns, Official (Govt. and Trade) sources, Authoritative (Govt. and Trade) sources, Official (Protester) sources, Authoritative (Protester) sources, and Unknown Protester, were studied with a univariate analysis.

The two variables measuring framing patterns, "Frame of the Story," and "Valence of the story," were subjected to a chi-square test.

RQ1 asked whether there was a significant difference in sourcing and attribution between press coverage of the Vietnam anti-war protests in Washington, D.C., in October 1967 and the anti-WTO protests in Seattle in November-December 1999. Anti-WTO protest coverage used significantly more official sources than the Vietnam anti-war protest coverage. The anti-WTO protest coverage also used significantly more authoritative sources than the Vietnam antiwar protest coverage.

No significant difference was found, however, in the use of official (protester) sources between the anti-WTO protest coverage and the Vietnam anti-war protest coverage. Similarly, no significant difference was found in the use of authoritative (protester) sources between the antiWTO protest coverage and the Vietnam anti-war protest coverage.

Finally, no significant difference was found in the use of

"unknown protester" sources between the anti-WTO protest coverage and the Vietnam anti-war protest coverage.

RQ2 asked whether a significant difference existed in "framing" between press coverage of the Vietnam anti-war protests and the antiglobalization protests in Seattle. The two variables that measured the framing patterns in the coverage, "Frame of the Story" and "Valence of the Story," showed no significant difference between the coverage given to the two protests. For "Frame of the Story," the anti-WTO protest coverage had 63 stories with a thematic frame, 103 with an episodic frame, and 46 stories in which the frame was mixed. The Vietnam anti-war coverage had 56 stories with a thematic frame, 138 stories with an episodic frame, and 38 stories with a mixed frame.

For the "Valence of the Story," the anti-WTO protest coverage had 42 stories with Valences supportive of protesters, 57 stories with Valences supportive of government/ trade (the target of the protesters), and 103 stories in which the Valences were neutral. The Vietnam anti-war coverage had 65 stories in which the Valences were supportive of protesters, 58 in which the Valence were supportive of the target, and 109 in which the Valences were neutral.

RQ3 and RQ4 inquired into the Internet's influence in the sourcing and framing of coverage of WTO protest. However, these data showed limited use of the Internet by journalists. The number of stories identifying an Internet role was very small and therefore not viable for statistical analysis. For a sample of the size picked for this study, the lack of an Internet focus or role is in itself quite revealing.

DISCUSSION

Clearly, the most significant finding of this research is that journalists today seem to be citing official and authoritative sources more than journalists did in the 1960s, at least as far as protest coverage is concerned.

These findings acquire even more significance in helping understand present-day journalism's treatment of social movements and social protest, for two reasons. First, it can be argued that from what we know about the Vietnam war and its key players, sources like the U.S. president and the U.S. administration, in particular, were unquestionably more indispensable to war coverage than they would be to coverage of the anti-WTO protest, given the considerations of nationalism and national security.

Therefore, journalists could be expected to approach those sources substantially more often for coverage of a war than for coverage of free-versus-fair trade issues. The exact opposite seemed to be the case.

Second, it is important to note one fact about the particular Vietnam anti-war protest sampled in this study- The March on the Pentagon. It took place in October 1967, which is noted by political scientists and media scholars as being before public opinion turned against the war. This should be considered in the context of analyses of the mass media's role in the Vietnam war era.

While it was once popularly believed that the mass media were pivotal in turning public opinion against the war, mass media scholars later argued that the media at first ignored opposition to the war and, after the My Lai massacre and the Tet offensive in 1968 and 1969, respectively, merely followed public opinion when it became too large to ignore.

So, during the coverage of The March on the Pentagon in 1967, the credibility of official sources was not already an issue for journalists, at least not as much as after 1968. One could, therefore, expect greater reliance at the time on official sources.

Vietnam era journalists like Walter Cronkite and David Brinkley have, in hindsight, explained this reliance as resulting from the lack of official dissent. Brinkley, who is noted as critiquing America's role in the Vietnam war as early as in 1963, has said, "I don't think that many people did disagree (with America's role in the war). And those that did, didn't want to go public."

In the case of the anti-WTO protests in 1999, however, national security was not an issue; journalists did not need to index announcements or decisions from government administration.

The increase in reliance on official sources in the WTO protests over the Vietnam antiwar protests, then, signifies a growing and almost reflexive dependence on "the official" as the dominant and primary source.

One example of this was the quoting of a public speech by President Bill Clinton, who had arrived in Seattle for the WTO meetings.

The Seattle Times led its report with: "President Clinton today referred to the 'interesting hoopla' surrounding the WTO protests, condemning people who came to Seattle to 'break windows, hurt small businesses and stop people from going to meetings to have their say.'"

However, even when there was no press conference or speech mandating coverage (for instance in a multi-part, serialized news analysis by the New York Times), stories were focused overwhelmingly on reactions from official and authoritative sources (city officials, merchants, WTO delegates, international governments) with little or no perspectives from protesters. This intensification of reliance on official sources, in particular, indicates that journalists today, more than in the sixties.

It is important to acknowledge, however, that journalistic reliance on official sources during the WTO protests may be explained by the fact that the target for these protests was a more diverse group of institutions, albeit one that included government and trade sources. Journalists may not have been questioning the credibility of these official sources as much as in the case of The March on the Pentagon, where the target was clearly the government and military.

The findings also showed, however, that the significantly greater dependence on official and authoritative sources from within the establishment is not matched by a corresponding increase in sourcing and attribution of official and authoritative sources from the other side of the issue. The New York Times series discussed above is also a good example of this.

Similarly, journalists today are no more willing to quote "unknown protesters," i.e., street protesters who are not protest leaders or officials of protest organizations and are not sought out for their "quote-worthiness." This is consistent with the literature on social protest coverage over the decades: journalists feature unusual participants but ignore the rank-and-file demonstrators.

Next, the lack of a change in the frames given to the two protests further indicates that coverage of social protest does, in fact, follow a pattern.

Journalists have traditionally been criticized for favoring episodic over thematic frames, using their own frames and filters to the detriment of the movement message, and rarely exposing casual readers and viewers to the rationale behind the movements' arguments.

Such a continued prevalence of thematic stories using episodic frames with a negative valence, citing "quote-worthy" protesters and employing descriptions of colour, costumes, and mayhem, is typified in the words of journalist Kenneth Klee in the Newsweek cover story titled "Seattle Under Seige," on December 13, 1999: " The protests drew an equally wide array of groups, from stilt walkers to beefy Teamster mechanics to a guy in a get-up that made him look like J.P. Morgan with a sinister mosquito beak. Where was he from? 'Planet Earth.'"

This also serves as an example of episodic coverage prevailing despite a thematic format-this was a "news feature" magazine article, where thematic discussions are better facilitated than in news reports in daily newspapers.

A social movement like the anti-globalization movement, which is relatively new, with diverse and dispersed issues, is more challenging for a reader/audience member to immediately recognize.

For media coverage to form public opinion on it, more thematic coverage may in fact be necessary. To have it played out in the mainstream media as episodic news of "disorder" and "deviance," increasing the media's reliance on sources such as the police, fire officials, owners of damaged property, and other such official sources once again points to a pattern of protest coverage with templates of delegitimization built into reporters' coverage decisions. This brings the discussion to the other key focus of this study, the role of the Internet. While the findings above are consistent with the literature on the coverage of social protest, and contribute to that literature some contemporary and comparative perspective, the limited use of the Web by journalists speaks to the continued discounting of protester sources.

Given the multiple points of access to the movement's discussions available via the Internet, journalists could actually have moved beyond reliance on (and suspicion about, and ethical concern with using) protester press releases, meetings, or other material.

This apparent non-impact of the Internet on protest coverage is consistent with the literature, particularly a 1994 study on journalists' Internet use, which found that "the forms of information retrieval may be different, but the same organizational power structures, sources, and news frames are still evident."

In the context of the celebration over the networking power of Internet-mounted social protests, however, this becomes even more revealing. One study using in-depth interviews with journalists who covered the anti-WTO protests has found that journalists did refer to the Internet but, ultimately, not only relied on old patterns of protest coverage but also used the Internet predominantly for the same sources that they would have referred to anyway, albeit offline.

We cannot conclude, however, that all journalists all the time are dismissive or resistant to accessing protest sources over the Internet or directing their readers/audiences to information and debates available on Web sites.

For one thing, 1999 was really only the beginning of the Web age, which can explain the limited Internet role in WTO coverage. While protesters were using the Web in new and creative ways to mobilize, journalists were still acquiring the skills and the savvy to use the Web without compromising credibility.

This study, therefore, may be viewed as a foundation for

the systematic and continued analysis of journalists' use of the Web and Internet in providing voice and context to stories such as social protest, civil action, and people's movements. Obviously, this content analysis did not sample online media to determine what was there in 1999.

This was because the content analysis was designed to compare periods-the antiWTO protests with the Vietnam anti-war protests. The Vietnam anti-war protests, of course, were not covered online.

Future research, therefore, might involve a study of online coverage using the same modes of analysis (i.e., sourcing and framing) to explore journalists' use of the Internet and their distribution of Web site information and hypermedia links within their stories; studies of hyperlinking by online journalists are now emerging.

Future research should include not only quantitative analyses but also qualitative analyses, through in-depth interviews and surveys, with journalists who covered the anti-WTO protests and other protests (such as the protests against the war in Iraq, especially since these grew out of the anti-globalization protests with some of the same groups and, indeed, the same Web sites), to inquire into the reality and reasons for the choices journalists made in their sourcing, framing, and Internet use.

It is possible, for instance, that these journalists did, in fact, use online resources but did not cite them in the stories, thereby making them invisible to a content analysis.

It becomes important to acknowledge here that this study is an attempt to track early impact and use of the Internet by journalists. While network activists were early adopters of the Web for coalition building and mobilizing for the WTO protests, journalists in 1999 were likely resistant to using the Web and the Internet as overt, attributable sources of information.

This suspicion about the credibility of the Web is one possible explanation for the fact that journalists were more likely to write stories about activists' use of the Web/Internet than they were to use these technologies themselves.

Moreover, in 1999 journalists also viewed these information technologies as emerging competition to their own role as sources of information. This study's focus, therefore, is situated in the early era of somewhat "tentative" Internet use in the newsroom.

It is this very vantage point, however, that makes this study intriguing as a backdrop against which to track emerging information-gathering practices in the newsroom. Documenting the use of the Internet during its early years might provide insights into its current and future use.

For instance, much is likely to have changed between 1999 and the present in terms of journalists' reception of information from alternative voices over the Internet, such as blogs.

One significant question to ask would be: In their use of the Internet, have journalists begun using Web sites, blogs, or people cited on these, as primary sources? Some new studies have suggested that even though some journalists stay resistant to using Internet technologies, and report skepticism of social movements' Web sites, they do seem receptive to corporate and public relations organizations' Web sites, and even interact online with these organizations. One study has shown that even bloggers continue to work within existing discourses about the war in Iraq, primarily employing pro-war and anti-war frames.

To summarize, this chapter's findings on how journalists use the Internet, and its disuse for certain types of coverage, points even more strongly to what scholars have called a selection bias.

It also alerts us to the need to study patterns of "gatekeeping" in journalists' use of the Internet. This study contributes to the study of the sociology of news production in an Internet age, as well as the reception of new social movements by the press. Other studies on the political communication strategies of social movements, particularly during social protests, may help build a body of theory for the study of Internet-age social protest and press coverage.

In recent years, anabolic steroid use among professional

athletes has received significant coverage in print and broadcast media. As an example, when the late baseball player Ken Caminiti told Sports Illustrated in 2002 that about half of all major league players use steroids to enhance athletic performance, mainstream sports journalists and government officials demanded that professional baseball institute drug testing procedures, which it did in August of that year.

More recently, in March 2005, a veritable all-star team of current and former players testified before the Committee on Government Reform in the U.S. House of Representatives about continued steroid use in professional baseball.1 Following that hearing, the committee called on officials from the National Football League, and in subsequent months, a separate committee heard from officials representing professional basketball, hockey and soccer.

Steroid use, in sum, has emerged and remained on the policy making agenda, if only as a consequence of political opportunism (i.e., the chance for elected officials to help "clean up" professional sports) stemming, in part, from dramatic media reports.

Because adolescents frequently idolize professional athletes, whom they observe earning millions of dollars and living glamorous lifestyles, they might be inclined to experiment with the drugs professionals have been known to use.

Through mass communication, they also may develop inaccurate perceptions of health risks, as well as perceptions of normalcy about drug use in sports. Drawing on data gathered by the Inter-University Consortium for Political and Social Research (ICPSR) at the University of Michigan in 2003, this chapter explores attitudes of high school seniors toward the use of anabolic steroids, with specific emphasis on the potential effects of mass communication in helping to shape those attitudes.

The 2003 Youth Risk Behaviour Surveillance System, administered by the Centers for Disease Control and Prevention, found that 6.8% of adolescent males and 5.3% of adolescent females had experimented anabolic steroids at some point in their lifetime. Yet, while scholars have examined relationships between exposure to mass communication and attitudes toward alcohol, cigarettes, and illicit drugs, very few studies have included the use of steroids, and none have focused solely on that subject.

Studies that have examined relationships between exposure to mass communication and attitudes of adolescents have focused largely on perceptions of ideal body image. Generally, where young women often develop unrealistic expectations of how thin they should be, young men often develop unrealistic expectations of how muscular they should appear.

With respect to mass communication, young women observe emaciated models on the covers of magazines such as Cosmopolitan and Glamour, while young men often peruse the photographs in Muscle & Fitness and Flex. Members of both sexes often seek to emulate those they observe in glossy magazines-or in other venues of pop culture. Movies feature hypermuscular action stars, and television offers sporting events, as well as pseudo-sporting events such as professional wrestling, almost nonstop. In recent years, many participants in "legitimate" sports have joined their wrestling counterparts in appearing somewhat cartoonish relative to the average person.

Apropos to cartoons, the physical dimensions of both Barbie and G.I. Joe have become more unrealistic in recent years, with Hasbro even introducing the extraordinarily muscular G.I. Joe Extreme. As Luciano (2001) observes, "If the original G.I. Joe had been life-size, he would have had a thirty-two-inch waist, forty-four-inch chest, and twelve-inch biceps; his successor would flaunt thirtytwo-inch biceps, dimensions that even Arnold Schwarzenegger wouldn't be able to attain".

Adolescent males enter puberty, then, having been inundated throughout childhood with unrealistic, yet idealized, versions of physical size. Given the pressures of adolescence (i.e., fitting in with others, but at the same time, seeking to develop a unique identity), some young men may seek to appear "untouchable" when it comes to muscularity. A substantial portion of these individuals actually may not participate in competitive sports, nor seek to participate; they merely want to appear as muscular as possible and are willing to take their chances with anabolic steroids in pursuing that look.

Thus, in conceptualizing the problem of steroid use by adolescents, one must appreciate that even at a relatively young age, individuals may have very different reasons for using steroids. One young athlete may seek to earn a college scholarship, while another may seek to develop a physique that he believes his peers will admire.

Additionally, contrary to what one might intuit, steroid use is increasing fastest among young women-not young men-with increased muscle tone a primary motivator. As more young women participate in both recreational and competitive sports, and as universities continue to expand scholarship opportunities for female athletes, steroid use will likely hold steady, if not increase, in that demographic.

In sum, whether adolescents of either sex obtain steroids from an Internet source, from a friend at the gym, from a visit to Tijuana, Mexico, or even from a physician, large amounts of these drugs are available for those who seek to try them.

The challenge for the present study is to identify quantitative relationships among (a) key demographics, (b) participation in athletics, and (c) exposure to mass communication, and attitudes toward anabolic steroids. Ideally, such relationships will shed light on how the perceptions of adolescents may be shaped by mediated sources of information, which may then lead to behaviors such as experimentation.

The following section describes the theoretical framework guiding quantitative analyses used in this study, as well as a brief review of the socio-historical context in which data were gathered by the ICPSR.

As a theory of mass communication, agenda setting asserts that while media may not tell us exactly what to think, they frequently tell us what to think about, when the issues at hand do not otherwise obtrude into our lives. As an example, while media need not tell us to consider war or the price of gasoline, they might tell us to consider an issue such as performance enhancing drug use in professional sports. As an extension of that theory, second level agenda setting asserts that the attributes of issues emphasized in media reports can affect how we think about those issues.

Where agenda setting tends to focus on objects, McCombs and Reynolds explain, second level agenda setting considers the characteristics, or attributes, of those objects. Thus, in reports about anabolic steroids, foci might include health risks, illicit use among professional athletes for performance gain, policy enactments, rule violations, or availability of the drugs, among other emphases.

The fact that data used in the current study were gathered in 2003 makes a review of emphases observed in 2002 especially relevant.

In 2002, a retired major league baseball player and former MVP named Ken Caminiti told Sports Illustrated in a highly publicized exposé that about half of all professional baseball players use anabolic steroids to enhance performance. As Denham reported, mainstream sports journalists responded in large numbers to the revelation (or allegation), demanding that major league baseball do something about drug use. Members of Congress also took an interest, calling on professional baseball to include a drug-testing programme as part of collective bargaining talks that year.

About three months after the Sports Illustrated article appeared, and following a barrage by other media outlets, an agreement reached between players and owners in August 2002 included the introduction of drug testing.

When the ICPSR gathered its data in 2003, it appears likely that high school seniors who attended to sporting news in 2002 and into the new year would have been exposed to considerable criticism of not only professional baseball, but all sports from which reports of performance enhancing drug use emerged. Large media companies tend to support dominant social norms, values, and ideals, and they do so by expressing support for fair play as well as advocating penalties for those who break the rules.

In recent years, athletes have broken the rules in sport by using the likes of amphetamines and steroids to enhance performance.

Thus, in the context of the present study, one might expect heavy media reliers to (a) estimate higher levels of steroid use in professional sports and (b) express more negative attitudes about the use of steroids to enhance performance, following a year in which sports journalists pulled few punches in blasting professional baseball and other sports affected by drug use.

Yet, in theorizing about the relationships between mass communication and adolescent attitudes toward anabolic steroids, one might expect athletic participation to be a significant predictor in statistical equations as well, perhaps controlling the effects of other variables.

Athletes may be more likely to get the "scoop" on steroids from other athletes, as opposed to media sources, and through social learning, or emulating the behaviors of those they admire, they may perceive a "need" to meet other athletes on the same figurative playing field.

In short, steroid use may be viewed by even the youngest of athletes as merely a part of modern-day competition. Shildrick (2002) has written on factors associated with the "normalization" of illicit drug use among young people, and while the author concluded that normalization theory presents an overly simplistic explanation of illicit drug use, peers nevertheless stand to influence risky behaviors. Ultimately, with demographic controls and athletic participation in the equation, the present study advances the following hypotheses:

H1: A significant relationship will emerge between exposure to mass communication and estimated use of illicit drugs by professional athletes, with higher media reliers expressing higher estimates.

H2: A significant relationship will emerge between exposure to mass communication and attitudes toward the use of anabolic steroids, with higher media reliers expressing more negative attitudes.

In addition to asking high school seniors to estimate the prevalence of drug use in professional sports and to express their attitudes toward such use, the ICPSR also asked students to estimate the amount of self-inflicted harm that steroid users cause themselves. To this end, Denham conducted a content analysis that may shed light on the relationship between exposure to mass communication and assessment of health risk.

Bibliography

Emery Edwin, and Joseph McKems. AEJMC: 75 Years in the Making. Journalism Monographs, no. 104. Columbia, SC: AEJMC, 2001.

Emery Edwin, and Michael Emery. The Press and America: An Interpretive History of the Mass Media. 6th ed. Englewood Cliffs, NJ: Prentice-Hall, 2004.

Failing Lynn. "The Changing Scene in Communication Education." Media Asia 13, no. 4 (2002).

Fischer Heinz-Dietrich and Otto B. Roegele, eds. Ausbildung für Kommunikationsberufe in Europa: Praktiken und Perspektiven. Düsseldorf. Droste Verlag, 2003.

Lee A., and Norman Soloman. 2002. Unreliable Sources: A Guide to Detecting Bias in News Media. New York: Carol Publishing Group.

Lichtenberg Judith, ed. 2004. Democracy and the Mass Media. Cambridge, England: Cambridge University Press.

Schudson Michael. 2002. Discovering the News. New York: Basic Books.

Siebert Fred S., Theodore Peterson, and Wilbur Schramm. 2002. Four Theories of the Press. Freeport, N.Y.: Books for Libraries Press.

Stanley Robert H., and Charles S. Steinberg. 2003. The Media Environment. New York: Hastings House.

Wicker Tom. 2000. On Press. New York: Berkley Publishing.

Willis Jim. 2004. Journalism: State of the Art. Westport, Conn.: Praeger Publishers.

Wilson Clint C., II, and Felix Gutierrez. 2004. Minorities and Media: Diversity and the End of Mass Communication. Beverly Hills, Calif: SAGE Publications.

Index

applied to the analysis of a real-life rhetorical environment. I refer to Manchester's famous depiction of the "general atmosphere of hate" that prevailed in Dallas when President Kennedy made his ill-fated visit in November of 1963. What Manchester did was to trace the antecedents of this "atmosphere of hate," that is, [illegible] in the history and culture of Dallas.

Research norms that the historical approach is congruent with the position advocated some years ago by a political scientist who has specialized in the study of organizations, [illegible] Mohr. In his book *Explaining Organizational Behavior* [illegible] challenged the value of constantly multiplying conventional studies that accomplish no more than add dozens of variables to an already huge and bewildering accumulation, from which very few really robust generalizations have emerged. He urged researchers to devote closer attention to the study of dependent rather than independent variables. One obviously important way of doing this is the retrospective investigation of antecedents.

One obvious implication of the foregoing suggestion is that we should explore ways of undertaking long-term studies, in which observations are made and data gathered over periods of several years. Would such an endeavor require generous funding? It most certainly would. Probably something on the order of magnitude of the 20 million grant that Walter Annenberg announced just a few months ago, to the University of [illegible] for the establishment of [illegible]

[illegible]

[illegible] environment, we need [illegible] to undertake